# GENOCIDE

Selected Titles in ABC-CLIO's
# CONTEMPORARY
# WORLD ISSUES
Series

For a complete list of titles in this series, please visit
**www.abc-clio.com**.

Books in the Contemporary World Issues series address vital issues in today's society, such as genetic engineering, pollution, and biodiversity. Written by professional writers, scholars, and nonacademic experts, these books are authoritative, clearly written, up-to-date, and objective. They provide a good starting point for research by high school and college students, scholars, and general readers as well as by legislators, businesspeople, activists, and others.

Each book, carefully organized and easy to use, contains an overview of the subject, a detailed chronology, biographical sketches, facts and data and/or documents and other primary-source material, a directory of organizations and agencies, annotated lists of print and nonprint resources, and an index.

Readers of books in the Contemporary World Issues series will find the information they need to have a better understanding of the social, political, environmental, and economic issues facing the world today.

# GENOCIDE

## A Reference Handbook

Howard Ball

## CONTEMPORARY WORLD ISSUES

 ABC-CLIO

Santa Barbara, California • Denver, Colorado • Oxford, England

**Library of Congress Cataloging-in-Publication Data**

Ball, Howard, 1937–
   Genocide : a reference handbook / Howard Ball.
      p. cm.—(Contemporary world issues)
   Includes bibliographical references and index.
   ISBN 978-1-59884-488-7 (hbk. : alk. paper)—ISBN 978-1-59884-489-4 (ebook) 1. Genocide. 2. Genocide—History.
3. Crimes against humanity. 4. International offenses. I. Title.
   HV6322.7.B35       2011
   364.15′1—dc22          2010035195

ISBN: 978-1-59884-488-7
EISBN: 978-1-59884-489-4

15  14  13  12  11    1  2  3  4  5

This book is also available on the World Wide Web as an eBook.
Visit www.abc-clio.com for details.

ABC-CLIO, LLC
130 Cremona Drive, P.O. Box 1911
Santa Barbara, California 93116-1911

This book is printed on acid-free paper ∞

Manufactured in the United States of America

*To my grandchildren Lila and Nathan Bernhardt*
*and Sophie Ball-Dolan*

# Contents

# Preface

> "The President will not authorize the use of force. England and Russia are rattling their sabers, but the political will in Parliament and the Duma just isn't there. The leadership in the House and Senate have also indicated they aren't willing to defend the . . . Treaty with American lives." "So that's it?" Juan said with disgust. "We call ourselves a moral nation, but when it comes to fighting for an ideal the politicians ram their heads into the sand." (Cussler 2010, 266)

Although these words are uttered by fictional characters in the Cussler novel *The Silent Sea*, they reflect the truth about the essential dilemma that confronts the civilized world community in the 21st century. *Realpolitik*, not humanitarian intervention to save lives, is still the operative term to describe international politics. It is a clear consequence of the continued and powerful presence of the sovereign nation-state system in international affairs. *Genocide: A Reference Handbook* tries to explain the reasons why the most vicious crime in all of human history, genocide, as well as the creators and perpetrators of this crime of crimes, (1) is allowed to run its course without outside interference and (2) why the leaders who ordered the genocide have never been stopped and most have never been punished by an outside world community for crafting and then carrying out their nefarious policy. We live in an age of impunity, an era where national leaders can order genocide without fear of punishment. And it is a world of nation-state publics that see the genocide occurring but, evidently, *lack the will* to intervene to stop the murderous path taken by a genocidal policy maker.

Genocide, the planned, intentional extermination policy of a state that is implemented against a group of persons based on their religion, their nationality, their ethnicity, or their race has an ancient history. Although the term itself, genocide, was formed in the 1940s, functionally the policy has been implemented throughout human history from the ancient Greeks to the expansionist imperialist societies of the past few centuries. History is replete with examples of "superior" societies acquiring new territory in Africa, the Americas, the Middle East, and Asia, through a policy of intentionally exterminating indigenous peoples who lived in these coveted regions. North American Indians, the Mayans in Central America, the Herreros in Africa, and Aborigines in Australia and New Zealand are but a few of the native societies destroyed, in whole or in part, in human history. Justifications abounded for such actions: Manifest Destiny, Survival of the Fittest, *Lebensraum*, and the creation of a Greater Serbia or a New Cambodia are a few names used to justify mass destruction of human beings because of their inferior and worthless race, religion, ethnicity, or nationality.

*Genocide: A Reference Handbook* looks at a number of critical issues and questions that flow from the reality of mass murder, crimes against humanity, and genocide throughout human history. Why does one group of people kill another group of people without any remorse or misgivings? Who are the perpetrators who commit these brutal acts against innocent men, women, and children? Why hasn't genocide been prevented or stopped by the bystanders—in the nation and by outraged world publics? (*Can* such planned state-ordered exterminations *ever* be stopped?)

*Genocide: A Reference Handbook* looks at the half century of nonuse of the 1948 Genocide Convention; the treaty stressed the obligatory actions of the nation-states that ratified the document to proactively respond to a perceived policy of exterminating a targeted group. However, these obligations were ignored until the 1990s. However, the actions that were taken in the 1990s were efforts that attempted to punish those responsible for genocidal actions *only after* the genocide had occurred. Why was there this hysterical blindness on the part of the nation-state bystanders? Surely the leaders of these powerful nations and international institutions *knew* about the murders of Rwandans, Burundians, Congolese, Somalians, Bosnians, Cambodians, Chinese, Russian, Bengalese, Sudanese, East Timorese, and others who were slaughtered by antidemocratic regimes or who disappeared. As this book shows, news coverage, television coverage, films and documentaries, and other media coverage showed, in full color and instantly, the results of most 20th and 21st-century genocidal actions.

The reasons for such genocidal actions are pieced together and chronicled in a genocide timeline in Chapter 4 (see also brief biographies in Chapter 5). Critics of the institutions responsible for (not) responding to genocide (primarily the UN Security Council and powerful nation-states such as the United States, Russia, China, the United Kingdom, and France) have tried to suggest steps the international community can take to *substantially* change the ways the "bystander" nations react to genocide. *Genocide: A Reference Handbook* looks at the various criticisms and suggestions and presents the ideas, the organizations, the solutions that they suggest.

Most of the suggestions and developments in response to actual genocides deal with possible actions *after* the genocide has ended. *Genocide: A Reference Handbook* describes these post-genocide proposals and practices, which are essentially legal ones. These include the creation of ad hoc international criminal tribunals, national criminal courts, truth and reconciliation commissions, the granting of amnesty to perpetrators, a permanent independent international criminal court, and additional treaties and conventions that attempt to clarify and strengthen existing prohibitions against genocide. *Genocide: A Reference Handbook* also contains a set of documents—treaties and conventions—that lay out the (as yet unfulfilled) hopes of the international community.

Two leading genocide scholars have written the following:

> It is painfully clear that we—humanity and members of the international community—do not yet have the "answer" as to how genocide can be prevented. What humanity is in most need of in this respect is how to cast off the addiction to *realpolitik*, the lack of political will to act, and, ultimately, the lack of real care about "others" who face annihilation at the hands of mass murderers. . . . We have not found the humanity that is needed to prevent genocide from reappearing, time and again, like a horrific nightmare (Totten and Parsons 2009, 2).

This assessment has come at a time when a radical suggestion has been posited by some critics of the status quo and realpolitik. There must be the *replacement* of the United Nations, which they believe has done little to prevent or stop genocides, with a new international institution with the clear *responsibility* to intervene in the sovereign affairs of a genocidal nation-state with enough force to stop the genocide. *Genocide: A Reference Handbook* also shows that many hundreds of nongovernmental organizations have advocated such a radical change in international law and politics. To realize the values of human integrity and justice, these advocates maintain, there must be the overcoming of realpolitik through the creation and employment of such a humanitarian intervention organization.

Will such a radical change occur in the new century? A central underlying theme of *Genocide: A Reference Handbook* is that there cannot be any true world peace unless there is effective humanitarian intervention to stop the genocide, followed by judicial processes to punish the perpetrators. "Never Again" has been a term used since the World War II holocausts. Instead, since 1945, the world has seen "Again and Again." The task for those committed to ending genocide is a daunting one. It must, however, be one acted upon by newly committed societies unwilling to deny the reality of genocide.

Howard Ball
June 2010

# References

Cussler, C., with Jack Du Brul. 2010. *The Silent Sea*. New York: G. P. Putnam's Sons.

Totten, Samuel, and Parsons, W. S. 2009. *Century of Genocide: Critical Essays and Eyewitness Accounts*. 3rd ed. New York: Routledge.

# 1

# Background and History

It was always easier to think of evil as the work of individuals rather than the successful and well-planned
efforts of societies and organizations operating with a
mandate. [Mad killers] were not created simply by their
environments. Auschwitz and the Nanking massacre
did not happen in a vacuum. (Burke 2009, 389)

James Patterson is a very popular writer of mystery fiction. His
major actor in many of his novels is a Washington, D.C., detec-
tive Alex Cross. In the 2008 novel *Cross Country*, Patterson has
Cross traveling to Sudan in Africa in search of a killer called Tiger.
His description of the genocide taking place in that nation, where
the Janjaweed (Arabic, means "man with a gun on horseback"),
Sudanese Muslim Arab militias, working on behalf of the government, were slaughtering black Sudanese who were living in the
Darfur region, I believe, is a somber introduction to a book on
genocide.

Since 2003, hundreds of villages have been destroyed by the
Janjaweed, and more than 100 refugee camps were created to
house the survivors of these massacres. There was no housing,
little food, and a tiny number of medical facilities to treat the sick
and the dying black Sudanese. And all the camps were vulnerable
to continued attacks by the Janjaweed.

In the book, an associate of Cross described what was
occurring:

"The Janjaweed burn everything they can—food, stores,
livestock. They put human and animal carcasses down

the wells, too. Anything to ensure that no one comes back." These were the Arab militias, widely believed to be supported by the current government in a vicious campaign to make life as unsafe as possible for black Africans in the region. An unthinkable two million people had already fled their homes and more than two hundred thousand had died. Two hundred thousand that we know of.

. . . There was no disguising the horror—especially against women and children, thousands of whom were raped, then branded to increase their humiliation. "Rape has become such a cruel weapon in this civil war. Americans have no idea, Alex. They couldn't possibly.

"Sometimes the Janjaweed will break a woman's legs first so she can't possibly escape and will be an invalid for the rest of her life. They like to flog victims; to break fingers one by one; to pull out fingernails," Adanne said in a voice that barely got above a whisper.

It was Rwanda all over again. In fact, it was worse. This time the whole world was watching and doing almost nothing to help.

In these sentences, one gets a sense of the brutality of genocide in the 20th and 21st centuries. The Janjaweed are attempting to eradicate an entire ethnic and religious culture in Sudan. It is a methodical, programmed, and coordinated slaughter aimed at the entire black Sudanese population through torture, murder, rape, destruction of habitat, and starvation. The Janjaweed are agents of the government, implementing a policy created by the political leaders of the nation. Unlike warfare between nations or a civil war between the government forces and insurgent armed forces, civilians are the sole target of the Janjaweed. (Note: Rwanda is a small African nation, formerly a colony of Belgium, where there exists, side by side, two different tribes, the majority Hutus, the minority Tutsis. In just three months, in 1994, the Hutus killed more than 800,000 Tutsis with axes, machetes, and other primitive tools.)

Finally, although the whole civilized world sees the slaughter, the murderers act with impunity because the world's bystanders have not interfered with the murders taking place in a sovereign nation and a member of the United Nations (UN). Unfortunately, the Darfur region of Sudan brutality is the reality in the

21st century to this point in time. (Although there has been some movement toward resolving the merciless slaughter of persons in the Sudan, the problem still continues. A nongovernmental organization, the U.S. Institute for Peace, issued the following in January 2010:

> With Southern Sudan's referendum on whether to remain part of Sudan or secede approaching, it is vital that the international community encourage and support negotiations on postreferendum arrangements, which include issues ranging from wealth sharing to citizenship rights to security arrangements. Good coordination among the international community will be essential:
>
> - A single mediator with a clear and strong mandate should lead negotiations on postreferendum arrangements, supported by a contact group or group of friends that can insert targeted pressures and incentives into the process. The mediator needs to be strong enough to prevent "forum shopping" and contain or co-opt spoilers.
> - States and nonstate actors that wish to play a central role in negotiations on postreferendum arrangements should demonstrate a long-term commitment to Sudan and to overseeing implementation of any agreement.
> - Negotiations on postreferendum arrangements and the ongoing negotiations on Darfur should be kept separate.) (US Institute for Peace, 2010.)

In February 2010, an e-mail sent by Martha Bixby for the Save Darfur Coalition to activists contained a statement about the events in Sudan (reprinted with permission of Martha Bixby and the Save Darfur Coalition):

> Brutal dictator Sudanese president Omar al-Bashir may still be held accountable for committing genocide in Darfur. Today, the International Criminal Court reversed an earlier decision not to charge Bashir with genocide. With Bashir already wanted for crimes against humanity and war crimes in Darfur, the court will now

reconsider whether to charge Bashir with the crime of genocide.

This strikes a blow to Bashir at the same time his regime *refuses to guarantee basic political freedoms for self-determination*: the freedoms of association, movement, assembly and speech; freedom from arbitrary searches, detentions, beatings and arrests; and freedom of the press.

And without scrutiny by the Obama administration and the international community, the elections will deliver the sort of legitimization that Bashir desires. Justice and accountability must be essential components of the comprehensive solution required to finally end the crisis in Darfur.

Both nongovernmental organizations (NGOs) implicitly voice concern about the unwillingness of the international community to do more than diplomatic overtures and sanctions to try to end mass murder and genocide. Their hope is that concerned people will

Send a letter to President Obama today and demand that without these freedoms, the United States and the world must not recognize the results of an illegitimate electoral process. Tell President Obama not to recognize the results of an illegitimate election. Send an email directly to the White House now and let them know you think the United States should lead the world in making sure brutal dictator Bashir is not allowed to claim legitimacy from a rigged election.

It is a sad commentary about the international community's inaction in the face of genocide when concerned NGOs can do no more than encourage people to write protest letters to their political leaders (also reprinted with permission of Martha Bixby and the Save Darfur Coalition).

This chapter will present (1) the definition of the crime of genocide formulated by the United Nations after World War II, (2) some emergent issues that the world faced after 1948; and (3) brief examples of inhumane practices before (in cases of genocide) and during war (genocide and crimes against humanity) that have occurred during the 20th and 21st centuries.

# A Brief History of the Events of the 20th Century That Led to the Concept of Genocide

Mass murder has occurred throughout history. The growth of the nation-state has led to new behaviors and immunity from action by other nations to prevent or stop genocide. Modern nations (from the 19th century onward) and their political and religious leaders, in the ideological effort to purify their society, or expand their territory, took efforts to rid the nation of unhealthy, diseased members of the sovereign nation. It certainly continued, with devastating horror and cruelty, in the 20th century and continues into the 21st century. The world community has not been able to prevent these actions taken by the leaders of sovereign nation-states against groups within the nation's borders nor has mass murder been stopped when national leaders invade other states and take steps to round up, isolate, and then exterminate targeted groups. The following segments examine why, in the 20th century, mass murder committed with the intent to destroy a group or groups is different from earlier epochs, in great part because of the modernity of the nation-state.

## The Sovereign Nation-State and Genocide

In the modern world, from the 1850s to the 21st century, the hallmark of this era is the sovereign nation-state. As will be shown, nation-building has become the impetus for 20th-century genocides.

Some states are based on religious nationalism and racist beliefs that groups in their society are inferior and therefore dangerous to the health of the nation. For the nation's continued, improved health, such less-than-human groups must be restrained and then disappear in order for the nation to achieve its destiny.

In the 20th century, for the first time in world history, mass killing and genocide became a massive state effort that required a state-sponsored policy and the use of the technology of the modern nation-state. "Mass killing is a huge endeavor that required the mobilization of enormous human, material, and administrative forces. It needs incitement, organization, guile and denial, often simultaneously" (Kiernan 2007, 34).

Given the technological strengths of the modern state, the mass production of arms, poison gas, dynamite, and other innovations brought about large-scale destruction, and radio, telegraph, and mass transportation by rail, road, and air all brought unspeakable violence into the civilian life of the nation-state (Gellately and Kiernan 2003, 21, ff). Also, if there was genocidal racism foisted by the political and religious leaders, two things occurred: (1) the state's technological strengths overwhelmed the targeted victims and steps taken, as forecast in the national policy, that did ultimately lead to extermination of that group, and (2) because of the strength of the universal concept of the inviolability of state sovereignty in the modern world, global justice actions are not taken by other, often horrified nations.

According to international law, if a nation begins to act on the final solution, the genocide of the targeted group, the civilized world is responsible, under the terms of the 1948 Genocide Convention, to take action against the perpetrators that will prevent or stop the genocide from taking place and to try those perpetrators for committing universal crimes against innocent individuals. Sadly, however, for most of the 20th century, genocide trumped justice.

Genocidal policy of the nation's political leaders needs racial hatred in the language of the society, the ability to have and use superior brute force to carry out the genocide policy, and "a cult of antiquity glorifying a lost history, a vision of ideal land use, and its deployment as justification for territorial aggression" (Kiernan 2007, 27). In world history, given the primacy of the nation-state system, colonial expansionism by the major nation-states was the natural order of events and *nothing* was done to prevent indigenous peoples from being nearly wiped out in Africa and Asia by these powers. Instead, there existed the doctrine of nonintervention in the internal affairs of a nation-state: a doctrine that still has a prominent place in international *realpolitic*.

Indeed, the first international treaties were written and signed by the major nation-states in the last half of the 19th century and these focused on the humane treatment of soldiers in wartime.

## Treaties and Conventions to Restrain Military Action during Wars

From the middle of the 19th to early 20th century, the civilized world realized the horrible destruction that *total war* produced—to military personnel and civilians in the path of the destruction. The concept of total industrialized war was introduced in international affairs in the middle of the 19th century. Unlike wars fought by nation-states prior to the American Civil War, this new type of war drew upon the entire society's resources to defeat the enemy. In total war there is the mass mobilization of the entire population and its resources to fight such wars across the globe.

Also, the distinction between civilian populations and the armed military forces of the nation-state dissolved. Unarmed civilians became targets of the armed enemy and, by the time of the Second World War, more civilians were killed than military forces. Winston Churchill spoke about this new type of warfare in a radio speech he gave to the nation, from the House of Commons, on August 20, 1940: "There is another more obvious difference from 1914, the whole of the warring nations are engaged, not only soldiers but the entire population, men, women, and children. The fronts are everywhere to be seen. The trenches are dug in the towns and streets. Every village is fortified. Every road is barred. The front lines run through the factories. The workmen are soldiers with different weapons but the same courage."

The First World War, for the first time in world history, brought civilians into warfare "in all-encompassing new ways." Women began to work in factories and in a limited number of military positions, mostly behind the lines of war. This age of patriotic nationalism brought entire populations into political life as both agents and victims. In that war, the German "Hun" was seen as a baby-slaughterer and vile rapist of women in occupied territories.

In humane efforts to restrain warring sides from unnecessary cruelty in war, the world community wrote treaties that tried to limit inhumane behavior in war. Included in the 1907 Hague Treaty were the following:

- limits on the treatment of the wounded on the field of battle;
- guidelines for the treatment of prisoners of war;
- restrictions on new and innovative techniques for killing the enemy, or causing "superfluous injuries";
- limits on the use of poison gas;
- banning of showing "no quarter" to captured or wounded soldiers in and after battle;
- "wantonly" destroying enemy cities or "caused devastation not justified by military necessity";

- "improperly using the flag of truce;"
- "willfully damaging institutions dedicated to religion, charity, and education, the arts and sciences, and works of art and science;"
- attacking soldiers who had laid down their arms;
- using aerial bombs;
- violating a nation's neutrality;
- using dum-dum bullets against the enemy;
- and committing to prevent the killing of civilians and the destruction of nonmilitary targets (Ball 1999, 15–16).

Both the 1899 and 1907 Hague treaties also focused on the "duty owed by a belligerent occupant to citizens of the overrun nation." This meant that the occupier "shall take all the measures in his power to restore and ensure, as far as possible, public order and safety, while respecting, unless absolutely prevented, the law in force in the country" (Ball 1999, 16).

The primary theme at the heart of all these treaties was that "the right of belligerents to fight war is not unlimited." However, although there emerged—over one-half century—an enumeration of "war crimes," no enforcement mechanisms were ever built into the various international rules of military behavior and into the international treaties to punish those who violated these rules of war. (See, for example, Francis Lieber's Rules of Engagement and Treatment of Prisoners of War for the Union Armies, 1864 [(emulated by the Confederate Army and then by various European nations]; Hague Convention, 1899; Hague Convention, 1907; Versailles Treaty, 1919; the Geneva Conventions, 1925, 1949, 1977; and Kellogg-Briand Pact, 1928.)

## The Definition of Genocide, 1933–1948

There was no word to define the mass murders that took place throughout history until the Nazi government was created in 1933 with Adolf Hitler as *der Führer*, the leader, of Germany. "Genocide," writes Adam Jones, "is one of history's defining features, overlapping a range of central historical processes: war, imperialism, state-building, and class struggle" (Jones 2006, xxi).

Scholars note that the first genocide in world history was Rome's siege and eventual destruction of Carthage at the close of the Third Punic War (149–146 BCE). At least 150,000 Carthaginians out of a population of more than nearly 2.5 million were killed by the Romans (Jones 2006, 5–6, passim).

However, it was not until one Polish-Jewish legal scholar Raphael Lemkin, living in America in the early 1940s, began chronicling the cruel, horrible era of Nazi occupation of the conquered nations of Europe that the word was created.

For Lemkin, who was obsessed with mass killings in history and the question of why such evil takes place (Jones 2006, 9), there was a fundamental difference between war crimes and genocide. Genocide, he wrote, was "not only a crime against the rules of war, but a crime against humanity itself." "The immorality of a crime such as genocide is not a war crime," Lemkin argued, "and should not be confused with the amorality of war" (quoted in Destexhe 1995).

## Lemkin's Original Definition of Genocide, 1933

Although mass murder of groups took place in world history, the word "genocide" did not exist before 1944. Its creator, Raphael Lemkin, had the germ of the thought to prohibit such actions when, in 1933, he presented a paper to an international conference in Madrid, Spain (The International Conference for Unification of Criminal Law). His goal, in 1933 and later, was to have international law recognize a general crime: the destruction of national groups. The laws of war were inadequate to recognize such a general plan of eradication. For Lemkin, such a crime "was not normal warfare, nor was it an excess of war, but a capital enterprise that went beyond war" (Shaw 2007 24–25).

In that document, he wrote about the need for the international community to prohibit "Acts of Barbarity," that is, actions that attempt to exterminate human groups, and "Acts of Vandalism" that attempt to destroy a national group's cultural heritage, whether in peacetime or in war because of their religious, ethnic, political, social status, and cultural views. The text of the Lemkin proposal read as follows:

> Article 1. Whoever, out of hatred towards a racial, religious or social collectivity or with the goal of its extermination, undertakes a punishable action against the life, the bodily integrity, liberty, dignity or the economic existence of a person belonging to such a collectivity, is liable, for the offense of barbarity. . . .

Article 2. Whoever, either out of hatred towards a racial, religious, or social collectivity or with the goal of its extermination, destroys works of cultural or artistic heritage, is liable, for the offense of vandalism (Lemkin 1933).

Given that the world had not yet witnessed the brutality of the Nazi regime's efforts to destroy Jews and other groups, Lemkin's proposal to make these two concepts a part of the international criminal law was not accepted at that time.

Forced to leave Poland when the Second World War began in September 1939, he escaped death at the hands of the Nazis by fleeing across Russia to his final destination, the United States. There, he taught law at Duke University and served as a consultant for the U.S. War Department. Through his European contacts and his research, Lemkin saw the wanton killings of large groups of civilians—Jews, Gypsies, and Poles—and made a continuing effort to inform the U.S. State Department about these mass murders.

### Lemkin Creates the Term "Genocide" in 1944

By 1944, with mountains of research on the actions of the Nazis when they occupied a nation, Lemkin wrote an important book, *Axis Rule in Occupied Europe: Laws of Occupation, Analysis of Government, Proposals for Redress,* about the Nazi occupation of Europe and its methodical killing of millions of Jews living in Europe. In response to Winston Churchill's view that was happening across Europe by the Nazi hordes "was a crime without a name," in his 1944 book, Lemkin provided these horrendous crimes alluded to by Churchill with a name: *genocide* (see Chapter 6, Documents). He formed the word by combining *geno-* from the Greek word for race or tribe, with *-cide,* the Latin word for murder. Lemkin wrote in the 1944 book that genocide ". . . is a conspiracy aimed at the total destruction of a group and thus requires a concerted plan of action. It is a coordinated plan of different actions aiming at the destruction of essential foundations of the life of national groups, with the aim of annihilating the groups themselves." However, although the word began to be used descriptively by the Allies, it had no force of law until 1948.

### The UN Narrowly Defines Genocide, 1948

On December 9, 1948, three years after the trials of the leading Nazi and Japanese leaders began and after years of negotiating behind the scenes by delegates, the UN approved the Convention on the Prevention and Punishment of the Crime of Genocide. Lemkin was the leading advocate of such a treaty, and his life from 1944 to 1948 was spent successfully convincing representatives of the nations that made up the UN that such a treaty had to be drawn up and be made a crucial part of international law. The treaty itself established genocide as an international crime, and the nations who signed it pledged to "undertake to prevent and punish." However, it is important to note that for centuries, the nation-state and its leaders were immune to international pressure.

The sovereign nation-state, wrote Jones, "trumped everything. The state [had] an immunity to do what it wanted with its own citizens." There was, and continues into the 21st century, the concept of state sovereignty (Jones 2006, 9). As another scholar wrote: "the movement for global justice has been a struggle against SOVEREIGNTY, the doctrine of non-intervention in the internal affairs of nation-states asserted by all governments which have refused to subject the treatment they mete out to their citizens to any independent external scrutiny" (Robertson 2002, xxx).

The international legal definition of genocide is found in Articles II and III of the Convention. Article II contains the two fundamentals of the crime: (1) the mental element, which is the "intent" to commit the crime, must be shown, and (2) a description of the tangible acts that constitute the crime. The concept ". . . brings together a whole class of violent and humiliating actions against members of [a targeted] collective; it was a general charge that highlighted the common elements of many acts that, taken separately, constituted specific crimes. The common feature: their threat to the existence of a collectivity and thus to the social order as well" (Shaw 2007, 18).

Genocide, for Lemkin, was a destructive process, not just the physical destruction of a group. Although different in some ways from war, genocide is like war "because it involves the development of strategies, moments of preparation, organization, supply, and deployment. Genocide, like war, involves political, economic and ideological and military power" (Shaw 2007, 36).

Genocide does not mean the immediate destruction of a group; it is a coordinated, comprehensive process of different actions aiming at the total destruction of a group over time. The aim is to ultimately "annihilate" the targeted group (Shaw 2007, 19–20):

> Article II. In the present Convention, Genocide means any of the following acts committed with *intent* to destroy, *in whole or in part,* a national, ethnical, racial, or religious group, as such: killing members of the group; causing serious bodily or mental harm to members of the group; deliberately inflicting on the group conditions of life calculated to bring about its physical destruction in whole or in part; imposing measures intended to prevent births within the group; forcibly transferring children of the group to another group.
>
> Article III. The following acts shall be punishable: Genocide; Conspiracy to commit genocide; Direct and Public incitement to commit genocide; Attempt to commit genocide; Complicity in genocide.

Because of the central role Lemkin played in bringing the world's leaders to accept the idea of crafting such an international law, in 1946, the secretary general of the UN asked Lemkin to write the first draft of the Convention. In his original draft, Lemkin included *all* types of national human groups, including political and social groups, in Article II. In a resolution written by him and passed by the UN in December 1946, genocide was defined as "a denial of the right of existence of *entire human groups*":

> Such denial of the right to existence shocks the conscience of mankind, results in great losses to humanity in the form of cultural and other contributions represented by these groups, and is contrary to moral law and the spirit and aims of the United Nations. Many instances of such crimes of genocide have occurred when *racial, religious, political or other groups* have been destroyed, entirely or in part. The punishment of the crime of genocide is a matter of international concern. The [UN] General Assembly therefore, affirms that genocide is a crime under international law, which the civilized world condemns, and for the commission of which principals and accomplices—whether private individuals, public officials or statesmen, and whether the crime is committed on religious, racial, political,

or on any other grounds—are punishable. (Quoted in Staub 2007, 7–8, my emphasis)

However, after two years of debate in the UN, which consists of sovereign nation-states, and with the start of the Cold War between Stalin's Soviet Union and the West a reality, at Stalin's insistence "political" and "social" groups were removed from discussion regarding possibly placement in Article II. (As later chapters will show, by 1948, Stalin's policy of purging his political and social enemies could be considered genocidal actions.) Although many nations believed that additional groups should be identified in Article II (cultural, economic, and political groups), this, however, did not happen.

Three events that took place between 1948 and 1949 (The Universal Declaration of Human Rights, December 10, 1948; the Genocide Convention, December 11, 1948; and the four 1949 Geneva Conventions) "were the high water marks of the UN movement for human rights. . . . [However,] it proved powerless to move politicians or diplomats to prevent genocide across the world until the 1990's" (Robertson 2002, 37). It was an "appalling failure" of will (Robertson 2002, 37).

By 2009, more than 135 nations had formally ratified the Convention and more than 70 nations have made provisions or passed legislation making the punishment of genocide part of their domestic law. By the end of the 20th century, *genocidal murders were more than double the number of soldiers killed: 61 million military deaths in wartime versus at least 127 million victims of genocide* (Goldhagen 2009, 33), although one scholar believes that only 61 million genocidal deaths occurred in the 20th century (Waller 2007, 15–16).

From the extermination of the Herreros by the Germans in 1904 to the slaughter of Bosnian Muslims and Rwanda Tutsis (1992–1995 and 1994, respectively), the killing of civilians because of their race, ethnicity, or religion has gone on without interference by outside nations until the 1990s. Since 1904, there has been no time when the world was free from ongoing mass annihilation and genocide. "Our time," writes Goldhagen, "has been the age of mass murder" (Goldhagen 2009, 55).

Jones has deconstructed the essence of genocide in the following manner.

Genocide's agents: state and official authorities;

Its victims: social minorities who are essentially defenseless;

Its goals: destruction/eradication of victim group and its culture;

Its scale: From targeting victim group in its totality downward to its psychic and finally, its physical extermination;

Its strategy: develop and implement a coordinated plan of different actions to exterminate targeted group;

Its intent: it is committed with the intent to destroy the minority group in a deliberate, organized, and systematic manner (Jones 2006, 19, ff).

Another scholar has written that the ideology of genocide means "a set of symbols, rituals, stereotypes, and partially concealed assumptions that dehumanize a people as a whole, justify the use of military power to destroy them, and are in turn reinforced by the economic, political, and military beneficiaries of that destruction" (Sells 1998, 28).

Because U.S. policy makers were concerned that the Convention might be used against Americans, the nation refused to ratify the Genocide treaty for more than four decades. However, during the administration of Ronald Reagan, the U.S. Senate ratified the treaty in November 1988. Before doing so, however, conservative senators added so many caveats to the legislation that it was nearly unenforceable. (See Chapter 3 for American policy makers' concerns about such international law voiced from 1918 to the present time.)

## The Legal Manifestations of Genocide

As defined by Lemkin and incorporated into the 1948 Genocide Convention, genocide

is the ultimate crime against humanity because it is legally defined as the targeting of people for destruction on the basis of inherited, or genetic, or religious shared group characteristics that the victims cannot divest. Whereas political party affiliation or social classes are not the same for one can move from bourgeoisie to another social class or political party—they have none of the impossibility of transforming one's racial background. Nor were they covered in the 1948 Genocide Convention (Gellately and Kiernan 2003, 17).

Although genocide became, with ratification, a major universal crime, until the 1990s it *never* became the basis for legal actions against perpetrators who ordered and those who committed genocide. Since 1948 the meaning of genocide has been "mired in disagreements, misuse, and controversies. The common thread? Each of these controversies stands in the way of meaningful action to end genocide, once and for all" (Human Rights 2008).

One critical element for such historical inaction, *intent* to act to destroy a group, in whole or in part, *must be shown* before any action could be taken by a national or a regional legal entity. Intent must be evident before an action can be labeled genocide. The intent of the Nazis to destroy, in whole or in part, Jews, Gypsies, and Poles was clearly seen when the regime's documents are read by jurists. There was clearly stated policy indicating intent to destroy the groups—whether in Hitler's book, *Mein Kampf,* or in published laws and regulations and military orders that clearly laid out the final solution for dealing with the targeted populations. For Hitler, the presence of the Jew in Germany despoiled the purity of the Aryan nation, and therefore these "deadly bacilli" had to be destroyed.

However, the critics maintain that the German habit of chronicling such deeds is unusual. In most cases of genocide in the 20th and 21st century, there has not been such clear intent shown, and this gives other nation-states and the UN an excuse for not calling the actions genocidal. However, although intent must be present, even if inferred by actions against a group taken by the government, the *motive* for such genocidal actions is not part of the legal definition of genocide (Kiernan 2007, 18–19).

Another reason was the fact that the Genocide Convention was insufficiently broad: it excluded two national groups—political and social/economic—and, according to some scholars, it did not specifically give a range of number of persons killed before any action could be labeled genocide—assuming intent was also present.

Finally, critics point out that the focus in Article II of the Genocide Convention is physical destruction of the group, but not a group's cultural destruction. For example, in the Bosnian War, 1992–1995, genocide was motivated and justified by religious nationalism. Destruction of Bosnian centers of culture—major libraries, manuscript collections, museums, and more than 1,400 Mosques—were destroyed by the Serbian religious nationalists (Orthodox Christians) as well as the Croats (Catholics). This  cultural destruction was accompanied by the murders or expulsions of Bosnian Muslims, which totaled more than 500,000 civilians after four years of war (Sells 1998, xiii, 10, passim).

Ironically, Lemkin, in 1933, called such actions by a nation to destroy a group's cultural heritage, "acts of vandalism." However, the 1948 Convention did not define such actions as one of the characteristics of genocide. Therefore, for example, post–World War II Chinese Communist government efforts to destroy Tibetan culture, as well as Brazil's and Paraguay's destruction of the culture of their indigenous tribes, are not genocidal actions. (With respect to physical destruction of a group, rape of the group's women was initially not enumerated as a characteristic of genocide. Only in the past two decades have such actions been considered genocidal.)

Although many journalists and political leaders use the term to describe *any* occurrence of human suffering, the irony is that the UN and individual nations "have been notoriously slow in recognizing and responding to genocide. . . . [Until the 1990s there was no] political will to intervene in actual cases" (Human Rights, 2008).

Serbia's nearly successful effort to create a "Greater Serbia" by occupying and committing genocide against the Bosnian Muslims and Croats was, for nearly one-half decade ignored by the world's onlookers. Boyle points out, "[T]he West's reluctance to recognize the commission of genocide in Bosnia, and the unwillingness to act against it, is the root cause of the prolonged agony of the people of Bosnia-Herzegovina." Because of their inaction for such a long period of time, 1991–1995, more than 200,000 Bosnians were exterminated by Serbian troops and Bosnian Serbian paramilitary units (Boyle 1996, viii). Why was there no effort to stop the exterminations and rapes and forced marches? For Boyle, a strategic reason for nonintervention in the first European genocide since the Nazi actions was because the Bosnians were Muslim and there is a prejudice against that group by Western nations (Boyle 1996, ix–x). As America's Secretary of State Baker stated in 1991: "[W]e do not have a dog in the hunt."

## Early 20th-Century "Genocides"

Imperialism (colonialism), wars, racism, agrarianism, and social revolutions are inextricably linked to the crime of genocide. These events can "facilitate" genocide of hated or unwanted groups in a society. Any one of them can "predispose" a government, its leaders, and their followers to more easily see genocide as a governmental policy (Goldhagen 2009, 40–41). The crime of genocide "transcends political labels." It has been associated with the following types of societies: expanding colonialism; shrinking empires; religious communalism; atheistic dictatorships; unfettered capitalism; national socialism; communist revolution; postcommunist nationalism; national security militarism; and Islamic terror (Kiernan 2007, 37, ff).

The first genocide in the 20th century—because of expanding empire and racism—was carried out by the German military in 1904–1907 in present-day Namibia in Southwest Africa, which was at the turn of the 20th century a German colony. The Herrero natives were herdsmen who moved their livestock and set up their homes in the 17th and 18th centuries in the territory that was colonialized by the Germans in the late 1800s. In 1885, the Herrero territory was annexed into German Southwest Africa. After the Herreros began attacking the settlers and the military, a German policy was established and implemented that exterminated four-fifths of the Herrero population, including women and children. Those who survived the killings were removed from their homes and forced into the desert.

To control the region, the Germans literally wiped out the native Herreros. Colonialism is the establishment and maintenance (through the use of military force), for an extended period of time, of a major power's rule over a native group that is separate and subordinate to that power, socially and geographically (Jones 2006, 39–40, ff).

Prior to—and even after—the World War II era, there existed a "culture of impunity" for a nation's leader who undertook destructive actions against national groups and indigenous groups whose territory was occupied by the nation. The men who ordered war crimes and crimes against humanity or what we now call genocide were never punished for their behavior; neither were those followers who obeyed these illegal orders and war policies and wantonly killed targeted civilian populations.

However, worse than genocide committed on behalf of colonial imperialism as a cause of genocide, is war. "Genocide and war are the Siamese Twins of history," wrote Jones (2006, 48, ff). "[War] accustoms a society to mass violence; greatly increases the quotient of fear and hatred in a society; eases genocidal logistics by making it easier to mobilize the resources for genocide; provides a smokescreen for genocide; fuels intracommunal solidarity and intercommunal enmity; stokes grievances and a desire for revenge" (Jones 2006, 48, ff).

World War I was the apex of total industrial war. Genocide, noted Kiernan, requires superior technological and material power over a sizable population. "The nation's technology overwhelms the victims" (Kiernan 2007, 21, ff). In that war, the second "genocide" took place. The extermination of nearly two million Christian Armenians living in the remnants of the Ottoman Empire, were targeted by the Young Turk Islamic government. The leadership took advantage of the war to commit genocide against the Armenian minority living in the nation.

The slaughters began soon after World War I began, which saw Turkey allied with Germany. In April 1915, Armenian soldiers serving in the Turkish army were removed and then murdered. Armenian civilians living in the nation were forced into deportation marches—after Armenian men and boys were murdered by Turkish police and military. Like the German colonial military in Southwest Africa, the Turkish strategy was to force march the women and children over mountains and into the desert.

During these marches, the Armenian women were systematically raped, tortured, and mutilated by Turkish perpetrators. The marchers were constantly attacked while on the road; they were not provided with food or water. Hundreds of thousands of them died during the long march. In the final analysis, more than half of the Armenian population in the Ottoman Empire (more than 1.5 million) was exterminated by the Young Turk government. Although the peace treaty called for trials of the leaders of the government for their policy of mass murder, opposition to the treaty in Turkey led to no action taken against the leaders of the nation who ordered the extermination of the Armenians (see Ball 1999). To this day, modern Turkey refuses to acknowledge that the government's actions against the Armenians were genocide.

World War II exhibited the "barbarization of warfare," as seen in Japanese actions against the Chinese and Nazi extermination of six million Jews, as well as the slaughter of Gypsies, Poles, Russians, and others, including Germans who were not worthy of life (Jones 2006, 52–54).

Since 1945, there have been more than 250 wars and civil wars. Since the end of World War II, the civilian-to-military casualty rate has been reversed, from 10 to 1 military casualties to 10 to 1 civilian deaths (Goldhagen 2009, 517).

Finally, genocide has occurred during social and political revolutions where the winner in the civil war committed genocide against their enemies. This occurred after the Russian Revolution of 1917, especially Soviet efforts to kill the Kulaks, which took place in the Chinese Communist revolution that began in the 1930s. Revolutions, notes Jones, create conditions for genocidal movements to gain power (Nazis in Germany, Fascists in Italy, Communists in Russia and China, Communists in Cambodia). Revolution makes possible the imposition of radical ideologies and new orders that legitimized genocide: social mobilization of low-class or despised groups that helped make them targets of genocide and the development of genocidal state policy against a group (Jones 2006, 55–56).

## International Military Tribunals in Germany and Japan, 1945–1948

With the ad hoc International Military Tribunals convened in Nuremberg and Tokyo by the victors in the years between 1945 and 1948, a new reality seemed to emerge in international law: the ending of a "culture of impunity"; leaders and major followers were put on trial for their actions and, after mass of evidence was presented by the prosecutors, they were found guilty, and most were sentenced to death.

At the Nuremberg trial of the major Nazi political and military leaders, 22 men were charged with waging aggressive war, war crimes, and crimes against humanity. A few defendants committed suicide, and three men were acquitted. Most of the others were sentenced to death (see Ball 1999). In the countries occupied by the Nazis during the war, national tribunals tried and found guilty many hundreds of Nazi perpetrators.

Tokyo war crimes tribunal, begun in 1946, saw 25 military and political leaders tried before a panel of 11 judges (each jurist represented each nation occupied by Japan or who were wartime enemies of the Japanese Empire). All were found guilty of waging aggressive war, some were found guilty for the inhumane treatment of prisoners of war, and key military generals for deliberately and recklessly disregarding their duty to take adequate steps to prevent their troops from committing atrocities during the war. Seven of the 25 were executed, and as happened in Europe, many of the occupied nations indicted, tried, and punished lower level Japanese military leaders in their own courts.

One critical outcome was the creation of the Constitution of the International Military Tribune (the Nuremberg Charter) used by prosecutors in both major trials of the defeated enemies, Germany and Japan. This was followed, after the major German and Japanese trial ended, by the UN's adoption of the seven Nuremberg Principles, which were segments of the Constitution of the International Military Tribunals.

Compared with current problems regarding genocide, these post–World War II trials were relatively free of problems and controversies. Robertson wrote that Nuremberg's legacy was that there are no human rights without remedies for human wrongs: crimes against humanity and that Nuremberg

> . . . stands as a colossus in the development of international human rights law, precisely because its charter *defined* crimes against humanity and its *procedures* proved by acceptable and credible evidence that such crimes had been instigated by some of the defendants (Robertson 2002, 231).

The Nuremberg Charter (see Chapter 6) and the trial of the top Nazi leaders established in international law the concept of *universal jurisdiction*. Because of the severity of the crime against humanity committed by perpetrators, any court anywhere "is empowered by international law to try it and to punish it, irrespective of its place of commission or the nationality of the offender or the victims" (Robertson 2002, 254, ff).

# Key Issues Associated with Genocide

"Under what conditions do governments and their agents decide on the utterly utopian goal of destroying a problem population?" (Gellately and Kiernan 2003, 9). How can people kill other people, often neighbors and friends? Is the extraordinary evil in genocide committed by pathologically cruel sadists and madmen? As this segment will point out, *ordinary people*—doctors, lawyers, religious persons, academics, opera buffs, law enforcement officers—do the killing. How that happens is examined below. The principal keys to this reality occurring are (1) the collective called the nation-state and (2) the political leaders of nation-states.

## Why Do People Kill Other People?

In Greg Iles' book, *The Devil's Punchbowl*, one of his characters, a retired Texas Ranger, is attending a dogfight in rural Louisiana. He hears the screams and yells of the rednecks watching the bloody, cruel spectacle:

> Walt's stomach heaves, unable to tolerate the mixture of anger and disgust flooding through him. This is like standing in a room where prisoners are forced to fight or copulate for the pleasure of their guards. The Nazis did that, and the Japanese, and probably the jailers of all nations in all epochs of history. . . . The spectre of Abu Ghraib rises in his mind. The terrible truth is that *brutality is part of human nature*, and all the laws in the world can't neuter it" (Iles 2009, 477, my emphasis).

Genocide occurs many times when the nation is at war. During a total war, when national fervor and xenophobia are at their peak, it is easy for the leader to accomplish the "depersonalization" of all the members of the targeted group or groups. During war, the nation's population is eager to ignore the "personhood" of the individual members of that hated group and brutally kill them, "systematically and intentionally," without any mercy (Waller 2007, ix). Brutality, when certain conditions exist in a society, a part of human nature, is let loose. What are the influences that enable ordinary citizens to "unleash [their] extraordinary evil destructive capacities" and become genocidal perpetrators? (Waller 2007, xii–xvii).

There are three *proximate* cultural causes that explain *how* such behavior occurs in a nation's population: (1) the society's cultural construction of a worldview (reflecting the views of its political leaders), (2) the psychological construction of the "other," the group targeted for extermination, and (3) and the social construction of cruelty in that nation. Under certain conditions, "these converge interactively to impact individual behavior in situations of collective violence" (Waller 2007, xvii), and (the *why* for genocidal actions in a nation), there is an *ultimate* cause present, triggered by the nation's leaders, which is the rationale for proximate behavior to evolve into genocide (see Waller 2007, 139–258, passim).

Central in all these causes is the role of "language and imagery" in a nation-state. Goldhagen believes they are the

> ... specific beliefs that people, through language, relate to one another; the fundamental reality of how people, leaders and followers, become cognitively, psychologically, and emotionally prepared to give themselves to the elimination of others, and how people become mobilized to attack, dragoon, expel, or kill others (Goldhagen 2009, 313).

Language "dehumanizes and demonizes" the potential victims in the society. For example, in Nazi Germany, Hitler, and other Nazi leaders, sharing the general hatred of the Jew with the population, had no difficulty describing the Jew as criminal, as a demon, and as subhuman and not worthy of life. Killing such subhumans is both natural and necessary for the German state to regain its lost purity (Goldhagen 2009, 319). All other genocides *must and do* dehumanize the targeted group before proceeding to the next stages in the march toward genocide and mass killing. Examples of dehumanizing language actually used by genocidists include the following phrases: The victim is to be murdered because

> "To allow you to live is no benefit, to destroy you is no loss." (Cambodia)
> You are an "undesirable parasite." (Bosnia)
> You are a "rodent, vermin, or a disease carrier." (all)
> You are "less valuable than a pig, because a pig is edible." (Japan)
> You are "a sleazy cockroach." (Rwanda)
> You are "dog food." (Turkey)
> You are "unworthy of Life." (Germany)
> You are "wearing glasses." (Cambodia)
> Your murder "would create no greater moral weight than squashing a bug or butchering a hog." (Japan)
> (Ball 1999, 220)

Proximate Cause 1. The cultural construction of a nation's worldview is the background, the lens, through which its citizens interpret their social environment and base their actions on. Waller identifies at least three such models: a *collectivistic* model, where group values are the basis of an individual's behavior; an *authority* model, whose values order the social world and its people according to their power and position in the society's hierarchy; and the *social dominance* model, based on the development and maintenance of hierarchical values.

Proximate Cause 2. The psychological construction of the "other" in a society shows how a group or groups in a nation become the objects of the nation's actions through the process of *we–they* thinking. This proximate cause becomes the "social death of the victims—they are excommunicated from a common moral community and slowly become the objects of perpetrators' cruel actions" (Waller 2007, 197–198), and social death occurs daily in the victims' lives. It makes their lives meaningless because of the daily legal, social, and economic indignities and hardships they experience. It is the prerequisite step before deportation, expulsion, and the final solution for the nation: genocide.

This proximate cause enables the society to disengage itself from the group targeted for social death and ultimately physical death. Death of the victim group is necessary for the nation's survival. To do this over a period of time, there is the dehumanization process, which creates a psychological distance between the victims and the rest of society. They are not human; they are disease carriers, parasites, insects, and vermin. Such psychological distancing makes it easier to exterminate the victim group. Therefore, the society must do this in order to remain healthy and free of germs and the sickness brought on by these victims.

Proximate Cause 3. The social construction of cruelty is the final proximate cause. This proximate cause contains the factors that provide the perpetrators with a coping mechanism for their wanton cruelty toward the victims. This social construction is "an inverted moral universe in which right becomes wrong, healing has become killing, and life has become death." It explains how ordinary people, not sadists, become extraordinary evil killers. The killers in such a society lose their individuality, and the prime societal value is extraordinary evil. It is inherent in the law, in justice, and in all other communal values. There is, in short, the evolving repression of individual conscience in such a nation-state through conformity to peer pressure and rational self-interest.

The ultimate influence is the political leader's ability to activate the proximate causes—through control of the media, repeated propaganda—over and over again through time, and thus unleash the innate characteristics inherent in human beings: aggressiveness and other bad human instincts. It is the ideology of the nation's leaders' that enables them to identify domestic enemies and provides the nation with the solution to the problem: genocide.

Human beings are evolving animals; they do evil because they can and this impulse to do evil "qualifies as a human capacity. . . . We all have dark sides and given the confluence of contributing factors, we are all capable of terrible deeds" (Waller 2007, 160–161). These allow for, as Hannah Arendt suggested in her book about the Eichmann trial in Israel, the "banality of evil" to take place (Arendt 2006).

Underscoring the emergence of genocidal acts in a nation is the presence of politics. Politics is central in the genesis of mass murder and genocide. Genocide is a political act; it is a policy of the state (Goldhagen 2009, 68–69). Although the possibility of extermination of a hated religious or ethnic group is a nascent ideal held by members of the community, politics actualizes these thoughts of hatred and fear, and intentional acts of genocide occur. As Goldhagen observes, "The most virulent hatred of a group does not result in systematic slaughter unless political leaders mobilize and organize those who hate into a program of killing" (Goldhagen 2009, 69). When the nation is at war, the political leaders find it easier to mobilize the public to act against the target group.

## Perpetrators, Victims, and Bystanders

In his 1944 book, Lemkin wrote the following:

> The instigators and initiators of a genocide are cool-minded theorists first and barbarians only second. The specificity of genocide does not arise from the extent of the killings, nor their savagery or resulting infamy, but solely from the *intention*: the destruction of a group.

If German voters had not given the Nazis an electoral victory in 1933, if Hitler had not become der Führer, the leader, of the nation, the genocidal policy immediately begun by the Nazis in 1933—ordered by Hitler—would not have emerged. "If other people held power, if leaders had decided on other [nongenocidal policies], there would have been no mass murder of the Jews, Gypsies, and other groups" (Goldhagen 2009, 73–74). The

Germans would still have held onto their malicious views of the Jew but would not have taken any organized actions against that group if the political leaders had not developed a state policy of genocide against that religious/racial group.

The political leader of the state—a Hitler, or a Pol Pot, or a Stalin—is the critical factor in triggering actions and state policies that ultimately lead to genocide. The leader is "the prime mover of mass murder" (Goldhagen 2009, 78). Most genocidal leaders want to *purify* their society by getting rid of the groups that infect the social community. Identifying the leader's aspirations, views of the world, moral values, hatreds, and prejudices is the critical knowledge one needs to understand why some leaders move to genocide and others do not.

Once the "great man," the political leader, assumes power, the policy is developed through discriminatory laws, severe proscriptions against members of the targeted group. Although Hitler centralized control over the "Jewish" policy, local groups—the police, the military, the race haters—took the *pleasurable* initiative of interpreting and implementing the policies. Social death of the targeted group occurs daily: members of the group are barred from practicing and teaching law, from practicing their professional jobs, from selling goods to non-Jews, from serving in the civil service and the military, from marrying Germans, and from doing business with Germans.

All those who participate in the development of state policies that will ultimately lead to the social and then physical deaths of the hated group are perpetrators. All those citizens who implement these discriminatory policies against members of the group are perpetrators as well.

A perpetrator "is *anyone* who knowingly contributes in some tangible fashion to the deaths of others, or to injuring others as part of an annihilationist program" (Goldhagen 2009, 91). These perpetrators see the targeted group as vermin, lice, or disease carriers; because the victims are not human, it is the perpetrators solemn duty to exterminate them.

Once Hitler moved to implement the Final Solution to the Jewish problem (which occured after the social death of the Jews reached its apex), the military became the prime state organization tasked to carry out the policy. The perpetrators are the willing and obedient military leaders who develop the procedures, the institutions, and the logistics for the killings as well as the special military units tasked to implement the killing process.

The victims, the targets of the genocidal policies crafted by the political leaders, are murdered in a variety of ways: They are gassed, shot, starved, beaten, and tortured. Machine guns, clubs, machetes, knives, clubs, and rakes are some of the tools used by the perpetrators to exterminate the victims.

If a person in Germany approved of the extermination policy of the Nazi government, he killed the victims. If another person approved the genocidal policy but did not kill, he was not punished. Such persons were not "coerced" because, in Nazi Germany, there were many willing perpetrators. They were, as were most of the citizens living in Nazi Germany, a "supportive bystander" (Goldhagen 2009, 146, ff). (Given peer pressure in Nazi Germany, few men in the military or in police battalions used for extermination tasks refused to participate in the slaughter.)

## The Stages Leading to Genocide

There have been five principal types of actions that lead, ultimately, to a nation's intentional effort to exterminate one or more domestic groups in the society: (1) transformation, the destruction of the group's defining identity; (2) repression, reducing by violent methods the hated group's ability to harm others in the nation; (3) expulsion, the deportation of the hated group from the nation or territory; (4) prevention of reproduction by systematic rapes of women in the group or through sterilization; and (5) the final solution, extermination of the members of the targeted group by intentional actions of the state's agents, primarily the military (Goldhagen 2009, 14–18).

Summing up, there are no less than eight stages of an uninterrupted, implemented genocidal policy in a nation-state (Stanton 1998). Genocide is a policy developed by the political leader or leaders of the nation-state. The progression toward the final solution can be halted by change in leaders, revolution, or civil war, but not by the targeted groups themselves nor, presently, by actions of the international community.

As will be seen in Chapter 4, which describes 20th-century genocides, each one is different in terms of time, culture, and technological development. However, they all, some very quickly (the Rwandan genocide, 1994) and others more slowly (the Jewish genocide, 1933–1945), reach the final solution stage: the intentional murder of some or all of the members of that hated group.

The initial stage is the reality that all national cultures have language and values to distinguish and *classify* the various societal groups. Because of these psychological and sociological distinctions, one or more groups, because of their religion or ethnicity or their race, are historically labeled as different and *dangerous* to the larger body politic.

In the second stage, these classifications become visible symbols (Jews, Gypsies, Muslims, Blacks, Hindus, and Bantus) in the society, and if the culture has historically disdained the group, there has also emerged over time a hatred of these members. If the hatred is accompanied by political change in the society, where the new political leadership is committed to destroy these "nonhumans," social customs and laws are generated to discriminate against these unwanted groups. This is the beginning of the group's social death. Physical *symbols* are forced upon the targeted group to distinguish them from the "pure" citizens, and so Jews were forced to wear yellow Jewish stars on their clothing, and the targeted urban persons and religious minorities in Cambodia were forced to wear blue scarves.

The third stage in the march to genocide is the further continuation of the social death of the group through their *dehumanization*. Wartime hastens this movement because of the primacy of nationalism, ethnocentrism, and xenophobia. In all spheres of social life in that nation, the members are denied their humanity. They are called cockroaches, vermin, and disease carriers. They are forbidden entry into most professions in the society. Further, radio, film, theatre, and the press broadcast and print and speak hateful words about the group and its danger to the nation. Hate crimes begin to proliferate, and individual members of the hated group are beaten up and murdered randomly; their stores are desecrated, their houses of worship burned down, and all other elements of their lives are disrupted over and over again by members of the larger society.

Stage four is the state's *organization* of the nation's personnel, especially its police units and special military units, into perpetrators who strike against the targeted group. Other government bureaucrats plan for the eventual destruction of the group through deportation to ghettos and then transport them to concentration camps and killing centers. They determine how to organize the transportation system to move the group's members (which can reach millions of persons), and they also draw up various plans for the killing of these groups—efficiently and effectively.

In the fifth, stage, the *polarization* of the society's groups has taken place. Propaganda, however, continues to describe the targeted group in hateful ways. Members of the group continue to live in a heavily discriminated society, slowly losing their humanity and their lives because of the continued beatings, rapes, and murders that occur with impunity.

By the sixth stage in the march to the final solution, the *preparations* for the genocide have or are about to be completed by the political leaders and their local surrogates. Ghettos are identified, killing centers are built, transportation plans have been approved, roundups of the group's members are planned or already underway. There are no due process guarantees that can be used by the targeted group. They are the powerless victims of these societal actions against them. They live at the mercy of the state's perpetrators.

Then comes stage seven, the beginning of the *extermination* process. The plans are implemented by the perpetrators. The group is rounded up, segregated into ghettos, shipped to concentration camps and finally, to the killing centers. This intentional mass killing of the members of the group, solely because of their race, religion, or nationality, or ethnicity, is what Lemkin called genocide. The world community has viewed the movement toward this stage but, because of the concept of nonintervention into the domestic affairs of the nation-state, nothing is done. There is no intervention even though hundreds of thousands, millions, of innocent civilians are seen in ghettos and concentration camps and killing centers, and stories emerge from these regions about the fate of these people.

The eighth stage is the genocide denial phase. In this stage, "the perpetrators of genocide dig up the mass graves, burn the bodies, try to cover up the evidence and intimidate the witnesses. They deny that they committed any crimes, and often blame what happened on the victims. They block investigations of the crimes, and continue to govern until driven from power by force, when they flee into exile" (Stanton 1998). They also argue that, as good soldiers, they were merely following the orders of their political and military leaders.

At any of the stages leading to genocide, the international community—either through the UN or through actions by the major powers—could intervene and stop genocide from occurring.

The history of the 20th century, however, indicates that this did not happen. The next chapter examines this tragic reality.

# References

Arendt, H. 2006. *Eichmann in Jerusalem: The Banality of Evil*. New York: Penguin Classics.

Ball, H. 1999. *Prosecuting War Crimes and Genocide*. Lawrence, KS: University Press of Kansas.

Boyle, F. A. 1996. *The Bosnian People Charge Genocide: Proceedings at the International Court of Justice concerning BOSNIA V. SERBIA on the Prevention and Punishment of the Crime of Genocide*. Amherst, MA: Alethia Press.

Burke, J. L. 2009. *Rain Gods*. New York: Simon and Schuster.

Destexhe, A. 1995. *Rwanda and Genocide in the Twentieth Century*. New York: New York University Press.

Gellately, R., and B. Kiernan 2003. *The Spectre of Genocide: Mass Murder in Historical Perspective*. New York: Cambridge University Press.

Goldhagen, D. J. 2009. *Worse than War: Genocide, Eliminationism, and the Ongoing Assault on Humanity*. New York: Public Affairs Press.

Human Rights. 2008. Five Controversies on Genocide (. . . but not the only five). http://humanrights.change.org/blog/view/5_controversies_on_genocide_but_not_the_only_five.

Iles, G. 2009. *The Devil's Punchbowl*. New York: Scribner's.

Jones, A. 2006. *Genocide: A Comprehensive Introduction*. New York: Routledge.

Kiernan, B. 2007. *Blood and Soil: A World History of Genocide and Extermination from Sparta to Darfur*. New Haven, CT: Yale University Press.

Lemkin, R. 1933. *Acts Constituting a General (Transnational) Danger Considered as Offences against the Law of Nations*, report presented at the 5th Conference for the Unification of Penal Law, Madrid, Spain, October 14–20, 1933. http://www.preventgenocideinternational.org.

Patterson, J. 2008. *Cross Country*. New York: Vision.

Robertson, G. 2002. *Crimes against Humanity: The Struggle for Global Justice*. London: Penguin.

Sells, M. 1998. *The Bridge Betrayed: Religion and Genocide in Bosnia*. Berkeley: University of California Press.

Shaw, M. 2007. *What Is Genocide?* Malden, MA: Polity Press.

Stanton, G. H. 1998. *The 8 Stages of Genocide*. (Originally presented as a briefing paper at the U.S. State Department in 1996.) http://www .genocidewatch.org/aboutgenocide/8stagesofgenocide.html.

Staub, E. 2007. *The Roots of Evil: The Origins of Genocide and Other Group Violence*. Cambridge, MA: Cambridge University Press.

Temin, J. 2010. United States Institute of Peace. Negotiating Sudan's post-referendum arrangements. http://www.usip.org/resources/ negotiating-sudans-post-referendum-arrangements.

Waller, J. 2007. *Becoming Evil: How Ordinary People Commit Genocide and Mass Killing*. 2nd ed. New York: Oxford University Press.

# 2

# Problems, Controversies, and Solutions

The goal of the 1948 Genocide Convention was to modify international law so that the United Nations (UN) or the nation-state, facing the prospect of genocide and mass murder in another nation, will devise strategies to stop, or intervene quickly, and provide justice for the victims and the perpetrators who planned and ordered the genocide. It was a reflection of the reality of Nazi and Japanese crimes against humanity during the long Second World War and would be an action that would enable the UN and nation-states to *aggressively act* to make sure genocide never emerges from any nation-state or territory.

Throughout world history, social conflict, including mass murder of innocent civilians, has been "ubiquitous." Wars erupted constantly in history. The 20th century was no exception. Genocides emerge during wartime and after "extreme social and political crisis, where normal rules of behavior are suspended and violence is honored" (Gellately and Kiernan 2003, 56).

Even after Nuremberg and Tokyo War Crimes Tribunals and the appearance of the Nuremberg Principles, the Genocide Convention of 1948, and the four Geneva Conventions of 1949, the next four decades unfortunately did not deviate from prior world history. There were more than 200 wars (including civil wars), involving more than 60 nation-state members of the UN. There were only 26 days of world peace during those years (Waller 2007, xiv). "Until [the war in] Bosnia, the world pretended that Nuremberg never happened, the precedent it established was ignored" (Robertson, 2002, 220).

**31**

The international community was at fault for its inaction over these decades. It did not prevent mass murder and genocides; justice was sacrificed in the name of national sovereignty. As Goldhagen states: "The international community must become more than a fiction: it is now a loose collection of individual states that come together to agree or disagree" (Goldhagen 2009, 570).

This chapter presents some of the reasons for this state of affairs. It also discusses a variety of efforts taken by the international community to try to figure out *how* to prevent or intervene and then to punish the perpetrators of these universal crimes, including two UN-created ad hoc tribunals (Yugoslavia and Rwanda), national tribunals, and, in 2002, the formal beginning of the world's first permanent International Criminal Court (ICC) created by the UN.

# Fifty Years of Nonuse of the 1948 Genocide Convention, 1948–1998

Unfortunately, after the trials of the major Nazi and Japanese leaders ended, the principle of sovereign impunity reemerged. Until the Bosnian War, 1992–1995, "the world pretended that Nuremberg never happened; the precedent it established was ignored" (Robertson 2002, 219–220). The ". . . intervening half century [after 1948]," commented Samantha Power, "had not been kind to the term [genocide]" (Power 2002, 478).

Although there have been many mass exterminations and genocides committed since 1949, until genocides were committed in the former Yugoslavia (Bosnia), 1992–1995; Rwanda, 1994; and Sierra Leone, 1997, no action was taken to either stop the genocidal actions or try and then punish, if found guilty, the perpetrators.

Some examples of genocides committed with impunity during this time include Pol Pot's slaughter of urban Cambodians and small religious groups; Stalin's mass murder of the Russian Kulaks; the Chinese Communist (Mao Tse-Tung) policy of exterminating Chinese and Tibetans; Pakistan's General Tikka Khan's genocide of the Bangladeshi Bengali Muslims; General Suharto's (Indonesia) mass murder of domestic communists; Guatemalan presidents Garcia and Montt's mass murder of the indigenous Naya; Ethiopia's murder of Ethiopians; the Argentina junta's "dirty war" against their domestic enemies (socialists, communists); Chile's Augusto Pinochet's murdering domestic enemies; Syrian president Hafez Al-Assad's extermination of the Hamas; Iraq's Saddam Hussein's use of poison gas to murder Iraqis, Iranians', and Kurds'; and Sudan's president Omar al-Bashir's effort to exterminate South Sudanese and black Arabs in the Darfur region of the nation. Those political and military leaders responsible for these actions have acted with near-absolute impunity until the last decade of the 20th century.

Ruth-Gaby Vermot Mangold, the president of the Society for Threatened Peoples, said recently: "I've looked at the list of all the genocides of the past (20th) century. One just follows the other [citing genocidal events on Cambodia, Rwanda, Bosnia-Herzegovina, and Darfur]. The international community has failed to prevent genocides, which is the main aim of the convention" (*Human Rights Tribune* 2008).

The reasons for such dramatic disuse of the Genocide Convention were alluded to in Chapter 1. This chapter further explores the problems that have led the world to this ongoing tragedy.

However, with the conviction of Bosnian Serb General Kristic in the International Criminal Tribunal for the former Yugoslavia (ICTY) in a courtroom in The Hague, for war crimes and genocide of Bosnian Muslims in Srebrenica, in August 2001, some internationalists saw the beginning of the path to enforcement of the Genocide Convention. The defendant, Kristic, was sentenced to 46 years in prison (Power 2002, 479, ff). That event, the first person convicted of genocide in the ICTY, came after unpunished genocides in Iraq and Cambodia—the genocide of Kurds by Saddam Hussein in 1988 and the 1975–1979 tragedy in Cambodia—led some nations and dozens of human rights nongovernmental organizations (NGOs) to demand that a criminal court be created to indict and try these genocidist leaders. The wars in the former Yugoslavia was the event that led to some legal action by the UN. (The world's very first conviction for the crime of genocide came in the International Criminal Tribunal, Rwanda [ICTR] in September 1998 when Jean-Paul Akayesu, the mayor of Taba, Rwanda, was found guilty of genocide and crimes against humanity.)

Critics of the ICC and the UN were not convinced that the age of impunity was ending that suddenly.

## Critics of the Genocide Convention

Since 1948, many scholars and critics, because of the politicized birth of the Genocide Convention, have insisted that the Convention is too narrow to be used as a deterrent to state actions that it labeled "genocide." The 1948 Genocide Convention contains no effective enforcement mechanisms. As Juan Mendez, an Argentinian lawyer and president of the International Center for Transitional Justice said in 2008: "The [1948] convention calls for the prevention of genocide, but it doesn't say how" (*Human Rights Tribune* 2008).

The most severe criticism focuses on the definitional problems with the concept of genocide. It excludes political, social, and economic groups. The Convention "does not define genocide, or include objective criteria (such as threshold number of people killed); as a consequence when mass murder takes place, nations avoid labeling the action as genocide" (Goldhagen 2009, 236, ff).

Still other critical observers believe that the term itself has lost Lemkin's original meaning and has become "dangerously commonplace" (quoted in Destexhe 1995). To shock the conscience of the civilized world, genocide "has been misused as synonymous with massacre, oppression and repression, overlooking that what lies behind the image it evokes is the attempted annihilation of the entire Jewish race." The "inevitable consequences of such misuse" (describing a human disaster such as a tsunami that kills hundreds of thousands of innocent persons as a holocaust) are a loss of "intrinsic meaning" and the trivialization of the word itself.

The other side of the genocide concept has also been quite common since the 1940s: *underuse* or *nonuse* of the word itself, and with underuse comes inertia—nonintervention—by the world community when genocides do occur. This silence in the face of mass murder continues to foster impunity for those leaders and perpetrators of genocide into the 21st century.

As one scholar wrote: "In full view [of the mass murders and concentration camps] in Bosnia, the world allowed genocide to be carried out with impunity" (Sells 1998, 25). Another scholar, with respect to the events in Bosnia in the 1990s, asked and answered the question of *why* the Western powers ignored their legal obligations under the Geneva Convention and did nothing to stop Serbia from genocide in Bosnia. The West stood silent, he claimed, for the following reasons:

Geopolitical considerations;
Lack of political will to act;
Political expediency;
State sovereignty and the national security concept;

Fear of the domestic impact in Western nations of their
   soldiers dying for Muslims; and
Prejudice against Muslims by the West. (Boyle
   1996, xix)

Two important omissions in the final version of the 1948
Genocide Convention were the rejection of political and social
groups from the definition of targeted groups. Critics believe that
such an intentional omission has allowed political leaders to murder their opposition after taking power.

In *all* dictatorial nations, the political leaders, whether a
Hitler, a Josef Stalin (Russia), or a Mao Tse-Tung (China), have
*always* targeted their political opponents for extermination. Hitler
targeted the Social Democrats and the Communist Party political
opponents as soon as he became chancellor in 1933. Massacres of
the *political* and *social* opposition in Russia, from the 1920s to the
1940s, and in China, from the 1930s to the 1980s, exterminated
more civilians than did the revolutions themselves in those two
nations. According to the definition of genocide finally approved
after 1948, the intentional targeting and murder of political, economic, and social groups does not constitute genocidal action,
and therefore there was no effort to initiate actions to stop these
millions of executions from taking place over decades.

The weakness of the international political system itself has
been a target of some of the critics. The politics that takes place in
the UN is mostly self-serving activities that do little to deal with
serious problems such as mass murder and genocide. Some critics
argue that the organization should be done away with because "it
is illegitimate and ineffectual and corrupt, and does far too little
to coordinate the world's countries to alleviate misery, including
genocide" (Goldhagen 2009, 592).

Given the continued power of the sovereign nation-state,
there is continual nonintervention *unless* it is in the nation's self-
interest to intervene. Political leaders in these nation-states are
reluctant to place their military in a combat scenario unless it
serves the foreign policy of the nation. Soldiers will be killed in
such an intervention, and the political leaders must explain to an
angry public why their sons and daughters, mothers and fathers,
were killed. The national security explanation holds the criticism
in abeyance for a while.

For example, the deaths of less than two dozen American military in Somalia in 1993, who were there to carry out peacekeeping

functions of the UN, led to a hasty American exit from that war-torn nation. President Clinton and the military refused to sacrifice American armed forces on behalf of the UN's effort to try to control the violence in Somalia. It was not in America's national interest.

After the American military disengaged from Somalia, the new Clinton administration policy was to *deliberately* avoid using the word "genocide" in reference to Rwanda and the former Yugoslavia, even though, in Rwanda, 800,000 civilians were murdered in three months (CBC News 2006). It was not until 2004, when then secretary of state Colin Powell appeared before the U.S. Senate Foreign Relations Committee, that the word "genocide" was uttered by an American political figure.

Talking about the brutal murders of black Sudanese in the Darfur region of the Sudan, he told the senators that the U.S. officials found a "pattern of atrocities committed by the *Janjaweed* and government forces. . . . The evidence leads to the conclusion that genocide has occurred and may still be occurring in Darfur." However, he did not suggest that the United States intervene to stop the genocide although, he said, "the U.S. is doing everything we can to get the Sudanese government to act responsibly" (quoted in CBC News 2006).

## No Enforcement Mechanism to Intervene to Stop Genocide or Apprehend Genocidists

At the present time, there is no enforcement mechanism to intervene in a nation-state where genocide is occurring nor is there a standing military presence to go after the genocidists. Critics belabor this failing: "There is a need for a standing, permanent military force to stop genocide—and [to provide] real punishment of the perpetrators of genocide" (Waller 2007, 284). A person indicted by an ad hoc tribunal or by the new ICC must be apprehended, even if the person is a national leader still in office.

In March 2009, the ICC indicted the sitting president of the Sudan, Omar al-Bashir, but he is still in power and there still has been no interference by the outside world to end the genocide. Although he is careful about his movements, he knows that enforcement of ICC indictments is serendipitous. Therefore, he did not travel to Turkey to attend a conference of Muslim nations in Istanbul. Even though the host nation does not recognize the authority of the ICC and is not a signatory, al-Bashir, cautiously, decided not to attend.

Apprehension of indicted genocidists is extremely difficult, if not impossible, because of the immunity the nation-state provides its citizens and the willingness of the UN and nation-states to accept the inviolability of national sovereignty. Some alleged genocidists escape justice by taking refuge in "friendly" states, protected there by their own security forces and those of the host nation.

In World War I, the German Kaiser sought refuge in Belgium. Even though the Allies wanted him to face trial for waging war in defiance of the Hague Conventions of 1899 and 1907, the Belgian government simply refused to hand the German leader over.

The UN recognized this problem in the early 1990s, about the time the ad hoc tribunals for Yugoslavia and Rwanda were being discussed. In 1993, there was a proposal put forward in the UN for the creation of a Rapid Reaction Force (RRF), "essentially a standing UN multinational military force that would be used to enforce the UN Security Council's peacekeeping responsibilities."

However, although the newly elected U.S. president Bill Clinton enthusiastically supported the idea of an RRF, the military leaders, led by the then chairman of the Joint Chiefs of Staff, Army general Colin Powell, just as strongly rejected the notion. The president bowed to their belief that such a standing force, with foreign generals issuing orders to American forces, would place the American military in jeopardy. Furthermore, in a speech Powell gave in September 1993, he clearly enunciated the Pentagon's unwillingness to participate in a UN multinational military force:

> We have a value system and a cultural system within the armed forces of the U.S. We have this mission: *to fight and win the nation's wars*. . . . Because we are able to fight and win the nation's wars, because we are warriors, we are also uniquely able to do some of these new missions that are coming along [Iraq and Afghanistan]. But we never want to do it in such a way that we lose sight of the focus of why you have armed forces—to fight and win the nation's wars (Powell 1993, 31–59, passim).

At the same moment in 1993, Anthony Lake, President Clinton's foreign affairs advisor, put this policy in even more blunt terms: "Let us be clear: peacekeeping is not at the center of our nation's foreign and defense policy. Our armed forces' primary mission is not to conduct peace operations but to win wars" (Lake 1994).

After Powell and the U.S. generals quashed the idea, the U.S. delegation to the UN informed the secretary general that, although the RRF was needed, the American leaders rejected the creation "at this time": "The U.S. does not plan to earmark forces or assign troops to the UN Security Council permanently under Article 43 of the UN Charter. Given the immediate challenges facing UN peacekeeping, these options are impractical at this time" (Wisner 1993, 69). (Article 43 calls for "all members of the UN to undertake and to make available to the Security Council, on its call and in accordance with a special agreement or agreements, armed forces, assistance, and facilities, including rights of passage, necessary for the purpose of maintaining international peace and security.")

There is, in the 21st century, still no standing military force that can carry out the legal orders of the UN's ad hoc tribunals or of the ICC. Without armed forces' intervening—crossing into the territory of a nation-state, either to stop the ongoing genocide or to arrest those persons indicted by the prosecutor—the impunity concept is the reality. Unless a government voluntarily turns over to the tribunal the indicted defendant (as the Serbian government did when it transported former president Slobodan Milosevic to the ICTY located in The Hague for trial), there is nothing that can be done to the perpetrators of genocide. Although an optimist might argue that the "veil of sovereign statehood has been lifted far enough," to date that seems to be the voicing of hope, not reality (Robertson 2002, 221). The age of impunity has not yet ended.

## Lack of Political and Diplomatic Will by the UN and Major Western Powers

Since the trials of the Nazi and Japanese leaders in the 1940s, the UN, individual nations, and regional organizations have *never* acted to prevent—or stop—a genocide from taking place. (See Chapter 4, which presents a chronology of genocides and mass murders that occurred during these decades.)

For example, the UN peacekeepers in Rwanda were not allowed to suppress the nascent conflict before the genocide took place (Durch 1996, 3–7, passim). In May 1998, four years *after* the genocide ended, UN secretary general Kofi Annan landed in Kigali, the capital of Rwanda. He was not greeted warmly because of his and his organization's role in not intervening when the genocide began. "Instead of finding forgiveness, he received an outright hostile reception from the Rwandan leaders."

The nation's foreign minister, Anastase Gasana, accused the organization of not heeding the clear warnings about the upcoming genocide "and then lacking the political will to intervene once the massacres started. We are interested in knowing who was behind this *lack of will*" (Ball 1999, 187, my emphasis). He was looking at the primary UN official responsible for the inaction. Kofi Annan, in 1994, was the UN's head of peacekeeping and issued the orders to UN commanders in Rwanda not to intervene!

The president of the United States, Bill Clinton (D-1993–2001), also visited Rwanda in 1998. Unlike Annan, he came to apologize for the world's failure to stop the genocide:

> The international community . . . must bear its share of responsibility for this tragedy. We did not act quickly enough after the killing began. We did not immediately call these crimes by their rightful name: genocide. . . . All over the world there were people like me sitting in offices, day after day after day, who did not fully appreciate the depth and the speed with which you were being engulfed by this unimaginable terror (Clinton 1998).

Although the UN Charter gives the Security Council "the primary responsibility for the maintenance of international peace and security" (see "Chapter 7, UN Charter," in Chapter 6, Documents), that organization's leaders rarely implemented this peace enforcement responsibility. The UN "proved powerless to move politicians or diplomats to prevent genocide across the world" until it created the two ad hoc tribunals to examine the events that took place in the former Yugoslavia and Rwanda *after the genocides ended*. Only then, in the mid- and late-1990s (Robertson 2002, 37; see also Waller 2007, 282) was anything done—however minimally—to indict, arrest, and try alleged genocidists.

The crisis in Darfur in the Sudan illuminates this dilemma. Nigerian ambassador Baba Gana Kinaibe spoke with a Canadian Broadcasting Company reporter David McGuffin in September 2006 about the ongoing genocide in that region. At the time, he served as head of the African Union's (AU) Mission in Sudan (AMIS) peacekeeping mission in that nation. After describing the continued bleakness of the situation facing the 7,000-member peacekeeping AU force, he spoke about the weakness of the UN and of the Western powers in helping the AU resolve the problem:

> The AU is committed to staying the course in Darfur. Why we have to leave is simply because we cannot stay. The operation costs us $25 million a month just in terms of allowances and feeding and so on, not to talk of logistics and infrastructure and so on. So, the deal with the international community was that Africa would provide the manpower and the international community will provide the necessary logistics and funding to sustain the operation. *The international community have reneged on that. . . .* So we are caught between the rock and the hard place, as the UN and the government of the Sudan carry on their disputation, the AU force is stranded. . . . *The international community has left Darfur to its fate; they have left the people of Darfur to their fate* (CBC News 2006, my emphasis).

# Possible Solutions to the Weaknesses Associated with Enforcement of the 1948 Genocide Convention

One scholar has argued that, in the last two years of the 20th century, there has been "a revival of the Nuremberg legacy" (Robertson 2002, xxv). He points to a number of events that occurred in that time frame, including the ICC statute agreed to by nearly 120 nations in Rome, Italy, in 1998; the arrest of General Augusto Pinochet, former leader of Chile when thousands of his political enemies "disappeared," in London, England, in October 1998; NATO forces and air power used in Yugoslavia to end the mass killing of Kosovars in 1998; East Timor genocide by Indonesian military stopped in 1999 by interference of the UN; the Hague tribunal's hearing cases involving the genocide and war crimes in the former Yugoslavia begins to receive indicted individuals captured by NATO forces in 1999; Slobodan Milosevic, the former president of Serbia during the 1991–1995 wars, is turned over to the Hague tribunal to face charges of war crimes and genocide; the Lockerbie Agreement between Libya and England signed, and the two defendants allegedly responsible for the air disaster over Scotland are surrendered to stand trial for their alleged terrorist activities in Scotland; and, also in 1999, the crisis in Sierra Leone seemed to be under control as the UN established a war-crimes tribunal (see Robertson 2002, xxvi–xxvii).

For Robertson, all these events suggest the weakening of the concept of state sovereignty and the gradual acceptance by the world community of the concept of the *universal jurisdiction* of the crime of genocide and crimes against humanity. If the crime committed is genocide or a crime against humanity, universal jurisdiction posits that any court anywhere is empowered by international law to try the alleged perpetrator and to punish the person if found guilty, "irrespective of its place of commission or the nationality of the offender or the victims."

The arrest of the Chilean dictator Augusto Pinochet in England after he was indicted in Spain, and the unwillingness of genocidal leaders such as indicted (by the ICC) President al-Bashir to leave the safety of his country, Sudan, for fear of arrest, gives hope for some observers of the international political arena. They hope that the era of impunity from the consequences of such shocking crimes seems to be eroding with these actions by the UN and by individual nation-states.

A review of the types of actions taken by the world community to deal with the consequences of genocide tends to exhibit the opposite reality. Reviewing these actions over the past four decades, suggests other scholars, reveals the continuing strength of the sovereign nation-state. It leads many observers to be less optimistic than Robertson and to maintain that all the domestic and international mechanisms created to respond to the reality of genocide "remain woefully inadequate and extraordinarily controversial" (Human Rights 2008). Although there have been a number of efforts to address the consequences of mass killings and genocide, none of the efforts have been able to resolve the dilemma discussed earlier: the lack of a rapid response military effort to stop the genocide and to capture the persons indicted for their actions. Until this dilemma is resolved in a substantive fashion, the world will continue to witness genocides and mass murder and will be powerless to intervene. For the creators of these possible structures that address the horrors of genocide, there is an effort to balance the need to achieve justice and redress for the victims of genocide with the equally valid need for truth telling by the perpetrators and the victims for the historical record.

## Amnesty

Amnesty is one response to genocide and crimes against humanity that occurred in a nation. After a genocide ends, the new political leaders forgive the perpetrators rather than press for justice. For the new Cambodian leaders, after Pol Pot's genocide, where more than two million Cambodians were executed between 1975 and 1979, a series of trials of the leaders would not allow Cambodia to get beyond that horrible past. "If we bring them to trial it will not benefit the nation, it will only mean a return to civil war. . . . If we put them in prison will this benefit the society or lead to civil war?" said the new Cambodian political leader, Hun Sen (quoted in Mydans 1998).

Said one former Khmer Rouge leader who turned himself in to the new government because of the offer of amnesty: "We must forget the past in order to reach national reconciliation, peace, and stability so we can rebuild our country" (quoted in Mydans 1999). After Pol Pot's death in 1998, other Khmer Rouge leaders came forward to accept amnesty. Prime Minister Hun Sen welcomed them, in his own words, "With bouquets of flowers, not with prisons and handcuffs" (Mydans 1998). To date, although there have been calls for an international tribunal to deal with those who led the genocide in Cambodia, there has been no such action.

The Cambodian response to the genocidal actions of the Khmer Rouge turns justice into a fungible concept, not a universally needed ideal. There are not too many defenders of the amnesty approach to the genocide, although the concept of truth and reconciliation commissions, actually used in South Africa and nearly two dozen other nations, is a close enough concept. However, both, argue the critics, do not provide justice for the victims and for the national community. They maintain that "some degree of justice is increasingly a precondition of peace and reconciliation." If genocidists are immunized from prosecution for their intentional acts, as happened in Cambodia, the inaction "corrodes the fabric of society" (Stanley Foundation 1998, 11). If impunity from any punishment is a primary goal of international law, "expediency has been placed above both principle and pragmatism.

There will be no lasting peace without justice" (McDonald 1998, 33).

However, between 1998 and 2005, due to worldwide pressure on Cambodian leaders to do more than provide amnesty for the Khmer Rouge genocidist leaders, intense deliberations were held between the leaders and the UN. As a consequence, in 2005, a special court was created—with a majority of Cambodian judges sitting in judgment—to hear cases involving the actions of the Khmer Rouge leaders.

Under a 2003 agreement between the two sides, it was agreed that the trial would be held for a period of three years— after the UN raised the needed funds for the special court. From the beginning the court structure has been criticized by NGOs and nations because a majority of the judges and prosecutors are Cambodian. In April 2003, one major NGO, Human Rights Watch, said, "So long as the Cambodian government continues to exercise direct control over the Cambodian judiciary, any tribunal with a majority of Cambodian judges and a Cambodian prosecutor will fail the most basic test of credibility with Cambodians and the international community" (Dworkin 2005).

Although the world community wanted another ad hoc tribunal similar to the ones listening to cases in the Yugoslavia and Rwanda tribunals (see below)—where international jurists were hearing the cases—Cambodian leaders refused to move in that direction. They did agree, however, that "at least one international judge would be required for conviction." The trials were scheduled to begin in 2006; however, the first trial began in 2009 in the court called the Extraordinary Chambers in the Courts of Cambodia (ECCC) when the leader of the infamous Tuol Seng torture and death prison, Kaing Gech Eav (Duch) faced trial for crimes against humanity and genocide. (He was charged with ordering the torture and deaths of 12,000 Cambodian prisoners.) In late July 2010, the hybrid Khmer Rouge tribunal sentenced the convicted Duch to 35 years in prison for his crimes. However, the tribunal took into account time served and, with leniency, sentenced him to a commuted term of 19 years in prison (Chun Sakada, "Hun Sen Praises Tribunal Verdict in Duch Case," Khmer NZ, August 4, 2010, at www.khmernz.blogspot.com.).

Very few—five—Khmer Rouge leaders faced trial, however. The Cambodian coprosecutor opposed the effort by the international prosecutor to add six additional suspects for trial. He "cited Cambodia's 'past instability' and the 'need for national reconciliation' as the reasons for rejecting bringing charges against additional suspects" (Human Rights Watch 2009).

Whether or not there will be "political manipulation" by the Cambodian government is an unanswered question. However, most NGOs and the UN itself are not sanguine about the results of these trials. Without an independent judiciary, they believe that justice will not be reached for the victims of genocide.

## Truth and Reconciliation Commissions

Truth and Reconciliation Commissions (TRC) are a dramatic alternative to national and international tribunals. These commissions hear testimony from both victims and perpetrators in order to provide the nation with an accounting of the events that occurred during the genocide. They are not courts of law, and the commissioners do not have the power to imprison anyone. The final report presents recommendations to the new government that, hopefully, will repair the social fabric of the community and promote national reconciliation—without retribution against the perpetrators.

No other concern has dominated discussions of truth commissions, especially from legal scholars, as has the issue of justice. For many, the proper response to the perpetrators of human rights abuses, violence, ethnic cleansing, or genocide must be criminal proceedings by some sort of tribunal, a court of law duly authorized to render judicial dispositions: to establish justiciable facts of the matter, to render verdicts, and if called for, to punish. However, truth commissions (including the more ambitious TRCs) cannot by their nature deliver this sort of justice, and so a significant part of the literature is devoted to the delineation (and defense) of quasi-justice forms and entities, among them "transitional justice," "restorative justice," or "retroactive justice," most of which aim, in the end, to move away from criminal verdicts—retributive justice—and forward to "truth-seeking" and reconciliation. These alternative forms of justice mean that the work of truth commissions falls somewhere in the morally, politically, and emotionally fraught continuum between "vengeance and forgiveness." A great deal of the controversy, not to mention passion, that surrounds the workings and assessment of these commissions by different parties, has to do with the tension existing between the two poles of this continuum: the human impulses to wreak vengeance or to offer forgiveness, for terrible wrongs done. The tension has to do as well with arguments about whether notions of "justice" and "truth" are related.

More than 40 nations have chosen the TRC path after the blood of many thousands has been shed by the perpetrators in power at an earlier time. This large group of nations have opted for hopes for reconciliation rather than courts of law to deal with the perpetrators of injustice. The complete list of nations who have used, through 2009, some version of the TRC follows (where there was a specific focus of the TRC, it is noted below.):

Uganda, 1974, disappearances
Brazil, 1979
Bolivia, 1982
Zimbabwe, 1983
Argentina, 1983, disappearances
Peru, 1986, massacre of prisoners
Uganda, 1986, human rights violations
Nepal, 1990, disappearances
Chile, 1990, disappearances
Chad, 1990
Germany, 1992, communist dictatorship
El Salvador, 1992
Ethiopia, 1993
Rwanda, 1993
Sri Lanka, 1995, disappearances
Haiti, 1995
Germany, 1995
Burundi, 1995
South Africa, 1995
Ecuador, 1996
Guatemala, 1997, disappearances
Rwanda, 1999

Nigeria, 1999, human rights violations
Uruguay, 2000, violating the peace
South Korea, 2000, suspicious deaths
Ivory Coast, 2000
Panama, 2001
Peru, 2001
Serbia and Montenegro, 2002
East Timor, 2002
Ghana, 2003
Democratic Republic of the Congo, 2003
Chile, 2003, torture, political imprisonment
Algeria, 2003, disappearances
Paraguay, 2004
Morocco, 2004
Liberia, 2006
Ecuador, 2007, address the impunity issue
Solomon Islands, 2009
Kenya, 2009

Clearly, the whole area of reconciliation and forgiveness remains a contested one, raising many more questions in the literature than answers. One such question is this: Is contrition and forgiveness, and even reconciliation, adequate for a nation's "coming to terms with its past"? One premise of most truth commissions is to answer this question in the affirmative. Another is to argue that reconciliation, so crucial to peace and stability, is part of how these commissions successfully affect the transition from regimes based upon violent oppression to those operating under the democratic rule of law.

## Replace the UN with a Collective Humanitarian Intervention Organization

The UN international organization "is illegitimate and ineffectual and corrupt; and does far too little to coordinate the world's countries to alleviate misery, including genocide" (Goldhagen 2009, 592). One writer summed up this critical view of the UN in the following words regarding the bloodshed in Argentina: "The UN has rattled its vocal swords, threatening sanctions but ultimately sending out a watered-down resolution condemning human rights abuses that the ruling junta duly ignored" (Cussler 2010, 20).

As already briefly noted, some critics argue that the UN should be replaced because of its continuing inability to deal with mass murder and genocide until after the murders have been committed. The new organization must be able to provide order, through military humanitarian intervention, in the international community and to end the impunity of perpetrators because of the continuing dynamic of the nation-state. Clearly, this is a daunting task—perhaps an impossible one—and those who call for the liquidation of the UN are expressing their frustration at the continuing futility of the UN and its member nations in stopping or ending genocide and mass murder.

They point out that, on a number of occasions in the post-Nuremberg world, genocide *was stopped* by military intervention (see, for example, Jones 2006, 395–396). In 1971, India intervened in East Pakistan to end the mass murders that were taking place, and the Pol Pot genocide in Cambodia ended when Vietnam invaded Cambodia in 1979. Another case in 1979 was the halt of mass murder in Idi Amin's Uganda when the Tanzanian military crossed the border and ended his dictatorship. A final example, this time of a regional military intervention, was the NATO intercession that stopped Serb forces from continuing to murder Kosovo civilians in 1999.

Some maintain, given the genocides that occurred in Europe and the Far East during the Second World War and the 1948 Genocide Convention that made the crime of genocide one of universal jurisdiction, that "humanitarian" military interventions are required. A collective institution must be created to "effectively intervene not only after genocides are underway but also in *advance*—to anticipate and prevent genocide" (Nardin and Williams 2006, 4, my emphasis):

> [There is a shift in emphasis] from the permissibility of intervening to the *responsibility* to intervene. [There] is an emerging conviction that the response to humanitarian crises needs to be collective, coordinated, and preemptive—in a word, *institutionalized*. . . . [There is] a consensus that genocide, ethnic cleansing, and other atrocities are the world's business—as their inclusive name, "crimes against humanity," implies (Nardin and Williams 2006, 3, my emphasis).

This issue of preemptive military intervention by a state or a collective organization, to prevent or to halt the mass murder of innocent people who are citizens of another state, is one that will continue to be discussed so long as genocides fester and then brutally occur in the world, ending only when they run their brutal course or when war breaks out and the genocidists are defeated.

These UN critics, however, do not seriously address the great good that *agencies* of the UN have accomplished in the face of genocide and the massive uprooting of ethnic communities.

UN specialized agencies, such as UNICEF, The World Food Program, the Office of High Commissioner for Human Rights, and others, have been "extraordinarily effective" in responding to the effects of mass murder and genocide (Jones 2006, 394). Furthermore, the UN, although its leaders acknowledge that little has been done by the institution to stop genocide from taking place, has done a great deal to repair the damages after the bloodletting ends through its *peace-building* efforts. This new concept emerged in force in the 1980s. As stated by then UN secretary general Kofi Annan, peace-building is

> ... [t]he creation or strengthening of national institutions, monitoring elections, promoting human rights, providing for reintegration and rehabilitation programs, as well as creating conditions for resumed development. . . . It aims to build on, add to, or reorient such activities in ways that are designed to reduce the risk of a resumption of conflict and contribute to creating conditions most conducive to reconciliation, reconstruction, and recovery (International Commission on Intervention and State Sovereignty 2001, 40).

## National Legal Tribunals to Try Indicted Genocidists

National legal tribunals to try indicted genocidists seemingly have "certain advantages" over the ad hoc ICTs created in the 1990s (Jones 2006, 368). He points out a major disadvantage of such trials: "the infrastructure for administering justice [in Rwanda, the Sudan, Bosnia, Ethiopia, et al.] may be sorely inadequate." A nation's criminal justice system is in place; there are precedents to follow; there are prosecutors and defense attorneys and judges to handle the cases. They have been used by a few nations in order to *quickly* try, convict, and punish those involved in the nation's genocide. Because of the extreme slowness of the two ad hoc international tribunals to bring indicted persons to The Hague for trial, Rwanda, for example, used its judicial criminal law system to deal with the Hutu perpetrators. Justice could be meted out quickly and, unlike the UN-created tribunals, the death penalty was available as punishment for some of the leaders. Critics argue, however, that in many instances involving these courts—Rwanda and Ethiopia are two examples offered—there has been a lack of due process evidenced in court because of the evident eagerness to punish the perpetrators (Ratner and Abrams 2001, 29).

Ironically, Rwanda was the only nation to vote against the UN's creation of an ICT to deal with those Hutu leaders who were responsible for the 1994 genocide.

## Ad Hoc ICTs

Ad hoc ICTs to try indicted genocidists were created in 1993 and 1994 to deal with the horror of mass murders in the former

Yugoslavia (ICTY) and Rwanda (ICTR). These were the first ad hoc ICTs created since Nuremberg and Tokyo. However, as one scholar pointed out, "[I]t is one of history's ironies that the ICT for Yugoslavia was created to deflect accusations of Western complacency in the face of genocide" (Jones 2006, 366).

To date, they are the only such ICCs established to deal with the consequences of genocide in Bosnia and Rwanda. When the first defendant, Dusko Tadic, faced justice before the ICTY in 1996, some "viewed [it] as a deeply symbolic moment; the first sign of a seismic shift from diplomacy to legality, in the conduct of world affairs" (Robertson 2002, 222). However, these two ICTs have faced the same problems as have other legal efforts to deal with the consequences of genocide: many indicted defendants are still living in their nations or have fled to nations that protect them, with no real effort to turn them over to the courts.

Also, although it took time for the tribunals to establish principles and protocols, they have added precedents applicable to international law, especially with regard to the definition of genocide. The ICTR, in the *Akayesu* decision of 1998, defined rape as a form of genocide. This new addition to the concept of genocide "reflects decades of successful feminist mobilization around the issue of rape, including ground-breaking analyses of rape in war and genocide" (Jones 2006, 367–368).

## Hybrid ICCs to Deal with Genocidists

By the turn of the 21st century, another legal international innovation was introduced to try to provide justice for the victims of mass murder and genocide. It was a legal tribunal composed of national and international jurists. Their task was to apply international legal rules to deal with those who committed genocide. A majority of international judges sit, with domestic jurists in the minority (except for Cambodia), to hear cases. The first such hybrid international court was created to deal with the mass murders that had taken place in Sierra Leone during the decade of the 1990s.

A civil war led to the deaths of nearly 100,000 civilians and the departure of nearly 600,000 refugees to neighboring African states. In January 2002, the new government agreed to the creation of the special hybrid court. Its task was to apply the law to deal with mass murderers. Additionally, the new government created a TRC. It provided amnesty for the perpetrators for their actions between 1991 and 1996. (The special court dealt with actions by the rebels after the 1996 peace treaty was broken by them.) Article 26 of the Lome Treaty laid out the purpose of the TRC: "to provide a forum for both the victims and the perpetrators of crimes against humanity to tell their story, get a clear picture of the past in order to facilitate genuine healing and reconciliation." The TRC's major goal was to heal the wounds of the small nation after a decade of civil war.

In another part of the world, a second hybrid court to deal with genocide and mass murder was created. The UN–East Timorese Crimes Tribunal consisted of East Timorese and international jurists selected by the UN to try to mete out justice for the East Timorese who suffered and died at the hands of the Indonesian military and rogue paramilitary forces.

East Timor is a very small territory administered by Portugal until 1975. It lies between Australia and Indonesia in the Timor Sea. In 1974, civil war broke out between those who wanted independence and those who wanted to join the Indonesian nation. Because of the war, Portugal left in 1975, and Indonesian troops invaded East Timor, calling the territory the 27th province of Indonesia. For a quarter century, Indonesian troops occupied East Timor, and terror rained down on the local population at the hands of the military. Between 1975 and 1999, more than 25 percent of the population—nearly 400,000 persons—was murdered. Another 300,000 civilians fled their homes and found themselves in West Timor.

In 1999, Indonesia, pressured by the UN, agreed to have the remaining population choose between independence and local autonomy within the Indonesian nation. Although terror was used by the military to coerce the population to remain in Indonesia, 79 percent of the voters voted for independence. After the vote, there was more violence until a UN peace force was sent to the territory and restored peace. After these events, an International Commission of Inquiry, reporting to the UN, called for the establishment of a hybrid special court to deal with the murders, massacres, assassinations, rapes, other human rights violations, and deportations that took place after the vote in 1999. Ironically, although the tribunal issued indictments against a number of Indonesian defendants, Indonesia refused to extradite these indicted individuals to East Timor to stand trial.

In still another territory, Kosovo, a province of Serbia, the UN, after hostilities ended between the ethnic Albanians (Muslims) and the Serb forces (Orthodox) in 1999, created a peace plan that gave Kosovo "substantial autonomy within the Federal Republic of Yugoslavia" (essentially Serbia). Because of continuing violence between the ethnic and religious groups since 1999, the UN has remained to provide administrative, police, and humanitarian aid to the province. Furthermore, the court system has been internationalized in Kosovo, with international prosecutors and judges, including Americans, working to ensure that there is no ethnic bias in the administration of justice.

In two other areas of the world, Cambodia and Afghanistan, the UN and other nongovernmental agencies have tried to create hybrid courts to hear cases with impartiality. However, as noted, Cambodia has rejected such an arrangement for dealing with the Khmer Rouge leaders who received amnesty and Afghanistan's tribal leaders had already granted amnesty to Taliban leaders and followers.

In all these cases, there was no external intervention while the mass murders and genocide and other crimes against humanity were taking place. Only after the killings stopped were there efforts to provide some justice for the victims and the survivors. The dilemma remains in the international system: There is no enforcement of the international treaties; there is no stopping of the murders, rapes, and deportations while they are happening.

## Mediation between Warring Parties

This is the basic protocol the UN has been using since the late 1940s. Because the organization still cannot quickly introduce a rapid response military action to stop the genocide and has been extremely slow in creating ad hoc ICCs, the UN relies on diplomacy and negotiation to end the war and the genocide.

In Switzerland, in 2008, a conference, organized by the Society for Threatened Peoples, took place to assess the reasons for continuing genocides after 1948. Its president, Ruth-Gaby Vermot-Mangold, stated, [The Genocide Convention is thus far limited] "to mediation and peace initiatives with rebels, government, and getting the various parties sitting around a table—the Geneva Convention, despite everything, is still an instrument for that" Ruth-Gaby Vermot-Mangold, "Value of UN Genocide Convention Questioned," (*Human Rights Tribune*, December 17, 2008), in Institutional Center for Transitional Justice, www.ictj.org/en/news/coverage/article/2187.html.

Vermont-Mangold and other leaders of NGOs believe that "various ideas and creativity" can work to end genocide. She believes that negotiations with the perpetrators of genocide are necessary for an end to their actions. For example, in Darfur she has engaged women's groups to talk with "offenders' mothers to *try to get them to talk some sense to their sons*" (*Human Rights Tribune* 2008, my emphasis).

These creative ideas, however, reflect the ongoing weakness of the institution and its leading nation-states. There is no possibility of intervening to stop a genocide or mass murder; the institution can only provide peacekeepers when there is successful mediation between the warring sides or when diplomacy and sanctions work.

## The Permanent ICC, 1998, 2002

World history was made in 1998 when, in Rome, Italy, more than 160 nation-states and more than 200 NGOs, led by UN secretary general Kofi Annan, met to discuss the possibility of creating a permanent ICC. When the conference ended, there was a treaty that, when ratified by 60 UN member states, would have the ICC come into existence. This formal ratification occurred in 2002.

The modern movement toward the creation of such an ICC began after World War I ended. The 1919 Versailles Peace Treaty contained an article that called for the creation of such a tribunal in order to bring before the international bar of justice Germans accused of committing war crimes in violation of the 1899 and 1907 Hague treaties. However, the Americans opposed such a court and the victorious allies, "in the interest of regional stability and political agendas," went along with the American policy makers. Noting this change, one scholar bitterly wrote that the Allies

> exemplified the sacrifice of justice on the altars of international and domestic politics of the allies. [They] missed the opportunity to establish an international system of justice that would have functioned independently of political considerations to ensure uncompromised justice (Bassiouni 1997, 20–21).

In 1926, the newly established League of Nations—which the U.S. Senate rejected—initiated another effort to create a permanent international criminal court. However, it did not get acted on by the member states. After the Nuremberg and Tokyo trials ended in the late 1940s, there was once again renewed interest by UN member states in a permanent ICC that would hear only grievous cases involving waging an aggressive war, genocide, crimes against humanity, and war crimes. Article VI of the Genocide Convention provided that individuals accused of genocide "shall be tried in a competent tribunal of the State in the territory of which the act was committed *or by such international tribunal as may have jurisdiction*" (my emphasis).

Inherent in this language was an important international legal concept that became part of the 1998 Rome Treaty: *complementarity*. If the nation that experienced genocide was unwilling or unable to bring to justice the perpetrators, then an ICT could act in its stead.

The UN, at the same time the 1948 Genocide Convention was being drafted and debated, mandated that the International Law Commission (ILC) codify the Nuremberg Principles and draft a statute for the establishment of a permanent ICC. Drafts were introduced in 1951 and 1953 in the General Assembly, but no action was taken because of the recent onset of the Cold War between the Soviet Union and its allies and the United States along with its allies. It was not until the collapse of the Soviet Union in 1989 that the idea of an ICC once again emerged in UN debates. In 1992, the ILC was once again asked to prepare a working draft of a permanent ICC.

One month after a draft of the statute was presented in November 1994 to the UN, the General Assembly created an ad hoc committee to review the critical issues presented in the ILC draft. In 1995, the committee recommended the establishment of a UN preparatory committee (PrepCom) that would hold a series of meetings to refine and redraft the ILC draft.

Between 1996 and 1998, the PrepCom held six meetings with member states and a drafting committee began to meet in the Netherlands to redraft the treaty in light of PrepCom discussions. Their primary focus was the definition of core crimes that would be within the ICC's jurisdiction. These core crimes were those that had universal jurisdiction: war crimes, crimes against humanity, genocide, and wars of aggression. After addressing other controversial issues such as the relationship between national sovereignty and international court jurisdiction, as well as the relationship of this independent criminal tribunal with the UN Security Council, a final draft statute was presented to Kofi Annan, the new secretary general of the UN. The draft was almost 200 pages in length and included 13 parts and 116 articles.

The secretary general then announced that between June 15 and July 17, 1998, a Rome Conference on the establishment of a permanent ICC would meet to possibly finalize and then approve the statute. Of the then 185 member states of the UN, 161 nations sent representatives to Rome for this historic meeting. In addition to the 161 nations represented, there were 235 NGOs in attendance and who, after they all coalesced under the Coalition for an Independent Criminal Court (CICC), provided critical assistance in the month-long effort to agree on the language of the statute. However, in this endeavor, the concept of national sovereignty loomed over the sessions. As the London *Economist* editorialized:

> After four years of intense negotiations among some 120 countries, the effort to set up the world criminal court has run smack into the ambivalence that has always been felt by the world's biggest powers about international law: they are keen to have it apply to others in the name of world order, but loathe to submit to restrictions on their own sovereignty (New World Court 1998, 16).

The "heart of the debate" then—and now—was "the scope of the UN's Security Council involvement in deciding whether or not the ICC takes up a particular case." Could one of the five permanent members of the Security Council (United States, England, France, China, and Russia) have *veto power* over the ICC's ability to investigate and to prosecute war criminals and genocidists (Goldman 1998, 16)? In this regard, the role of the United States was very clear: There must be veto power over the ICC held by the five permanent members of the Security Council!

However, the U.S. position on the critical issues debated and incorporated into the Rome Treaty was always the negative one—and always in the minority when the votes were cast by the nations attending the Rome meeting. These controversial issues were found in Part 2 of the statute, containing 15 articles (5–20), all of them focused on "Jurisdiction, Admissibility, and Applicable Law."

Articles 5 and 12, the jurisdiction articles, stated that the ICC "shall be limited to the most serious crimes of concern to the international community as a whole (genocide, war crimes, and crimes against humanity). Seventy-five percent of the nations voted for *automatic jurisdiction* for all three core crimes. The United States, in the minority, voted for automatic jurisdiction only for genocide.

Article 15 addressed the power of the prosecutor. Eighty-three percent of the states voted for the prosecutor to have independent power to initiate an investigation and then, if necessary, to initiate actions against the perpetrators. Article 13 enabled the Security Council or a state that is party to the treaty (termed a "State Party") to refer cases to the prosecutor for possible action. The prosecutor was checked internally by having to gain approval for his actions by the Chambers (judges whose task was to review the case built by the prosecutor) at an early stage in the proceedings of the ICC. Article 18 allowed an "interested party" to challenge the admissibility of a case before the ICC at an early stage of the proceedings.

The Security Council, in Article 16, was able to defer ICC cases for one year when necessary for "peacekeeping purposes." Fifty-three nations voted for the one-year deferral; the United States and four other nations voted for the "unspecified number of years" Security Council option.

In order for the ICC to succeed in its effort to punish genocidists, the world's powerful nations, especially the United States, must support the general concept of such a permanent international judicial organization, accept the ICC's legal jurisdiction, and assist in the apprehension of persons indicted for crimes against humanity and genocide. This new court faces many challenges, most significantly the concept of national sovereignty. The ICC's opponents, especially the United States, argue that the court infringes upon the prerogatives of national sovereignty by placing their political and military leaders and their military forces "in jeopardy of being indicted for war crimes" (Ball 1999, 9). (Chapter 3 focuses on the problems American political and military leaders have with a permanently sitting ICC.) Robertson hopes that the ICC will succeed. However, it will "succeed once it teaches nation-states to live with the idea that justice, in respect to crimes against humanity [and genocide], is non-negotiable" (Robertson 2002, 307).

Critics of the ICC scoff at the views of the optimists. They are of the belief that the new creation is not strong enough to end nation-state impunity when its leaders order genocide against a minority group. Only armed force can prevent or stop genocide from occurring and the ICC does not have that mechanism built into the Rome Treaty. To disregard the vital role of the Security Council is a fatal flaw in the Rome Treaty and the ICC. If the ICC has any chance of success, it must reflect a balancing of international idealism with the *realpolitik* of the still very potent nation-state system.

The major opposition to the ICC and other suggested innovations that would strengthen international criminal law was the United States, after the fall of the Soviet Union, the world's only superpower. Chapter 3 examines this issue, looking at some of the strategies used by the United States to nullify the impact of the ICC.

While the U.S. policy makers in the White House, Congress, and the Pentagon sought to weaken or destroy the ICC, by 2009 there were 110 member countries. More than six years after opening its doors, the ICC began its first trial in The Hague. Thomas Lubanga, a Congolese warlord, was in the dock, charged with war crimes, "including commandeering children under the age of 15 and sending them into war to maim and kill."

The reasons for the long delay in getting down to business were "the turf wars within the court, bitter legal squabbles and irritation among trial judges [that] had almost torpedoed the case" (Simons 2009, A1). In addition to the charges against Mr. Lubanga, ICC prosecutors have also filed charges, in 2009, against war crimes suspects in Sudan, Uganda, and the Central African Republic, and an arrest warrant was issued in March 2009 for Sudanese president Omar Hassan al-Bashir. Furthermore, the ICC's investigators are conducting preliminary examinations regarding alleged war crimes incidents in Kenya, Sri Lanka, Colombia, the Ivory Coast, and Gaza.

In the summer of 2010, the ICC will have had its first review conference. In addition to the grave problems the United States has created for the ICC, the chief prosecutor of the ICC, Luis Moreno-Ocampo, an Argentinean jurist (who taught law at Harvard Law School), has been responding to criticisms that the Court only goes after rights violators in weak countries. Critics of the ICC have raised concerns that the institution has done little to "build a stronger international justice system" and that the ICC should expand its purpose ("ending impunity for war crimes") to helping weak nations develop their own national court systems (Franchi 2009, 1).

Furthermore, a recent ICC action that is sure to anger NATO forces, especially the American commanders and their troops, concerns Afghanistan, one of the 110 nations to ratify the Rome Statute. Moreno-Ocampo has noted that because Afghanistan is a member state, the ICC has "normal jurisdiction" and that the court's investigators are conducting preliminary investigations regarding "collateral damage" incidents and allegations of torture committed by NATO forces.

## The *Gacaca* Trials in Rwanda

The *gacaca* trials in Rwanda have been taking place since 2005 to bring the perpetrators of genocide some kind of justice—as well as moving the nation beyond its recent, bloody history. After the 1994 genocide, the new government detained more than 100,000 persons suspected of involvement in the genocide. However, the Rwandan courts were not capable of hearing these cases because of the huge mass of suspects held in jails across Rwanda. The solution to the crisis was an age-old Rwandan judicial custom that was reworked to end the human bottleneck the government faced. The solution was a modern version of the *gacaca* trial.

> For centuries, Rwandans would select well-respected elders in their community who would sit on *umucaca*— covered ground—to resolve disputes among certain members of the community. *Gacaca* is a derivative of that word. It means "on the hilltop," referring to these venerated open air community courts. In 2001, the government began using this mechanism to deal with its overcrowded prison population of suspected genocidists (Jones 2006, 370). In its modern form, more than 260,000 lay judges were elected from within the community to sit on nine-member panels in *gacaca* sessions "with the mission not of settling petty disputes, but of hearing and recording testimonies from community members who saw and witnessed what happened during the genocide; who killed who, who stole what, and so on" (Rwanda Development Gateway 2010).

After gathering and reviewing this information, the judges— both Hutu and Tutsi, who come from different levels in society—sit in their respective villages and preside over trials of genocide suspects, depending on the category of their crime. In 1996, two years after the slaughter of Tutsis, the Rwanda parliament enacted and voted a genocide law dividing genocide suspects into four categories:

1. Suspects whose deeds during the genocide put them among the planners, organizers, instigators, leaders, and supervisors of the genocide
2. Suspects who participated in physical attacks that resulted in the death of the victim
3. Suspects accused of terrible assaults that did not result in the death of someone, and
4. Suspects accused of looting, theft, or other crimes related to property.

"Gacaca courts have jurisdiction over genocide suspects that fall between categories 2 and 4. Each gacaca jurisdiction is made up of a general assembly, a coordinating committee, a seat and a president. A gacaca court general assembly is comprised of every adult (18 years and above) who resides within a cell in which that particular court sits" (Rwanda Development Gateway 2010).

The trial is a version of a TRC. Victims and perpetrators confront each other and speak about the event that occurred in 1994. However, there is no death penalty if persons are found guilty of participating in the genocide. Instead, the sentences received by persons found guilty "emphasize redress through service to the community: helping to build homes, . . . repairing schools and hospitals, and performing agricultural work" (Jones 2006, 371). The government's goal was to provide some kind of justice to victims and move the nation beyond its brutal history. In 2005, thousands of these courts began to hear cases in the effort to end the problem and reconcile the nation's population.

# The Critical Role of International Nongovernmental Organizations in Encouraging and Drafting International Human Rights Conventions and Taking Actions to Prevent Genocide

Claude E. Welch Jr. wrote about a significant change in international politics: "*State sovereignty has been persistently and progressively undermined by NGOs. . . .* States have not been *displaced* by non-state actors; but, without question, they have been *supplemented*, often extensively, by them" (Welch 2001, 262–263, my emphasis).

Although it can be difficult to categorize NGOs by specific activities, they can be broadly classified as operational or campaigning. Campaigning NGOs influence the international political system to achieve large-scale change. Operational NGOs use direct projects to achieve small-scale change.

There has been an explosive growth of NGOs since the end of World War II. Prior to that time, there were few NGOs, and only one had reached worldwide attention: the International Committee of the Red Cross (ICRC). In 1956 there were 973 NGOs functioning in a different number of ways. By 1968, there were 1,899 such groups. In 1981, there were 4,265 nongovernmental actors at work in the world; in 1996, the number had increased to nearly 5,500 NGOs. In 2010, there are over 10,000 major NGOs functioning across the world. Including NGOs in nearly every nation-state, local as well as national and international, there are almost 50,000 agencies. For example, Amnesty International, housed in London, has 4,300 local groups and national sections in 55 nations, "some of them with 100,000 or more members" (Amnesty International 1999, 377).

NGOs serve a number of different functions that impact sovereign states, including authoritarian regimes. Disaster relief, developmental aid, and humanitarian assistance NGOs such as CARE and Oxfam, "generally cooperate even with rights-abusing governments in order to gain access and distribute relief" (Welch 2001, 270). Human rights international nongovernmental organizations (INGOs) such as Amnesty International, International Human Rights Law Group, International Commission of Jurists, and Human Rights Watch, who are concerned about and target civil and political abuses, reject any formal association and dependence on governments because, generally, the governments are the *targets* of these organizations.

Some scholars have identified at least six separate functions of NGOs:

> Standard setting for human rights both locally and globally;
>
> Providing information through research, information gathering and documenting abuses;
>
> Evaluation and disseminating of their findings through reports;

Lobbying against governmental actions that infringe human rights and trying to transform public opinion on these human rights issues;

Provide assistance to victims, legal and emergency humanitarian relief; and

Moral condemnation or, less often, praise for state actions (Scoble 1984).

One example of lobbying by an NGO is the following Internet message from Amnesty International USA. It concerns a particular human rights issue regarding open and fair trials, even for those who are allegedly terrorists. It advocates action that would impact governmental actions. It also raises funds for its continuing efforts in addressing human rights injustices. Part of one message to the public, sent in an e-mail, states

The White House is playing political football with the 9/11 terror trials. Don't let our government cave in to fear. Give Amnesty the firepower it needs to raise the public outcry in defense of justice.

For human rights groups, the first *major task* is standard setting, that is, trying to do what sovereign states have done in the past—"establishing international norms for state behavior, set forth in legally binding treaties that have been negotiated and ratified by governments" (Welch 2001, 3). For example, two norms that have been targeted for decades by NGOs is to have an international treaty that defines and prohibits torture (The Convention Against Torture and other forms of Cruel Inhuman or Degrading Treatment or Punishment, 1984) and to create a treaty that bans the use of land mines globally (The Convention on the Prohibition of the Use, Stockpiling, Production, and Transfer of Anti-Personnel Mines and on Their Destruction, 1997). This effort led to the awarding of the Nobel Peace Prize to the person and NGO responsible for successfully drafting and lobbying successfully for such a ban (although the United States has still not signed the treaty). In all, more than 1,200 NGOs took part in the passage of the Anti-Landmines Convention.

The second major task is monitoring, researching, disseminating, and promoting information they have collected regarding a human rights abuse. The third task is *advocating for change*: the establishment of norms, then the research and documentation and reports, and finally, advocacy and lobbying by NGOs until the civil or political abuse is addressed by a nation-state or an international organization such as the UN. As already seen, more than 300 human rights NGOs attended and vigorously participated in the 1998 Rome Conference that led to the passage of the statute creating the ICC.

To accomplish their goals, the NGOs must have financial and human resources. There a number of ways these nongovernmental agencies raise the money needed to continue their work: donations from individuals, governments (although human rights NGOs eschew this source of funding), foundations such as the Ford Foundation and the Rockefeller Foundation, and money generated through the payment of membership dues.

There are, however, limitations to the success of NGOs. For example, Welsh has written, "the severity of abuses [to indigenous Maya] in Guatemala and the seemingly minimal impact of human rights NGOs during more than a decade of major repression seem to underscore their limitations: NGOs have generally proven far more effective in raising awareness about abuses than in directly resolving them" (Welch 2001, 14).

However, there has been a shifting of power in international relations since the full-blown emergence of the INGO after World War II. Through the research and dissemination and lobbying of these non-governmental organizations, international law has undergone some significant shifts in the effort to protect citizens from abuses by governments. Chapter 7 provides a great deal of information about the number and scope of NGO activity.

## Operational and Campaigning NGOs

Operational NGOs sustain their programs and projects by mobilizing resources: financial donations, materials, and volunteer labor. To organize these resources, these NGOs usually maintain a field staff and headquarters. For campaigning NGOs, fundraising is still necessary, but on a smaller scale. It symbolically strengthens the donors' identification with the cause. More important is persuading people to donate their time; successful campaigning NGOs have the ability to mobilize large numbers of people for certain issues and events (Willets 2002).

Fundraising, mobilization of supporters, organizing special events, courting the media, and managing a headquarters are activities common to both organizing and campaigning NGOs. Only the major actions, implementing projects or holding demonstrations, are different. In reality, however, these lines are often crossed. When projects are not making the expected impact, operational NGOs often move into campaigning. For example, an environmental operational NGO may support campaign networks. Similarly, campaigning NGOs often feel they cannot ignore the immediate practical problems in their policy domain. A human rights NGO may have programs assisting the victims of discrimination and injustice.

## Other Categories of NGOs

Other types of NGOs use variants of these two primary functions. Research institutes, for example, increase knowledge and understanding (a form of operational programming). They could promote an academic, nonpolitical issue and/or disseminate information for campaigning purposes. Professional associations, trade unions, recreational groups, and other organizations provide program activities for their members. Sometimes, these organizations also campaign to enhance their economic interests and status.

# The Perennial Clash between Justice and Sovereignty

At the core of all these international and national efforts to deal with the consequences of genocide and war crimes is the perennial clash between justice and national sovereignty. To date, the national sovereignty concept has been a successful tool to blunt efforts by internationalists to provide a working justice system to deal with some of the dilemmas brought on by war crimes, genocide, and crimes against humanity. However, especially since the 1970s, the proliferation of human rights INGOs has had an impact on the once-sacrosanct concept of state sovereignty. Advocating changes regarding human rights has become the norm across the globe. And there have been many success stories showing how NGOs can influence public opinion around the globe to call for adoption of the norms addressed by the nongovernmental organizations. However, as the next chapter will show, there are still powerful nations whose leadership continues to reject the standards called for by INGOs and other sovereign states.

The events of the 21st century, especially those triggered by the many hundreds of INGOs, as well as the impact of multi-national businesses and the shrinking of the world through the Internet, will determine the outcome of this clash of important yet conflicting values.

# References

Amnesty International. 1999. *Amnesty International Report 1998*. London: Amnesty International.

Ball, H. 1999. *Prosecuting War Crimes and Genocide*. Lawrence, KS: University Press of Kansas.

Bassiouni, M. C. 1997. From Versailles to Rwanda in Seventy-five Years: The Need to Establish a Permanent International Criminal Court. *Harvard Human Rights Journal* 10: 11–62.

Boyle, F. A. 1996. *The Bosnian People Charge Genocide: Proceedings at the International Court of Justice Concerning BOSNIA V. SERBIA on the Prevention and Punishment of the Crime of Genocide*. Amherst, MA: Alethia Press.

CBS News. 1998. Text of Clinton's Rwanda speech. Speech given March 24, 1998, in Kigali, Rwanda. http://www.cbsnews.com/stories/1998/03/25/world/main5798.shtml.

CBC News. 2006. The Genocide Convention. September 18, 2006. http://www.cbc.ca/news/background/sudan/genocide-convention.html.

Cussler, C. 2010. *The Silent Sea*. New York: G. P. Putnam's.

Destexhe, A. 1995. *Rwanda and Genocide in the Twentieth Century*. New York: New York University Press.

Durch, W. J. 1996. Keeping the peace. In *UN Peacemaking, American Policy, and the Uncivil Wars of the 1990s*, edited by W. J. Durch. New York: St. Martin's Press.

Dworkin, A. 2005. Cambodian War Crimes Tribunal Given Go-ahead. May 5. http://www.crimesofwar.org/onnews/news-cambodia2.html.

Franchi, H. A. 2009. International Court Eyes Role Beyond War-crimes Trials. *Christian Science Monitor* September 12, 1.

Gellately, R., and B. Kiernan, 2003. *The Spectre of Genocide: Mass Murder in Historical Perspective*. New York: Cambridge University Press.

Goldhagen, D. J. 2009. *Worse Than War: Genocide, Eliminationism, and the Ongoing Assault on Humanity*. New York: Public Affairs Press.

Goldman, T. R. 1998. A World Apart: U.S. Stance on a New ICC Concerns Rights Groups. *Legal Times* June 8, 16.

Human Rights. 2008. Five Controversies on Genocide (. . . But Not the Only Five). http://humanrights.change.org/blog/view/5_controversies_on_genocide_but_not_the_only_five.

*Human Rights Tribune*. 2008. Value of UN Genocide Convention Questioned. December 17. http://www.ictj.org/en/news/coverage/article/2187.html.

Human Rights Watch. 2009. Cambodia: First Trial to Test Tribunal's Credibility. February 14. http://www.hrw.org/en/news/2009/02/14/cambodia-first-trial-test-tribunal-s-credibility.

International Commission on Intervention and State Sovereignty. 2001. *The Responsibility to Protect*. Ottawa, Canada: International Development Research Centre. http://www.iciss.ca/pdf/Commission-Report.pdf.

Jones, A. 2006. *Genocide: A Comprehensive Introduction*. New York: Routledge.

Lake, A. 1994. The Limits of Peacekeeping. *New York Times* February 6, D17.

McDonald, G. K. 1998. The Changing Nature of the Laws of War. *Military Law Review* 156: 30–51.

Mydans, S. 1999. Two Khmer Rouge Leaders Spend Beach Holiday in Shadow of Past. *New York Times* January 1, 1.

Mydans, S. 1998. Cambodia's Leader Says Top Khmer Rouge Defectors Will Be Spared. *New York Times* December 29, 1.

Nardin, T., and M. S. Williams. 2006. *Humanitarian Intervention: Nomos XLVII*. New York: New York University Press.

A New World Court: American Objections to a Strong International Criminal Court are Misplaced. 1998. *The Economist* June 13–19, 16.

Powell, C. 1993. Testimony before U.S. Congress. U.S. Participation in UN Peacekeeping Activities. House Committee on Foreign Affairs.

Power, S. 2002. *"A Problem from Hell": America and the Age of Genocide*. New York: Basic Books.

Ratner, S. R., and J. S. Abrams 2001. *Accountability for Human Rights Atrocities in International Law: Beyond the Nuremberg Legacy*. Oxford, UK: Oxford University Press.

Robertson, G. 2002. *Crimes against Humanity: The Struggle for Global Justice*. London: Penguin.

Rwanda Development Gateway. 2010. About Gacaca. http://www.rwandagateway.org/gateway_new/?rubrique30.

Scoble, H. M. 1984. Human Rights Non-governmental Organizations in Black Africa: Their Problems and Prospects in the Wake of the Banjul

Charter. In *Human Rights and Development in Africa*, edited by C. E. Welch Jr. and R. I. Meltze, 177–194. Albany, NY: State University of New York.

Sells, M. 1998. *The Bridge Betrayed: Religion and Genocide in Bosnia*. Berkeley: University of California Press.

Simons, M. 2009. "International Court Begins First Trial," *New York Times* January 29, A1.

Stanley Foundation. 1998. The UN Security Council and the ICC: How Should They Relate. Conference at Arden House, New York, February 20–22. http://www.stanleyfoundation.org/publications/archive/Issues98.pdf.

Waller, J. 2007. *Becoming Evil: How Ordinary People Commit Genocide and Mass Killing*. 2nd ed. New York: Oxford University Press.

Welch, C. E., Jr. 2001. *NGOs and Human Rights: Promise and Performance*. Philadelphia, PA: University of Pennsylvania Press.

Willetts, P. 2002. *What Is a Non-governmental Organization?* http://www.staff.city.ac.uk/p.willetts/CS-NTWKS/NGO-ART.HTM#.

Wisner, F. 1993. Statement before U.S. Congress: International Peacekeeping and Peace Enforcement. U.S. Senate Committee on Armed Forces.

# 3

# Special U.S. Issues: The United States and the Creation of an International Criminal Court

U
ntil 1998, the United States was in the forefront of efforts to ameliorate crimes against humanity and war crimes and, after 1945, to punish those who fomented genocide before and during war. It was a major supporter of the ad hoc tribunals to try and then to punish those found guilty of such crimes in the former Yugoslavia and Rwanda. The Clinton administration called for a special criminal court to try the leaders of the Cambodian Khmer Rouge for ordering and committing genocide.

However, the United States opposed the creation of a permanent international criminal court and fought hard not to have the International Criminal Court (ICC) come into existence. This opposition was voiced by Democratic president Bill Clinton (1993–2001) and Republican president George W. Bush (2001–2009). This chapter will examine the opposition to the ICC by these administrations and examine the view of the ICC held by the administration of Democratic president Barack Obama (2009–2013). It is clear that for the ICC to be successful, the United States *must* be a forceful supporter of this international criminal tribunal.

# American Antipathy toward the Idea of an ICC, 1918–2010

Charges of war crimes and "crimes against civilized humanity" by the Allies—against Germany and Turkey—were made by them during and after the First World War ended in 1918. As early as 1915, the United Kingdom and Russia warned Turkish leaders that their actions against the Armenian minority were "crimes against civilized humanity" and those responsible would be punished at war's end.

In 1919, the report by the Allies' Committee of Enquiry into the Breaches of the Laws of War found that almost 1,000 German military and political persons, including the Sovereign, Kaiser Wilhelm II, committed serious war crimes and crimes against humanity. The Committee recommended the establishment of an international criminal court, composed of five judges (from the United States, France, the United Kingdom, Italy, and Japan) to try those identified by the Committee. Sections 227–230 of the Versailles Treaty established such a tribunal and set parameters for the criminal trials.

However, these *smachparagraphen* were never implemented because of the unwillingness of the United States. The American secretary of state, Robert Lansing, successfully argued that punishment for war crimes must be left to each nation's military tribunals—even the defeated nations. He argued that the creation of an international war crimes tribunal, an unprecedented idea, was not needed and that the idea was "an unchartered area of international law and a *frontal attack on the concept of state sovereignty*." Lansing said that the idea of such an international criminal tribunal "reflected a lack of precedent, precept, practice or procedure" (my emphasis) (quoted in MacMillan 2001).

Lansing also stated that a head of state, whether kaiser or president, is immune from any criminal charges because of the existence of the centuries-old international law concept of "sovereign immunity." He also rejected the new concept, in the Versailles Treaty, of "negative criminality," i.e., that the Central Powers leaders *failed* to prevent war crimes and crimes against humanity committed by their subordinates in the field.

The alternative, for Lansing and President Woodrow Wilson, was to democratize the defeated nations and to let them have their own legal and military law authorities provide criminal justice for those accused of war crimes. In 1922, the German Supreme Court, sitting in Leipzig, received the 1,000 charges against German military personnel from the Allies. The result: all but 12 cases were dismissed by the "democratic" court; only four cases, involving about a dozen military personnel, ended in guilty verdicts. All were sentenced to minor prison terms of two years or less.

During the interwar era, 1919–1939, there was some talk about creating an international criminal court but no action ensued. In 1926, for example, the League of Nations proposed the creation of an international criminal court, with jurisdiction over individuals accused of violating the laws of war. Nothing came of the proposal.

Even during the Second World War, 1939–1945, the United States was opposed to the creation of an international criminal law war tribunal to try the leading Nazi and Japanese leaders. President Franklin D. Roosevelt's view, shared by Winston Churchill, the United Kingdom's prime minister, was for *summary execution* of the top 5,000 military and political leaders without any trial whatsoever. As late as April 1945, one month before the unconditional surrender of Nazi Germany, Churchill wrote the following to FDR:

> His majesty's government is deeply impressed with the dangers and difficulties of judicial proceedings, and they think that execution without trial is the preferable course. A trial would be exceedingly long and elaborate, many of the Nazis' deeds are not war crimes in the ordinary sense, nor is it at all clear that they can properly be described as crimes under international law.

However, the winter 1944–1945 war crimes of the Nazis at Malmady and the late April 1945 discovery of the Nazi concentration and death camps led the Allies to create an ad hoc, not a permanent, international military tribunal to try the leaders of Nazi Germany and, later, the Japanese leaders, excluding the emperor. These actions led to the formulation of the Nuremberg Principles of 1946, which made waging aggressive war, war crimes, and crimes against humanity serious violations of the laws of war. In 1948, the United Nations (UN) defined "genocide" and, in the Genocide Convention of 1948, ratified in 1950, made genocide—whether committed in peacetime or during war—a major violation of the laws of war and international humanitarian law.

Article VI of the Genocide Convention called for the creation of an international criminal court to hear cases brought against individuals, including heads of state, charged with genocide, war crimes, crimes against humanity and/or waging aggressive war. In Article VI were two critically important innovations in international law: *"universal jurisdiction"* and *"complementarity."* The former suggested that there were certain crimes that fell under the concept of universal jurisdiction because every civilized society condemned them.

*Complementarity* is the concept suggesting that a civilized society should bring to national justice any person accused of a serious breach of international law but that, should the nation be *unable or unwilling to so act*, an international criminal tribunal could act in order to ensure justice and deny *impunity* to the accused.

In 1948, the UN created the International Law Commission (ILC) to look into the matter and to draft rules and guidelines for a permanent international criminal court. The ILC submitted drafts of the proposed ICC in 1951 and 1953; however, the Cold War between the Soviet Bloc and the West negated any discussion of such an international entity. It would not be until 1990 that the ILC once again began drafting a statute that would lay the foundation for a permanent international criminal court.

Between 1950 and 1990, there were 40 years of hot and cold war, of regional warfare, and of wars of revolution and independence. More than 200 "wars" occurred during this time frame, from Korea and Vietnam to Cambodia and Cyprus. However, by 1989–1990, the world community saw the collapse of the Soviet "empire," and the UN once again began to examine the ideal of a permanent international criminal court. Continuous work by the ILC and the Preparatory Committee (PrepCom) of the ILC—and nongovernmental organizations (NGOs) across the globe—led to the convening of 161 state delegations and 235 NGOs in Rome, Italy, in June–July 1998 to examine and possibly ratify the work of the draft statute committees.

By 1998, the world had seen the creation of two ad hoc International Criminal Tribunals (former Yugoslavia, 1993, and Rwanda, 1994). These were nonpermanent international courts created by the UN to try to bring to the bar of justice those who had committed war crimes, crimes against humanity, and genocide: (1) during the 1991–1995 wars in the former Yugoslavia (involving Croatia, Bosnia, and Serbia) and (2) during the less-than-three-month Rwandan civil war between Hutu and Tutsi where almost one million Tutsi were murdered by Hutu soldiers.

Although U.S. leaders supported the creation of the ad hoc tribunals, they were wary of the effort to create a permanent—and independent—international criminal court. Clearly, this was seen in the actions of the Democratic administration of President Bill Clinton (1993–2001) and those of the Republican administration of President George W. Bush (2001–2009).

# The "Two Roads Taken" by the United States before and during the Drafting of the Rome Treaty of the ICC, 1998: the Bill Clinton Years

The U.S. opposition to an ICC had been voiced for almost a century, from Wilson and Lansing in 1919 to contemporary U.S. opposition to the Rome Treaty and the ICC. Criticism has been voiced by Democratic and Republican administrations, by moderate presidents as well as conservative chief executives alike and by the nation's military leaders. Fundamentally, there is the perception that ceding legal and prosecutorial powers to an independent ICC is equivalent to turning over a segment of the United States' "national sovereignty" to the ICC and that American military personnel and their political leaders would become the targets for partisan prosecutors.

The U.S. Constitution is a set of sanctified, governing principles that prohibit a "surrender" of national sovereignty to an international prosecutor. This view of national sovereignty by American leaders was clearly enunciated before and during the Rome conference. For the chief American spokesperson at the conference, David Scheffer, there had to be substantive checks on the independence of the prosecutor's office, primarily through the intercession of the UN Security Council, where the United States has veto power.

For the Americans, a major fear was that an overzealous, anti-American, politically motivated prosecutor would use the discretionary powers of an independent prosecutor's office to try to bring U.S. military personnel and their leaders, as well as the political leadership of the United States, before an international criminal court for "frivolous" reasons. For Scheffer, absent Security Council veto power, the United States could not vote in favor of the creation of an ICC. "The Security Council," he said in

Rome, "needs to be a very significant player in the operation of this court" (Goldman 1998, 16–17).

The Security Council's role had to be that of a check on the actions of an independent prosecutor. Without the check and balance of the Security Council, there might be the horror of a prosecutor running wild—acting out of personal or political motivations. Scheffer concluded, "[The U.S. government] remains strongly opposed to giving an international prosecutor the right to initiate cases" (Crosette 1998, A1).

At the conclusion of the Rome meeting, the United States was on the losing side on the critical issues of prosecutorial independence and of the role of the UN Security Council in regard to the actions of the ICC. The Rome Statute was approved by 121 nations; only seven voted against the statute: China, Iran, Iraq, Israel, Libya, North Korea—and the United States. (The remaining state delegations chose to abstain from voting.)

Article 15 (1) of the Rome Treaty, which gave the prosecutor independent power to investigate allegations of serious breaches of international law and the discretionary power to initiate prosecutorial actions in the ICC, passed by a vote of 63–13. (Article 13 (b) and (c) also enabled the UN Security Council or a State Party to refer a case to the prosecutor for possible adjudication.)

Prior to and during the Rome meeting in June–July 1998, the U.S. leaders strode down two very different roads at the same time. Although President Clinton, his secretary of state, and the U.S. ambassador to the UN championed the idea of an ICC that was constrained by the Security Council, others in the administration, primarily the Defense Department, including the top echelon of the military establishment, took a different road: threats and intimidation.

Newspapers on the Continent reported that U.S. spokespersons were threatening poor nations with a cutoff of aid, and NATO allies were told that U.S. military aid would be jeopardized if they voted for the Rome statute (Jackson 1998, 19). For example, a paper prepared for the U.S. secretary of defense William Cohen, stated that "if Germany [voted for the statute], the U.S. might retaliate by removing its troops, including those in Europe" (Jackson 1998, 19).

As a practical matter, the United States was concerned about the direction the Rome meeting was taking. Said Scheffer,

[No] other nation matches the extent of United States overseas military commitments through alliances and

special missions such as current peacekeeping commitments in the former Yugoslavia. We constantly have
troops serving abroad on humanitarian missions, res-
cue operations, or missions to destroy weapons of mass
destruction. . . . Someone out there isn't going to like
it, but we're the ones who do it. . . . It is our collective
interest that the personnel of our military and civilian commands be able to fulfill their many legitimate
responsibilities without unjustified exposure to criminal
legal proceedings (Stanley 1998, A1).

In the end, the United States voted against the Treaty in July 1998;
its representative did not sign the document at the conclusion of
the Rome meeting.

Not signing the Rome Statute, "a largely nonbinding ges-
ture," meant that the United States could not participate in any of
the follow-up meetings of PrepCom to work on continuing issues
surrounding the formulation of standards for the ICC. However,
in the waning days of his administration, and on the very last
possible day that a nation could sign the Statute—December 31,
2000—President Bill Clinton signed the Rome Treaty on the ICC.
He signed, he said, "to reaffirm our strong support for international accountability and for bringing to justice perpetrators of
genocide, war crimes, and crimes against humanity. We do so
as well because we wish to *remain engaged* in making the ICC an
instrument of impartial and effective justice in the years to come"
(my emphasis).

However, in the attached statement, Clinton voiced again the
concerns of the United States about the ICC:

We are concerned that when the Court comes into existence, it will not only exercise authority over personnel
of states that have ratified the Treaty, but also claim jurisdiction over personnel of states that have not. With signature, we will be in a position to influence the evolution
of the Court. Without signature, we will not. . . . Court
jurisdiction over U.S. personnel should come only with
U.S. ratification of the Treaty. *The United States should have
a chance to observe and assess the functioning of the Court,
over time, before choosing to become subject to its jurisdiction.*
Given these concerns, I will not, and do not recommend
that my successor submit the Treaty to the Senate for

advice and consent until our fundamental concerns are satisfied. (my emphasis)

# America's Position after the Signing of the Rome Treaty, 2001–2009: the George W. Bush Years

After the delegations left Rome, the U.S. position was fixed: It would oppose the ICC as long as the Security Council's five permanent members did not have a veto power to restrain a partisan independent prosecutor. As will be seen, there was some movement toward working cooperatively with the ICC after 2006; however, no president, including Democratic president Barack Obama, has moved to bring the treaty to the U.S. Senate for ratification.

Although President Clinton was willing to wait and see how the ICC evolved and to have the United States participate in future discussions about the ICC, his successor, George W. Bush, took a totally different approach to the ICC—and to other multilateral treaties deliberated by members of the international community.

## President Bush's "Unsigning" of the Rome Statute, May 2002, and Other Actions in Response to the "Entry into Force" of the ICC, July 2002–2009

As soon as George W. Bush took the oath of office on January 20, 2001, the atmosphere in the political White House regarding the ICC changed radically. For the conservative Republican president, the ICC substantially impinged on the national sovereignty of the United States in a number of major ways:

1. The ICC claims jurisdiction over certain crimes committed in the territory of a State Party, including by nationals of a non-Party. Such a claim would entail ICC jurisdiction of U.S. citizens (U.S. Department of State 2002);
2. Although a "State Party" to the ICC treaty could "opt out" of crimes added by amendment to the ICC's jurisdiction, a non-State Party cannot so act;

3. The office of independent prosecutor would be subject to pressure that would lead to "politicized prosecutions";
4. The prosecutor is totally unaccountable to an elected body or to the UN Security Council. There are no "checks and balances" in place;
5. The ICC has usurped the role of the UN Security Council;
6. There is no trial by jury; therefore, there is a denial of due process of law.

Furthermore, the new president was categorically and ideologically unwilling to wait and see how the ICC would function over time once the requisite number of states (60) formally ratified the Rome Treaty, nor were Bush and his foreign affairs leaders interested in U.S. participation in future discussions about possible improvements and modifications in the ICC.

From the beginning of his administration, Bush saw the ICC as an "unchecked power" able to prosecute military soldiers and their leaders. Bush's under secretary of state, Marc Grossman, said: "We believe the ICC is built on a flawed foundation. These flaws leave it open for exploitation and politically motivated prosecutions." The Bush administration's ambassador for war crimes, Pierce-Richard Prosper, stated bluntly: "We [the United States] have washed our hands. It's over."

On May 6, 2002, after there were more than 60 nations that formally ratified the ICC Statute, for the very first time in U.S. diplomatic history, a president formally renounced previous U.S. support of an international treaty. In a letter to UN secretary general Kofi Annan, John R. Bolton, then the under secretary for arms control and international security, wrote: "This is to inform you in connection with the Rome Statute of the ICC, adopted on July 17, 1998, that the United States does not intend to become a party to the treaty. Accordingly, the United States has no legal obligations arising from its signature on December 31, 2000. The United States requests that its intention not to become a party, as expressed in this letter, be reflected in the depository's status list relating to this treaty."

For Bolton this was a most satisfactory action. Prior to the controversial 2000 electoral victory of Bush over his Democratic opponent, Al Gore, John Bolton, was vice president of the neoconservative American Enterprise Institute and advisor to Sen. Jesse

Helms. He was a most outspoken war hawk and vocal critic of the ICC. As Helms' advisor, he was instrumental in the early drafting of the American Service-Members' Protection Act (ASPA) of 2002.

The decision to "unsign" Clinton's ratification of the ICC Statute was, evidently, a controversial one in the Bush administration. The "unilateralists"—Vice President Dick Cheney, Secretary of Defense Donald Rumsfeld, and others—successfully battled Secretary of State Colin Powell and other senior State Department officials who believed that the May 2002 "unsigning" letter was unnecessary and symbolic but that it would "needlessly alienate European allies" (Lobe 2002).

However, once the decision was made, beginning on May 6, 2002, there was an orchestrated defense of the action as well as the positive position of the United States with respect to bringing to justice individuals who perpetrate genocide, war crimes, or crimes against humanity. Various high level officials in the U.S. Department of State participated in this public relations effort, including Secretary of State Colin Powell. In an interview broadcast on South Africa's radio stations, Powell said there was no reason to apologize for not ratifying the ICC treaty "because we hold our soldiers and our public officials to the very highest levels of accountability and responsibility. And we also have a constitutional system that says when one of our individuals who is serving overseas has done something wrong, we expect that individual to be dealt with under the Constitution of the United States."

Others who spoke out negatively about the ICC included Ambassador for War Crimes Issues Pierre-Richard Prosper (at a Foreign Press Center briefing in Washington, D.C.) and Under secretary for Political Affairs Marc Grossman (in remarks to the Center for Strategic and International Studies in Washington, D.C.).

In his prepared remarks, Grossman presented the essential principles of the Bush administration:

- justice and the promotion of the rule of law;
- those who commit the most serious crimes of concern to the international community should be punished;
- states, not international institutions are primarily responsible for ensuring justice in the international system; [and]
- the best way to combat these serious offenses is to build domestic judicial systems, strengthen political will and promote human freedom.

However, the ICC "does not advance these principles." Grossman then reiterated the litany of flaws in the ICC, ". . . flaws that leave [the ICC] open for exploitation and politically motivated prosecutions. . . . [For these reasons,] President Bush has come to the conclusion that the United States can no longer be a party to this process." He also stated that the United States does share a

> common goal—the promotion of the rule of law. Our differences are in approach and philosophy. In order for the rule of law to have true meaning, societies must accept their responsibilities and be able to direct their future and come to terms with their past. An unchecked international body should not be able to interfere in this delicate process. . . . We believe that there is common ground, and ask those nations who have decided to join the Rome Treaty to meet us there. . . . [We] believe that justice would be best served in creating an environment that will have a lasting and beneficial impact on all nations across the globe. . . . In the end, the best way to prevent genocide, crimes against humanity, and war crimes is through the spread of democracy, transparency, and rule of law. Nations with accountable, democratic governments do not abuse their own people or wage wars of conquest and terror. A world of self-governing democracies is our best hope for a world without inhumanity (Grossman 2002, 4–6 passim).

## The March toward Passage of the American Servicemen's Protection Act (ASPA), 2001–2002

In addition to these political, legal, and diplomatic actions taken by the Bush administration in the international arena, the president and his political advisors took domestic political actions— supported by two key Republican legislative leaders in the U.S. House of Representatives and the Senate—to buttress the administration's rejection of the ICC. In early August, 2002, President Bush signed the ASPA of 2002, a critically important amendment to the U.S. Defense Department supplemental authorization legislation.

The ASPA legislation began its 15-month trek to passage on May 8, 2001, when the archconservative, Rep. Tom DeLay

(R-Tex.), the House majority whip, introduced the ASPA as an amendment to H.R. 1646, the Foreign Relations Authorization Act. Passed in two days, it was sent to the Senate where, on May 10, 2001, Sen. Jesse Helms (R-N.C.), who was joined by Sen. Zell Miller (D-Ga.), introduced it as free-standing Senate bill S. 857, the ASPA of 2001. DeLay, in turn, introduced the same legislation in the House as H.R. 1794.

Although critics of the ASPA, led by Sen. Christopher Dodd (D-Conn.) and Representative Amo Houghton (R-N.Y.), unsuccessfully introduced legislation in support of continued U.S. engagement with the ICC, the ASPA moved inexorably toward passage. After the 9/11 attacks, on September 26, 2001, Senator Helms again introduced a revised ASPA (with administration support) as an amendment to the Defense Department (DoD) Authorization Act. After the revised ASPA was ruled nongermane, Helms in October 2001 again introduced another ASPA. On December 7, 2001, Helms reintroduced still another version of ASPA as an amendment to the fiscal year 2002 DoD Appropriations Act. That amendment passed the same day on a vote of 78–21.

The amendment was removed in conference committee on December 20, 2001. However, DeLay and Helms were unremitting in their effort to see the ASPA become law. On May 9, 2002, DeLay's ASPA, attached to a supplemental Defense Appropriations Act (H.R. 4775), passed, and in June 2002, Sen. Paul Warner (R-Va.) proposed the ASPA as an amendment to the supplemental DoD appropriations bill in the Senate. The text was identical to DeLay's House version of ASPA.

During the floor debate in the Senate, Senator Dodd introduced a second amendment that was incorporated into the final version of the supplemental appropriations bill. In the final version of the ASPA, the Dodd Amendment (Section 2015) states: "Nothing in this title shall prohibit the United States from rendering assistance to all international efforts to bring to justice Saddam Hussein, Slobodan Milosevic, Osama bin Laden, other members of Al Qaeda, leaders of Islamic Jihad, and other foreign nationals accused of genocide, war crimes, or crimes against humanity." In the conference committee deliberations, Sen. Patrick Leahy (D-Vt.) and Sen. James Byrd (D-W.Va.) urged the legislators to leave the Dodd Amendment in the final bill. Leahy said: "Congress wanted to be clear that the United States can cooperate with international efforts, including those by the ICC, to bring foreign nationals to justice."

The conference committee met in July 2002 and approved the ASPA with the Dodd Amendment added as Section 2015 of the legislation. On July 23–24, 2002, Conference Report 107-593 passed the House, and the following day, the Senate as H.R. 4775. On July 26, 2002, it was given to President Bush. On August 2, 2002, Bush signed the ASPA legislation, making it Public Law 107-206.

Among the provisions of the ASPA were ones that prohibited any cooperation between ICC investigators and other ICC employees and any federal or state or local law enforcement agency. Indeed, ICC investigators were prohibited from doing their work on American soil. The statute also prohibited any U.S. participation in UN peacekeeping actions unless there was a blanket waiver of any possible ICC action against American military personnel. Further, the act prohibited any military assistance to a nation that was a "State Party" to the ICC—except for NATO and major non-NATO allies. The major sections of the ASPA follow.

Section 2003 grants the president authority to waive restrictive sections of ASPA (Sections 2004, 2005, 2006, and 2007) for a period of one year. Section 2004 prohibits cooperation or support

- by any U.S. court, U.S. agencies, or state and local government with the ICC,
- for any investigative activity on U.S. soil by the ICC,
- of extradition of any person from the United States to the ICC, and
- from transferring any U.S. citizen or permanent resident alien to the ICC.

Section 2005 states that it is the policy of the United States to seek permanent exemption from the ICC for U.S. troops in every UN peacekeeping operation authorization. It also bars U.S. military participation in UN peacekeeping unless the president submits to Congress a "certification waiver" that one of three conditions has been met: (1) that the UN Security Council exempted U.S. forces in the resolution, (2) that the ICC does not have jurisdiction over the nations in which U.S. troops will operate, or that these countries have entered into Article 98 bilateral agreements with the United States, or, (3) that the "U.S. national interest," in the estimate of the president, justifies participation in the peacekeeping activity.

Section 2006 requires the president to develop procedures to ensure that there would be no direct or indirect transfer of classified national security and law enforcement information to the ICC. Section 2007 prohibits any U.S. military aid or assistance to any "State Party" to the ICC treaty. However, it does allow the president to waive the ban if, in a report to the Congress, the president deems it important to the "national interest" of the United States or if there is an Article 98 bilateral immunity agreement with a nation. Exempted from this restriction are (1) NATO members, (2) major non-NATO allies (Australia, Egypt, Israel, Japan, Jordan, Argentina, the Republic of Korea, and New Zealand), and (3) Taiwan.

If the ICC had the audacity to investigate and hold Americans at The Hague, its permanent home base, Section 2008 authorizes the president to use "all means necessary and appropriate to bring about the release" of these U.S. detainees—and allied persons if the detainees' nation makes such a request to the United States. It also authorized legal assistance for such persons if the ICC, located in The Hague, was not attacked by U.S. forces first.

Section 2011 grants the president, in the role of commander in chief (and consistent with the executive power of the president), authority to cooperate with the ICC or to provide national security information to the court, requiring only presidential notification to the Congress within 15 days of the president's action.

The United States made an even stronger statement against the ICC on July 13, 2004, when Congressman George Nethercutt, a Republican legislator from Washington state, introduced in the U.S. House of Representatives an amendment to the Foreign Operations Appropriation Bill. In December 2004, Congress adopted the Nethercutt Amendment. This legislation authorizes the loss of Economic Support Funds to all countries, including many key U.S. allies, that have ratified the ICC treaty but have not signed a bilateral immunity agreement (BIA) with the United States.

The Nethercutt provision was again debated in 2005 and was adopted in the joint appropriations bill for 2006. It was included in the fiscal year 2006 and 2008 budget authorizations (although presidential exemptions and waivers for certain allies, including NATO countries, were authorized).

For example, if an ICC member such as Peru declined to enter into one of these BIAs with the United States, then Peru would lose money earmarked, for example, for efforts to reduce coca production and fight drug trafficking. As pointed out, a number of America's allies declined to enter into these side agreements because they believed their obligations to the ICC prevented them from doing so. They were punished accordingly.

However, after the presidential election victory of Democrat Barack Obama in 2008, by 2010, the amendment was finally dropped out of the appropriations bill (Goldberg 2009). (More will be said about the Obama administration's views of the ICC below in this chapter.) Don Kraus, an official with the NGO, Citizens for Global Solutions, said,

> Thanks in large part to the work of House Foreign Operations and State Subcommittee chair Nita Lowey (D-N.Y.) and her staff, the language has been removed from the appropriations bill. Although her counterpart in the Senate, Patrick Leahy (D-Vt.) has successfully kept this language out of the Senate bill for many years, House Republican opposition ensured it remained in the final bill that went to President Bush. With the removal of the Nethercutt language, the [bi-lateral immunity campaign] is now officially over.

## The Bilateral Immunity Agreement (BIA) as Another Strategy of the Bush Administration to Weaken the ICC

The Bush administration, coming into office in 2001 as formal court approval by 60 nations neared, adopted an extremely active opposition to the new court. Washington began to negotiate bilateral agreements with other countries, ensuring immunity of U.S. nationals from prosecution by the court. As leverage, Washington threatened termination of economic aid, withdrawal of military assistance, and other painful measures. These exclusionary steps clearly endangered the fledgling court and might seriously weaken its credibility and effectiveness.

In late June 2002, the United States had successfully pushed for action within the UN Security Council to exempt its soldiers from legal action against them. The tack taken by the United States quickly led to the adoption of Resolution 1422 on July 12, 2002, less than two weeks after the "entry into force" of the ICC at The Hague. The actions of the United States were political hardball from the beginning. In June 2002, the United States vetoed the adoption of a resolution regarding the renewal of the UN's peacekeeping mission in Bosnia-Herzegovina. "The underlying [U.S.]

threat was to vote against all future resolutions establishing UN operations" unless American forces were excluded from the jurisdiction of the ICC (Zappala 2002, 117). The threat ended when the Security Council passed a resolution (1422) guaranteeing "exoneration" from ICC jurisdiction for all personnel of nations that are not a State Party to the ICC Statute who were involved in all authorized UN peacekeeping operations or missions (see Stahn 2003). In addition the U.S. Department of State began to develop BIAs with State Parties to the ICC Statute to exempt from ICC jurisdiction "all American citizens" (Zappala 2002, 115). By the end of the first decade of the 21st century, more than 100 bilateral agreements had been entered into by the United States.

Furthermore, in early 2002, the Bush administration warned foreign diplomats that their nations could lose all American military assistance if they became members of the ICC without pledging to protect Americans serving in their countries from its reach. The threat to withdraw military aid—including education, training, and help financing the purchase of equipment and weaponry—would be felt by almost every nation that has relations with the United States, though the law exempts many of its closest allies. The law gave the president authority to waive the provision and decide to continue military aid if he determines it is in the national interest. "The president welcomes the law—I can't underscore how important this is to us to protect American service members," said Philip Reeker, a State Department spokesman (Becker 2002, A1).

Another provision in the ASPA gives the president authority to free members of the armed services or other Americans who are in the court's custody by any "necessary and appropriate means," including use of the military. "It is easier to list what countries do not receive American military assistance than those that do," said Navy Lt. Cmdr. Barbara Burfeind a Pentagon spokesperson. "Virtually every country but Cuba, Iraq, Iran and the other countries on the terrorist list receive some military training or aid from us." Jonathan Grella, a spokesman for DeLay, said, "This is just an effective tool, and we have said numerous times that we have to do whatever it takes to protect our service members from this rogue court" (Becker 2002, A1).

Human rights groups condemned the administration's tactic of using the threat of withdrawing military assistance as a tool in the ICC discussions. "This makes the remote possibility of American prosecution by the court trump every other definition of national interest—it is fixation to the point of craziness," said Kenneth Roth, the executive director of Human Rights Watch (Becker 2002, A1).

Several foreign diplomats said they were angry and puzzled by this threatened cutoff of military assistance even to countries that provided valuable military cooperation to the United States in the world wars, the Vietnam War, the Gulf War and the current campaign against terrorism. "Why is this court so important that Washington would risk our military friendship?" asked one diplomat who represents a country that was a wartime ally of the United States (Becker 2002, A1).

Since passage of the 2002 ASPA, in capitals around the world, U.S. government representatives have been seeking BIAs, in an effort to shield U.S. citizens from the jurisdiction of the newly created ICC. These United States–requested agreements provide that current or former government officials, military and other personnel (regardless of whether or not they are nationals of the state concerned), or nationals will not be transferred to the jurisdiction of the ICC.

To date, several versions of these bilateral agreements have been proposed: those that are reciprocal, providing that neither of the two parties to the accord would surrender the other's "persons" without first gaining consent from the other; those that are nonreciprocal, providing only for the nonsurrender to the ICC of U.S. "persons"; and those that are intended for states that have neither signed nor ratified the Rome Statute, providing that those states not cooperate with efforts of third-party states to surrender U.S. "persons" to the ICC.

Although 105 governments have reportedly signed BIAs through 2008, less than 40 percent of these agreements have been ratified by parliaments or signed as an executive agreement. In fact, many legal experts argue that the executive agreements (which make up 18 percent of the BIAs) are unconstitutional and require the approval of parliament, and are thus not valid agreements. Furthermore, more than half of States Parties have resisted signing BIAs— despite large economic penalties imposed by the United States, and 54 countries continue to publicly refuse to sign (including Brazil, Croatia, Costa Rica, Ecuador, Kenya, Namibia, Peru, Samoa, South Africa, and Trinidad and Tobago). (See Chapter 6, Documents, for a list of nations who have signed BIAs with the United States.) With the election of Barack Obama, the BIA has become a nonissue in American foreign relations.

## The Status of U.S. Policy Regarding the ICC after the 2008 Election of Democratic President Barack Obama, 2009–2012

During the presidential campaign of 2008, most of the candidates spoke about the future of the ICC. John McCain, U.S. senator from Arizona and the Republican Party's candidate for president, said, in 2005, "I want us in the ICC, but I'm not satisfied that there are enough safeguards."

The Democratic candidate for president, U.S. senator Barack Obama, from Illinois, was just as circumspect in his response to questions relating to the U.S. future relationship with the ICC:

> The ICC has pursued charges only in cases of the most serious and systematic crimes and it is in America's interests that the most heinous of criminals, like the perpetrators of genocide in Darfur, are held accountable. The [ICC] actions are a credit to the cause of justice and deserve full American support and cooperation. Yet the Court is still young, *many questions remain unanswered about the ultimate scope of its activities, and it is premature to commit the U.S. to any course of action at this time.* (my emphasis)

During the campaign, in April 2008, Obama said: "the U.S. also needs to work with the ICC to ramp up the pace of indictments of those responsible for war crimes and crimes against humanity." His chief rival for the nomination was U.S. senator Hillary Clinton of New York. Although she voiced some of the misgivings her husband, President Bill Clinton, voiced in 2000, she did say, "Fortunately, some of the worst fears about the ICC have not been borne out. . . . Consistent with my overall policy of reintroducing the United States to the world, I will as President evaluate the record of the Court, and reassess how we can best engage with this institution and hold the worst abusers of human rights to account."

Although Barack Obama, as president since January 2009, has been cautiously positive in his statements about the court, it is reasonably clear that he does not share the outright hostility to the court that was seen at the start of the Bush administration.

Secretary of State Hillary Clinton has stated, "[W]hether we work toward joining or not, we will end the hostility toward the ICC, and look for opportunities to encourage effective ICC action in ways that promote United States interests by bringing war criminals to justice."

Obama has not explicitly stated a view on the extent to which the United States would be involved with the court stating that he "will consult thoroughly with our military commanders and also examine the track record of the Court before reaching a decision on whether the U.S. should become a State Party to the ICC."

In the run-up to the election, Mark Lippert, a foreign affairs adviser for Obama, said that he "has a wait-and-see, go-slow approach. The policy is unchanged from where he has been." The reactivation of the U.S. signature remains a viable option for the Obama administration, which could take place at any time, probably without significant repercussions. Furthermore, if the Obama administration should choose to provide information to the court or to attend the Review Conference scheduled for September 2010, this would, in fact, indicate a movement further in the direction of a wider and deeper relationship with the Court.

The progress of the court was noted by Hillary Clinton who stated in response to questions for the purpose of her confirmation as secretary of state by the Senate, "Now that it is operational, we are learning more about how the ICC functions. Thus far, the ICC has operated with professionalism and fairness—pursuing perpetrators of truly serious crimes."

Less than 10 days after Obama took the oath of office, the U.S. ambassador to the UN, Susan Rice, "signaled a shift in U.S. policy toward support for the ICC . . . in her first speech to the UN Security Council. [There is] a pledge by the United States to work together with the United Nations and international organizations such as the International Committee of the Red Cross, in a new era in support for international humanitarian law" (Varner 2009).

By March 2009, international law experts were saying that President Obama has dropped outright U.S. hostility toward the world's first permanent war crimes court, "but it is still a far cry from joining it. . . . Our policy on the ICC is under review," said a U.S. State Department official in May. The official voiced concerns shared by the military and conservative congresspersons: "Any look at the ICC has to include the basic fact that the United States has more troops deployed overseas than any other country in the world and that spurious charges against our troops could keep the court and the U.S. military tied up for decades" (*Agence France Presse* 2009).

Unlike the Bush administration's view of the ICC, the Obama experts do not stress the ICC's "political" threat to America's "national sovereignty." A month earlier in February 2009, the American Society of International Law recommended that the Obama administration adopt a policy of "positive engagement with the ICC." Other NGOs, including the Save Darfur Coalition, sent similar messages to the new administration urging greater cooperation with the ICC.

In August 2009, *The Guardian*, a respected British publication, printed a major story that suggested a major policy change was coming from the Obama administration regarding the ICC. It reported that Secretary of State Hillary Clinton, in Kenya, "has signaled a significant shift by the U.S. in favor of the ICC." Clinton was quoted as saying, "This is a great regret that we are not a signatory. I think we could have worked out some of the challenges that are raised concerning our membership. But that has not yet come to pass" (MacAskill 2009). (Clinton's shift was a personal one as well. In 2002, as a Democratic senator, she voted for the ASPA, the harshly negative reaction by Congress to the perceived ICC threat to American sovereignty.)

Noah Weisbord, a scholar and a former prosecutor at the International Criminal Tribunal, Yugoslavia, said that Clinton's words were "intriguing [and] marks an important moment in the courtship between the U.S. and the ICC" (MacAskill 2009).

However, although Clinton and others in the administration urge movement toward ratifying the Rome Treaty, the Obama administration is divided on the issue. There are military and congressional leaders who still have to be convinced that the ICC will not work against American foreign and military policies. They urge extreme "caution" in order to see how the new international court "evolves."

One response to Clinton's comments was published a week later in *The Washington Post*. John Bellinger III, wrote:

> Although the Obama administration will undoubtedly make greater efforts to engage with the court, the United States is unlikely to join the ICC anytime soon. . . . The White House will have a hard time convincing the U.S. military of the merits of joining the ICC unless the flaws identified by both Presidents Clinton and Bush are resolved,

and it is highly unlikely that 67 senators would approve the treaty without such changes (Bellinger 2009).

For Bellinger, the "thorniest issue for Obama will be how to approach the Rome Statute Tenth Anniversary Review Conference scheduled for next Summer in Uganda." Obama, like his two predecessors, believes that there must be changes in the ICC that provide "stronger protections for Americans" (Bellinger 2009) before there is the possibility of the Senate's ratifying the treaty.

However, in November 2009, Stephan Rapp, the U.S. ambassador at large for war crimes, announced that the United States would send representatives to The Hague "to explore issues involving the United States' possible participation in the ICC" (Carl 2009). In addition, Rapp confirmed that an American delegation would attend the 10th anniversary ICC meeting in Africa: "The United States will return to engagement with the ICC," he said. "For the first time in nearly eight years, the U.S. will participate in a conference with members of the ICC, a decision that signals growing U.S. support for a war crimes tribunal the Bush administration once shunned" (Lynch 2009).

However, Rapp repeated the fears of many legislators and military men: "There remain concerns about the possibility that the United States . . . and its service members might be subject to politically inspired prosecutions" (Lynch 2009). Underlining this concern was a story titled, "Prosecuting American 'War Crimes'" that appeared in the conservative daily, *The Wall Street Journal*, on November 26, 2009. The reporter, Daniel Schwammenthal, quoted the chief prosecutor of the ICC, Luis Moreno-Ocampo, who said that the ICC has jurisdiction to open preliminary investigations into NATO and American military actions in Afghanistan because that nation is one of the signatories to the Rome Treaty and also said:

> We have to check if crimes against humanity, war crimes, or genocide have been committed in Afghanistan. There are serious allegations against the Taliban and al Qaeda and serious allegations about warlords, even against some who are connected with members of the [Afghanistan] government. There are different reports about problems with bombings and there are also allegations about torture [committed by NATO] (Schwammenthal 2009).

For the reporter, these words are ominous ones and buttress the fears American political and military leaders hold about an independent ICC. Schwammenthal concluded his essay with the following words: "The fact that Mr. Ocampo mentioned the Sudanese perpetrator of genocide [President al-Bashir] in the same breath with alleged crimes of NATO soldiers shed light on *what the ICC may have in store for the U.S. in the future*" (Schwammenthal 2009, my emphasis).

Nonparticipation in the ICC, however, is not a new policy of American presidents and foreign policy makers, nor is it a purely Republican foreign policy position. It reflects "a deep-seated American ambivalence toward international institutions" that goes back nearly 100 years (Bellinger 2009).

# The Future of International Law in the Nation-State Universe

America's "toleration of unspeakable atrocities, often committed in clear view" of the world's people and their political leaders, clearly suggests that the United States "has consistently refused to take risks in order to suppress genocide":

> The United States is not alone. The states bordering genocidal societies and the European powers have looked away as well. . . . Despite public consensus that genocide should "never again" be allowed, the last decade of the twentieth century was one of the most deadly in the grimmest century in history (Power 2002, 508).

American military and foreign policy leaders, including the president, "did almost nothing to deter the crime." Because American "vital national interests" were not involved, the official American, as well as the and European, policy was reliance on negotiation and diplomacy. For many, as already noted, the *real reason* for American and European inaction ". . . was a lack of will. Simply put, American leaders did not act because they did not want to." These decisions were "concrete actions" by the government; they were not "accidental products of neglect" (Power 2002, 508).

Until America moves from idleness to vital support of the actions of the ICC, even if not a signatory to the Rome Treaty, there will continue to exist in the international community weakness in the face of war crimes, crimes against humanity, and genocide. Unless there is a mechanism available to prevent or stop genocide before slaughtered human beings are seen on nightly television and unless there are effective international efforts to make sure that "never again" will the world witness genocide, unfortunately the *era of impunity* and *national sovereignty* will continue in the 21st century.

Underscoring this pessimistic assessment of the future of genocide and ethnic cleansing in a world of sovereign nation-states is the latest explosion of violence in June 2010, this time in Kyrgyzstan, formerly of the Union of Soviet Socialist Republics. As has happened so often in the past 60 years, news headlines reported the first rumblings of another "ethnic cleansing."

*The New York Times* headline cried out: "Ethnic Rioting Ravages Kyrgyzstan" (Schwirtz 2010). *The Washington Post* headline read: "Ethnic Violence Spreads in Kyrgyzstan, Raising Fears of Humanitarian Crisis" (Pan 2010a). The attacks began a few days earlier when Kyrgyz mobs began murdering the ethnic Uzbek minority in the southern Kyrgyzstan city of Osh and surrounding villages populated by ethnic Uzbeks. Hundreds were murdered, stores were emptied of food and goods and then burned, and cars and Uzbek homes were set afire by the Kyrgyz. "There was," wrote the *Times* reporter, "a campaign of rage that moved from house to house through Uzbek neighborhood[s]." The recently installed— but unelected—provisional government, in power because they ousted the Kyrgyz president in April 2010, was simply unable to stop the "murderous mobs" (Schwirtz 2010; see also Pan 2010b). The Uzbek minority supported the new government, and Kyrgyz citizens saw a minority seize power in their nation. In a little more than a month, the ethnic cleansing began. As a consequence, the police and military had not been able to suppress the violence. While the Uzbek men remained to fight back and protect their property in the city of Osh, within a few days more than 150,000 women and children fled the area and relocated in refugee camps in neighboring Uzbekistan.

The hatred between the majority Kyrgyz and the Uzbek minority (only about 15 percent of the nation's population) has been a long-standing one in this central Asian nation with a mostly Muslim population of five million. Tensions were raw and clashes between the two ethnic groups had occurred repeatedly over land and water rights in the South. The problems, however, were never resolved; they were shelved until the next outbreak of violence.

In northern Kyrgyzstan, away from the violence, both Russia and the United States have military air bases. (The American air base in the embattled nation was a critical piece of the NATO mission in neighboring Afghanistan.) However, both did not immediately intervene to stop the killing and burning and looting in the South even though the interim government asked Russia to send in peacekeeping forces to restore order. Russian president Dmitry Medvedev "turned down the request, calling the violence *an internal matter*" (Pan 2010a, my emphasis).

Immediately, human rights NGOs including Human Rights Watch "urged the international community to intervene with the deployment of a UN-mandated force. . . . [In addition,] aid organizations (the International Committee of the Red Cross) described a growing refugee crisis" (Pan 2010a). However, as has been the case in so many other such ethnic cleansings and genocides discussed in this book, nothing has been done and nothing will be done by the international community other than the usual speeches decrying the murders and the destruction.

The UN has remained silent, except to observe that "the fighting was orchestrated, targeted and well-planned." A spokesman for the Obama administration in Washington said it was too early to speculate about military intervention. In addition, a regional intergovernmental organization (IGO), the Collective Security Treaty Organization, met at the call of its most powerful member, Russia, but concluded that it should not intervene in the internal affairs of the small nation.

The events taking place in Kyrgyzstan tragically highlight the core elements discussed in this book. There still is an unwillingness of nation-states to intervene in the "internal affairs" of a sovereign nation—even though tens of thousands of innocent citizens are murdered or become refugees, living in desperate squalor without medicine, food, and shelter. Although there are some human rights NGOs that call for concerted UN action, *including the use of military force to intervene*, nothing seems to budge the international community to take some kind of action to save lives. Even though "more than humanitarian aid is needed to stabilize the situation" (quoted in Pan 2010b), if the past is prelude to the continued reality of *nonintervention*, then nothing will happen in this latest outbreak of violence and ethnic cleansing.

# References

*Agence France Presse*. 2009. Under Obama, U.S. Drops Hostility to ICC: Experts. March 29. http://www.commondreams.org/headline/2009/03/23-24.

Becker, E. 2002. US Ties Military Aid to Peacekeepers' Immunity. *New York Times* August 10, A1.

Bellinger, J. B., III. 2009. A Global Quandary for the President. *The Washington Post* August 10. http://www.washingtonpost.com/wp-dyn/content/article/2009/08/09/AR2009080902093.html.

Carl, M. 2009. Obama May Put Americans under World Judges' Power. *World Net Daily* November 19, 2009. http://www.wnd.com/?pageId=116552.

Crosette, B. 1998. US Budges at UN Talks on a Permanent International Criminal Tribunal. *New York Times* March 18, A1.

Goldberg, M. L. 2009. Congress Reverses Bush-Era Policy on the ICC. March 12. http://www.undispatch.com/node/7837.

Goldman, T. R. 1998. A World Apart: U.S. Stance on a New ICC Concerns Rights Groups. *Legal Times* June 8, 16.

Grossman, M. 2002. American Foreign Policy and the ICC. May 6. http://www.amicc.org/docs/Grossman_5_6_02.pdf.

Jackson, D. W. 1998. Creating a World Criminal Court Is Like Making Sausage—Except It Takes Longer. *Texas Observer* June 30, 19.

Lobe, J. 2002. Bush "Unsigns" War Crimes Treaty. May 6. http://www.alternet.org/story/13055.

Lynch, C. 2009. U.S. to Attend Conference Held by War Crimes Court. *The Washington Post* November 17. http://www.washingtonpost.com/wp-dyn/content/article/2009/11/16/AR2009111603662.html.

MacAskill, E. 2009. U.S. May Join ICC, Hillary Clinton Hints. *The Guardian* August 6. http://www.guardian.co.uk/world/2009/aug/06/us-may-join-warcrimes-court.

MacMillan M. 2001. *Paris 1919: Six Months That Changed the World*. New York: Random House, 159–165, 167–203.

Pan, P. P. 2010a. Ethnic Violence Spreads in Kyrgyzstan, Raising Fears of Humanitarian Crisis. *The Washington Post* June 14. http://www.washingtonpost.com/wp-dyn/content/article/2010/06/13/AR2010061305069.html.

Pan, P. P. 2010b. Regional Bloc Led by Russia Plans to Send Equipment to Violence-torn Kyrgyzstan. *The Washington Post* June 15, 1.

Power, S. 2002. *"A problem from Hell": America and the Age of Genocide.* New York: Basic Books.

Schwammenthal, D. 2009. Prosecuting American "War Crimes." *The Wall Street Journal* November 26. http://online.wsj.com/article/SB1000 14240527487040130045745192530954440312.html.

Schwirtz, M. 2010. Ethnic Rioting Ravages Kyrgyzstan. *New York Times* June 13. http://www.nytimes.com/2010/06/14/world/asia/14kyrgyz.html.

Stahn, C. 2003. The Ambiguities of Security Council Resolution 1422. *European Journal of International Law* 14:85–104.

Stanley, A. 1998. U.S. Specifies Terms for War Crimes Court. *New York Times* July 10, A1.

U.S. Department of State. 2002. Fact Sheet. The International Criminal Court. Office of War Crimes Issues, Washington, D.C., May 6.

Varner, B. 2009. Obama's Envoy Voices Support for International Court. January 29. http://www.bloomberg.com/apps/news?pid=newsarchive&sid=aYK_ULgi3Ix0.

Zappala, S. 2002. The Reaction of the US to the Entry into Force of the ICC Statute: Comments on UN SC Resolution 1422 (2002) and Article 98 Agreements. *Journal of International Criminal Justice* 1:114–34.

# 4

# Chronology

This genocide chronology begins with actions taken by nation-states from 1900 to 2010. The timeline highlights significant events during this time and the great difficulty the world community faced trying to stop genocide and, after 1948, enforcing the Genocide Convention.

Each of the following entries presents a brief analysis of the importance of the event. The men who instigated and carried out these mass murders and genocides will be discussed in Chapter 5.

## 1904–1907—German South West Africa, Herreros

The Herreros were native African herdsmen who migrated to present-day Namibia in the 17th century. After Germany entered Africa as a colonial power in that region of Africa in the 19th century, the Herrero territory was annexed in 1885 as a part of German South West Africa. After a series of uprisings against the German colonial farmers, the German military, between 1904 and 1907, exterminated four-fifths of the Herrero population. The extermination policy did not exclude women and children. Although the world community read about the slaughter of the native tribe, nothing was done to prevent the killings. One hundred years later, the German government apologized for the killings.

# 1915–1923—Ottoman Turkey, Armenians, 1.5–2 Million Dead

The Christian Armenian genocide was carried out by the Young Turk government of the Ottoman Empire from 1915 to 1923. The ethnic Armenian population, part of the Ottoman Empire since the 16th century, was the last major ethnic group remaining in the Empire. In earlier decades, the Greeks, Romanians, Bulgarians, and Serbs had left Ottoman rule. When young Armenians, in the 1890s, pressed for political reforms, including a constitutional government, the response was brutal persecutions of these leaders. In two years, 1894 to 1896, more than 100,000 ethnic Albanians were massacred by the military. A new Turkish leadership emerged in 1908 and greatly limited the Sultan's powers. In 1913, three Young Turks seized control of the government and immediately became dictators with a plan for creating a new Turkish empire by expanding the borders of their nation eastward. Their new nation would be called Turan with one religion and one language. The major obstacle to the plan was the fact that the ethnic Albanians (10 percent of the population) lived on territory that blocked eastward expansion. The Armenians were labeled infidels because they refused to convert to Islam. After World War I began, the new Turkish government saw the opportunity to solve their "Armenian problem." They developed an extermination policy that targeted the large Armenian population, especially those who lived in the eastern sections of the Empire. In April 1915, the final solution began. Intellectual leaders, teachers, and local government officials were murdered. The 40,000 Armenians serving in the Army were disarmed, placed in labor battalions, and then murdered. Then came the mass arrests of all Armenian men aged 15 to 70 across the nation and their extermination by the military and local citizens. Finally came the deportations of one million women, old people, and children. They were driven in death marches southward, over mountains toward the Syrian desert. Many of the women were raped and tortured by the Turkish soldiers. Although many thousands of young children were kidnapped by Turkish officers and raised as Turkish Muslims (now referred to as "the leftovers of the sword,") nearly two million Armenians were murdered during this eight-year extermination era (Dan

Bilefsky, Secrets Revealed in Turkey Revive Armenian Identity. *The New York Times* January 10, 2010, 9). A public warning was issued by the Allies to the Turkish leaders: "The Allied governments announce publicly that they will hold all members of the Ottoman government as well as such of their agents as are implicated, responsible for such matters." Although the victorious allies tried to have the Turkish government try the leaders of the Young Turk government for their actions against the Armenians, the Turkish outcry against such war crimes trials forced the government to stop the effort. The three leaders of the Young Turk government fled to Germany where they had been offered asylum. German officials refused to send the leaders back to Turkey to face trial. Ultimately, by 1923, all the major leaders of the Young Turk government were assassinated by Armenian gunmen in Germany.

# 1932–1933—USSR, Ukraine's Forced Famine: 7 Million Dead

In 1917, with the collapse of tsarist rule, the Ukraine (about the size of France), declared itself to be an independent people's republic. For four years, the Ukrainians fought the new Soviet government's military until they were defeated in 1921. In 1924, Joseph Stalin became the dictatorial leader of the Soviet Union. Beginning in 1929, his forces rounded up more than 5,000 Ukrainian professors, as well as political, cultural, economic, and religious leaders, and had them murdered. In 1932, Stalin, ordered a system of harsh land management, called collectivization, in the Ukraine. All privately owned farmland and livestock was seized by the Soviet government. He also targeted for extermination a class of wealthy farmers, the Kulaks, whom Stalin believed would become the next set of insurrectionists. They were declared "enemies of the people" and stripped of all their possessions—from their land and homes to their kitchen utensils. It is estimated that 10 million Kulaks were transported to Siberia and that more than three million died in this process. By the spring of 1933, about 25,000 people in the Ukraine died daily of starvation. Deprived of the food the farmers were harvesting, nearly 7 million (including 3 million children) died due to the artificial famine created by the Soviet Union's leader, Stalin.

## 1937—Japan, The Rape of Nanking, China: 300,000 Dead Chinese

In another horrid slaughter of innocent men, women, and children, in December 1937, the Japanese Imperial Army conquered China's capital city of Nanking. The troops were ordered to kill all captives. In the succeeding six weeks, Japanese soldiers murdered half the city's population of 600,000 (including about 90,000 Chinese soldiers who had surrendered). They burned, stabbed, shot, and drowned their victims. Between 20,000 and 80,000 Chinese women were raped and then murdered by the troops. Less than two dozen foreign diplomats, in the effort to save the Chinese, created a 2.5-acre secure zone that enabled 300,000 Chinese to find sanctuary in that area. Even the Nazi consul participated in this humanitarian effort. He also wrote a letter to Hitler condemning the brutality of the Japanese. However, in a few years, after the attack on Pearl Harbor by the Japanese fleet, these two nations became allies in World War II.

## 1941–1945—The Nazi Holocaust: Approximately 6 Million Dead Jews, as well as Other Ethnic Groups and Nationalities: Roma-Sinti, Russians, and Poles

In 1933, the Jewish population across Europe stood at more than nine million Jews from Russia in the East to England in the West. Most of them lived in the 11 countries that the Nazis conquered and then occupied during the Second World War. In Germany itself, the Jewish population constituted only 1 percent of 55 million Germans. When Adolf Hitler came to power in 1933, the Jews began to suffer. In 1935, for example, their German citizenship was revoked. In 1938, *Kristallnacht* (the Night of Broken Glass) occurred, and more than 500 synagogues were destroyed as well as hundreds of Jewish businesses. Just before the war began in 1939, in a speech in Berlin, Hitler said that if there was a world war, it would result in the "annihilation of the Jewish race in Europe." In 1942, the executions began in the Nazi concentration camps and death centers. By 1945, about six million Jews had been exterminated in the Nazi government's Final Solution to the Jewish Problem. Although the Jew was the prime target of the Nazi killing operations across the continent, there were other victims. Tens of thousands of Roma (Gypsies) were murdered by the Nazis and millions of Russians and Poles were exterminated through starvation, torture, and murder. Millions more were used as slave laborers for the Nazi war industry. Most died because of poor diets, lack of medical treatment, and beatings and torture. There were also political and religious groups targeted for destruction by the Nazi regime, including Communists, Socialists, Trade Unionists, and Jehovah's Witnesses.

# 1945–1948 — International Military Tribunals Created in Germany and Japan at the Conclusion of the War

During World War II, the Allies called for unconditional surrender of the Axis Powers (Germany, Japan, and Italy). It was not until early 1945 that the Allies agreed to conduct international war crimes trials, with the leaders of the Nazi government and the Japanese Imperial government to be tried for their war crimes and crimes against humanity. The decision to bring them before the international bar of justice, charged with violations of the Hague and Geneva treaties, was to provide history with a written record of the enemy's extermination patterns used by both the Nazi and the Japanese governments against innocent civilians across the world. The International Military Tribunals (IMT) in Nuremberg, Germany, consisted of four representatives from the victorious nations: the United States, the Soviet Union, England, and France. The Tokyo IMT consisted of one jurist from the 11 nations who fought against and/or were occupied by Japanese troops during the Pacific War. Most of the defendants were found guilty, and a majority of them were executed by the Allies. In addition to these two major trials, there were literally hundreds of trials held in the nations who suffered human losses during the lengthy occupation of their homelands by the enemy. The defendants in these lesser-known national tribunals ranged from medical doctors to lawyers and judges, from those who ran the concentration camps to the military commanders who did not attempt to control the brutal actions of the troops under their immediate command.

## 1947–1948—UN: International Convention on Genocide Established

In 1947, while the trials of Nazi and Japanese defendants continued, the United Nations (UN) organized an ad hoc international convention to draft an international law that defined genocide as an action that had "universal" condemnation and described the characteristics that were exhibited in the term. Raphael Lemkin took a major role in the drafting of the proposed treaty. In December 1948, with considerable modifications reflecting the new realty of the Cold War between the Soviet Union and the West, it was ratified by the General Assembly.

## 1949—Communist China's Great Leap Forward: 27 Million Die of Starvation

The People's Republic of China came into being when, on October 1, 1949, Chinese Communist Party leader Mao Tse-Tung made the announcement and immediately began the Communist effort to systematically destroy the ancient Chinese social and political systems. A major goal of the leadership was the collectivization of the peasants in China. The policy was called the Great Leap Forward, and the hope was that there would be dramatic economic and technical development of the nation. The reality was that by 1958 the policy destroyed the agricultural system and led to a major famine in China in which 27 million Chinese starved to death.

## 1951—Genocide Convention in Force

By mid-1951, the requisite number of member states had signed the Genocide Convention, and the document "came into force" in the hope that genocide would "never again" occur.

## 1967–1970—Biafran War, Nigeria

Nigeria is a federation of states that are segregated by three major ethnic groups: the Ibo, Hausa/Fulani, and Yoruba. The northern tribes would not allow Biafra to secede from the federation. The Biafran War, 1967–1970, resulted in 100,000 military casualties. However, between 500,000 and 2 million Ibo civilians died from starvation during the war. On May 30, 1967, a formal announcement that Biafra would be an independent republic was announced. The reason for this was the Nigerian government's inability to protect the lives of the Ibo, and its collaboration in genocide forced them to secede from the federation. The independent republic failed, and Biafra was reintegrated into Nigeria after the cease-fire in January 1970.

# 1971 — East Pakistan, East Bengal

The genocide that took place over nine months in 1971 had its beginning when India achieved independence from the United Kingdom in 1947. This immediately led to the partition between India (mostly Hindu) and Pakistan (mostly Muslim). After the partition, there was a mass exodus of Hindus from Pakistan to India (more than 5 million) and Muslims from India to Pakistan (nearly 9 million). Pakistan was divided into West and East Pakistan at the time. East Pakistan was home for millions of Bengali Muslims. In all of Pakistan, Bengali Muslims were in the majority. However, the ruling Muslim elite saw the Bengalis as Hindu-leaning and vowed to act to "cleanse" them from Hindu influence. Because of this attitude, an autonomy movement, called the Awami League, developed in East Pakistan in the 1950s and became the political voice of the Bengalis. In the December 1970 general election in Pakistan, its first democratic election, the Awami League won 167 of 169 seats and more than 80 percent of popular votes in East Pakistan. Numerically, the Awami League had an absolute majority of seats in the Pakistan National Assembly (167 of the total 313 seats). Historically, East Pakistan was allocated only 36 percent of the total resources, and East Pakistanis occupied only 20 percent of the positions in the federal government in the United Pakistan. The outcome of the 1970 elections for the Awami League created an alternative power center for an already alienated people. In March 1971, however, the government postponed the opening of the parliament. The Awami leaders immediately declared their independence and called their new state Bangladesh. In response, on March 25, 1971, the Pakistani army, on President Yahya Khan's orders, initiated a campaign of terror that was to last till its final surrender to the Indian army on December 17, 1971. This terror campaign by the Pakistan army resulted in 10 million Bangladeshi refugees crossing over into India, 3 million Bangladeshi citizens killed, and 250,000 women and girls raped by Pakistani soldiers. The nine-month, bloody war ended in December 1971 with the Indian military assistance. In addition to the millions murdered and raped by the Pakistan military, 10 million Bengalis fled to India, and nearly 30 million Bengalis were displaced from the cities to the rural areas of the new nation-state.

## 1971–1979, Uganda's Killing Fields

Idi Amin seized power and ruled Uganda from 1971 to 1979. The economy was devastated by Amin's policies, including the expulsion of Indians, the nationalization of businesses and industry, and the expansion of the public sector. The real value of salaries and wages collapsed by 90 percent in less than a decade. The number of people killed as a result of his regime is unknown; estimates from international observers and human rights groups range from 100,000 to 500,000. Although jubilant at his success, Amin had the secret police redouble their efforts to uncover subversives and other imagined enemies of the state. State terrorism was rampant. Political opponents and Christian groups were brutally murdered. These atrocities were greeted with international condemnation, but apart from the continued trade boycott initiated by the United States in July 1978, verbal condemnation was not accompanied by action to stop the killings. In 1979 Amin was ousted from power by a group of Ugandan rebels, backed by Tanzanian soldiers.

## 1972—Burundi, 150,000 Hutus Executed in Two Months

On April 29, 1972, Hutu radicals in Burundi launched an uprising against the country's Tutsi-dominated military, massacring several thousand Tutsi civilians. In response, Micombero's government began a selective genocide, aimed at eliminating Hutu political aspirations for good. Any Hutu with any semblance of education was rounded up and killed. Estimates of the death toll range from between 200,000 and 300,000, up to 3 percent of the population. Hundreds of thousands more fled abroad. The international reaction was muted. Even the Hutu-dominated ruling party in neighboring Rwanda, which at various times had sought to characterize itself as the defender of Hutu interests against Tutsi domination, did not intervene.

## 1975–1979—Cambodian Khmer Rouge: 2 Million Dead Cambodians

From 1975 to 1979, the rebel Cambodian leader Pol Pot overthrew the government and led his Khmer Rouge army in a reign of violence, fear, and execution of nearly 2 million of his domestic enemies. Similar to China's failed "Great Leap Forward," Pol Pot's goal was to create a Communist peasant farming society of local communities. His policy called for the destruction of the Cambodian urban centers and the "reeducation" of all those who lived in the cities. This effort was to "purify" Cambodia of all Western culture, religion, foreign influences, and city life. Small ethnic groups living in Cambodia, all those who were members of the "old society," as well as Buddhist monks, intellectuals, and former government officials were exterminated. "What is rotten must be removed" was one of Pol Pot's many phrases that explained his goals. In the end, more than 25 percent (nearly two million civilians) of Cambodia's population was executed by the Khmer Rouge. After Vietnam invaded Cambodia in December 1978, Pol Pot's reign of terror ended. There was no effort to punish the Khmer Rouge leaders.

## 1977–1978—Ethiopian Red Terror

Never colonized by the European powers, Ethiopia was ruled by emperors until 1974, and the ethnically diverse feudal society was often characterized by regional, territorial, and religious discord. In 1930, Haile Selassie was crowned emperor of Ethiopia and established a more modern state by creating a structured, central bureaucracy, a judicial system with codified laws, and a constitution. Despite these accomplishments, however, revolts, rebellions, droughts, and famine marked Selassie's reign. The emperor's unresponsiveness to the economic development of the country and the political needs of his people, specifically his methods of dealing with (and concealing) the widespread famine that plagued the nation in the 1950s, 1960s, and 1970s, is what most scholars believe ultimately led to his downfall. Although Selassie ordered the importation of grain into Addis Ababa, other sections of the country were neglected and hundreds of thousands of peasants starved. The famine contributed to his downfall. By early 1974, strikes, protests, and demonstrations against the government were staged throughout the country. The government's unwillingness or inability to respond to these demands eventually led to the overthrow of Emperor Haile Selassie and the accession to power of the Dergue, a committee of nearly 120 military officers. It abolished parliament, suspended the constitution and arrested Selassie. All land, industries, and institutions were nationalized. However, power struggles within the new ruling elite led to the rise of a new leader, Mengistu Haile Mariam. As the undisputed leader of the Dergue and Head of State, he began a campaign to suppress the opposition groups that had begun to organize in response to the Dergue's more violent tactics and autocratic rule. Revolts by various right- and left-wing political groups demanding an elected government, and guerilla warfare by secessionist fronts spread throughout the country in the late 1970s.

In 1977, the Red Terror was officially unleashed. During this two-year campaign, tens of thousands of Ethiopians were arrested, tortured, and summarily executed. To assist in exterminating the Dergue's political opponents and "enemies of the revolution," Mengistu employed the secret police and issued arms to local government, or *kebele*, officials. Mengistu then turned on his former allies. In October 1977, an estimated 3,000–4,000 people were killed, and by the end of the year, opposition members had been removed from all high-level government positions. The murder of others in more rural areas continued as well. By the end of the 1980s, Mengistu's regime faced international criticism and dwindling financial and military support from the Soviet Union. In 1989, several long-standing liberation movements took the opportunity to consolidate forces and formed a united front called the Ethiopian People's Revolutionary Democratic Front (EPRDF). In February 1991, they launched new offenses against Dergue forces and were able to overpower the army, which had become divided and frustrated with the brutality of Mengistu's rule. On May 21, the EPRDF entered Addis Ababa and took control of the country. Today, the Federal Democratic Republic of Ethiopia is led by the EPRDF, and a number of political and economic reforms have been implemented.

# 1981–1983—Guatemala, Murder of the Indigenous Maya

The Guatemala genocide case arises from a period in that country's long civil war where violence against noncombatant, indigenous Mayans rose to the level of genocide. More than 200,000 Guatemalans were killed or disappeared during the 1960–1996 internal conflict. According to the UN-sponsored Commission on Historical Clarification (CEH), the Guatemalan military and paramilitaries indiscriminately targeted indigenous communities, labor leaders, students, clergy and other civilians under the theory that they formed a subversive "internal enemy."

The violence peaked in 1982–1983, when government forces launched a systematic campaign of genocide against the Mayan people. Drawing on an historical antipathy to the indigenous peoples of Guatemala, the State justified the extermination of an estimated 440 Mayan communities by claiming that they were part of a communist plot against the government. The army and its paramilitary teams—including "civil patrols" of forcibly conscripted local men—attacked more than 600 Mayan villages. They would cordon off a village, round up the inhabitants, separate men from women, and then kill them sequentially. Those who escaped were hunted from the air by helicopters. Extreme torture, mutilation, and sexual violence became commonplace, as was violence against children. This two-year period became known as the "Silent Holocaust."

# 1987–1991—Iraq, Anfal Campaign against the Kurds

The Anfal was the Iraqi government's organized attempt to eradicate the Kurds living in northern Iraq. Anfal means "the spoils." It is also the name given by the Iraqis to a series of military actions against the Kurds. There was an organized campaign incorporating prison camps, firing squads, and chemical attacks. The campaigns of 1987–1989 were characterized by mass summary executions and the disappearance of many tens of thousands of noncombatants, including large numbers of women and children, and sometimes the entire population of villages; the widespread use of chemical weapons; the wholesale destruction of about 2,000 villages, including homes, schools, mosques, and wells; the looting of civilian property; the arbitrary arrest and jailing in conditions of extreme deprivation of thousands of women, children, and elderly people; the forced displacement of hundreds of thousands of villagers; and the destruction of the rural Kurdish economy and infrastructure. The Iraqi regime, led by Saddam Hussein, committed the crime of genocide.

# 1992–1995 — Serbia, 200,000 Bosnian Muslims Killed

With the death of Yugoslavian leader Josip Tito in 1980, the nation slowly disintegrated into ethnic and religious units. Serbia, one of the larger segments of the former Yugoslavia, began an effort to create, beginning in 1990, a "Greater Serbia." In 1991, Croatia and Slovenia both declared their independence, which led to a brief (10-day) war between Serbia and Slovenia; also in 1991, Serbia attacked Croatia (which, unlike Slovenia, had about 12 percent Orthodox Serbs). In 1992, after Bosnia, with 32 percent Orthodox Serbs living there, declared its independence from the former Yugoslavia, Serbian military and Bosnian-Serb militias attacked Bosnia in the genocidal effort to "ethnically clean" Muslim Bosnia in order to protect the Serb minority (Orthodox Christians) living in Bosnia. Although it had been for centuries home to ethnic Serbs and ethnic Croats (most of whom were Catholic), Bosnia also was home to a Muslim population. Serbia, led by Slobodan Milosevic, tried to remove the Croats and the Muslims and bring Bosnia into the "Greater Serbia." Like earlier genocides in Turkey and Europe, the Serbs targeted for execution Muslim leaders, including government officials, religious leaders, teachers, and other intellectuals. Rape was used as a weapon to try to destroy the Bosnian Muslim culture. By 1995, when the fighting ceased because of pressure from Western nations, especially the United States, more than 200,000 Bosnian Muslims had been murdered by the Serbs and more than 2 million Bosnian Muslims became refugees during this time period.

# 1993 — UN Resolution 827 Creates International Criminal Tribunal, Yugoslavia

The UN Security Council, responded to the situation in the former Yugoslavia and established the International Criminal Tribunal for the former Yugoslavia (ICTY). On October 6, 1992, the Security Council established the Commission of Experts to investigate the possible violations of international humanitarian law. The Security Council in due course received the report of the Commission of Experts, which concluded that grave breaches of the 1949 Geneva Conventions and other violations of international humanitarian law had been committed in the territory of the former Yugoslavia, including willful killing, "ethnic cleansing," mass killings, torture, rape, pillage and destruction of civilian property, destruction of cultural and religious property, and arbitrary arrests. On February 22, 1993, by Resolution 808, the Security Council decided that an international tribunal should be established and directed the secretary general to submit specific proposals for the implementation of that decision. On May 25, 1993, in Resolution 827, the Security Council adopted the draft statute and established the ICTY.

# 1994 — Rwanda, 800,000 Tutsis Killed by Hutu Militias in Three Months

Rwanda, with only 7 million people, was formerly a colony of Belgium, and during the colonial period the two major ethnic groups—the more populous Hutus (who were farmers) and the minority Tutsis (who were chosen by the Belgian occupiers to be incorporated into the local government and bureaucratic structure)—were treated very differently. The much taller Tutsis were clearly the favored ethnic group of the European colonialists. After independence in 1962, the Hutus seized power and governed Rwanda. More than 200,000 Tutsis fled their homes and went into neighboring nations. There they formed a rebel guerilla army, the Rwandan Patriotic Front. Periodic fighting occurred between these two communities until 1990, when an agreement was reached where the two groups would share power. In April 1994, groups of ethnic Hutu militia, armed with farming instruments, including machetes, began a genocidal campaign against the Tutsi population and moderate Hutus. For nearly 100 days, the Hutus systematically targeted their enemy and executed them in the effort to wipe out the Tutsi population in Rwanda. The killings ended when Tutsi rebels, attacking from neighboring states, defeated the Hutus in July 1994. Although nearly 3,000 UN troops were present as peacekeepers in the nation when the exterminations began, they were not allowed to actively interfere with the Hutus in order to stop the genocide. In three months, 800,000 persons, more than one-tenth of the population, were killed and hundreds of thousands of Tutsis managed to flee their nation and settle in neighboring states.

# 1994—UN: Resolution 955, International Criminal Tribunal for Rwanda Created

Recognizing that serious violations of humanitarian law were committed in Rwanda and acting under Chapter VII of the UN Charter, the Security Council created the International Criminal Tribunal for Rwanda (ICTR) by Resolution 955 of November 8, 1994. It was established for the prosecution of persons responsible for genocide and other serious violations of international humanitarian law committed in the territory of Rwanda between January 1, 1994, and December 31, 1994. Identical to the protocols of the ICTY, the Rwandan Tribunal consists of three organs: the Chambers and the Appeals Chamber; the Office of the Prosecutor, in charge of investigations and prosecutions; and the Registry, responsible for providing overall judicial and administrative support to the Chambers and the Prosecutor.

# 1998–2007—Democratic Republic of the Congo

Since 1998, fighting, as well as disease and malnutrition resulting from armed conflict, have claimed an estimated 5.4 million lives in the Democratic Republic of the Congo (DRC). The decade of conflict has displaced a total of more than 3 million Congolese across eastern and southern DRC and hindered access to agricultural land and traditional markets. On October 7, 2009, U.S. chargé d'affaires Samuel V. Brock declared a disaster in response to the ongoing humanitarian emergency in the DRC. In fiscal year 2009, the U.S. government provided more than $191 million for humanitarian assistance in the DRC, including nearly $34 million in funding for agriculture and food security, economic recovery and market systems, humanitarian coordination and information management, health, nutrition, protection, shelter and settlements, including water, sanitation, hygiene programs, and the provision of relief commodities. The conflict in the DRC may be the world's most deadly crisis since World War II, and the death toll far exceeds those of other recent and more prominent crises, including those in Bosnia, Rwanda, Iraq, Afghanistan, and Darfur. Since 1998, 5.4 million people have died, and 45,000 people continue to die every month.

# 2003–Present — Sudan, Darfur: 400,000 Black Arabs Killed

Since February 2003, violence, destruction of hundreds of villages, and the murder of hundreds of thousands of black Sudanese has occurred in the Darfur region of western Sudan. Since that date, the Janjaweed, government-supported armed militias, have conducted a systematic campaign of slaughter, rape, starvation, and forced displacement of the population in Darfur. It is estimated that more than 400,000 persons have died because of the actions of the Sudanese government and its militias. Nearly 3 million persons have been forced from their villages, and more than 200,000 have fled their country by entering Chad, a neighboring state. All the displaced live in miserable camps in Darfur and Chad where they are systematically attacked by the Janjaweed. Beyond the murderous attacks, people are dying of starvation and lack of medical treatment. For the very first time, nations have labeled the actions of the Sudanese government as "genocidal," and the ICC has issued an arrest warrant for capture of its president, Omar Hassan al-Bashir. However, little has been done by the watchful world community to halt the genocide in Darfur.

# 5

# Biographical Sketches

This chapter provides the reader with brief biographies of two dozen major national leaders responsible for genocidal actions and mass exterminations during the 20th and 21st centuries. Most of these men have never been brought before a court of law, either national or international, to face charges of genocide or war crimes or crimes against humanity. A majority of them *were never indicted* for their genocidal actions.

## Hafez al-Assad (1930–2000)

Hafez al-Assad was born in rural Syria as part of the minority Alawite community. Because his family had no money to send him to university, al-Assad went to the Syrian Military Academy and received a free higher education. In 1951 he joined the Syrian military and was assigned to the Air Force division. Showing real aptitude, Assad was send to the Soviet Union to receive advanced training. Like many of Syria's young officers, al-Assad was politically active. At age 16 he had joined the Ba'ath Party and as he rose through the ranks of the military became an important figure. Al-Assad opposed the creation of the United Arab Republic and despite being stationed in Cairo worked with other officers to end the union between Syria and Egypt. In the chaos that followed the dissolution the Ba'athists seized power, and al-Assad was appointed head of the air force. Officially, the state was ruled by Amin al-Hafiz, a Sunni Muslim, but it was actually run by a coterie of young Alawites. In 1966 these Alawites launched a violent coup. Al-Assad became minister of defense and the true ruler of the country. After being discredited by the failure of the Syrian military in the Six Days War in 1967, al-Assad overthrew the civilian government and became ruler of Syria in 1970. Al-Assad ruled Syria through the power of the army. He did achieve some popularity because of his moderate reforms and the vast increase in Syria's military power, but was always mistrusted by the population for his secularism and his Alawite roots. Al-Assad ruled the country until his death in 2000 due to a heart attack while speaking on the telephone with Lebanese prime minister Salim Hoss. He was succeeded by his son Bashar al-Assad.

# Omar Hassan al-Bashir (1944–)

Omar al-Bashir is the current president of the Sudan. He came to power in 1989 when he led a group of military officers in a bloodless coup that ousted the government. He called his action the "salvation revolution." Once in power, he suspended all political parties and barred trade unions. He instituted Islamic law in parts of the nation (excluding the south, which was involved in a lengthy civil war with the Sudan government). In 1993 he ended military governance by naming himself president. In 1996, he won the election (he was the sole candidate for president). In 2004, he ended the Sudanese civil war with insurgents from South Sudan by granting the area limited autonomy. However, at about the same time, 2003, al-Bashir initiated a violent bloodbath in Darfur, in the western part of Sudan. Unlike the civil war that was to end, which was based on religious differences, the Darfur genocide was and remains an ethnic war between al-Bashir's Muslims and the Afro-Arab population in Darfur. Since 2003, nearly 400,000 residents of the Darfur region have been murdered by al-Bashir's Muslim militia, the Janjaweed. Millions more have been displaced from their villages and living in poverty in camps in Darfur and across the border in Chad.

Guerrilla warfare continued into the second decade of the 21st century. In July 2008, the International Criminal Court's (ICC) prosecutor, Luis Moreno-Ocampo, charged al-Bashir with genocide, crimes against humanity, and war crimes. The ICC issued an arrest warrant for al-Bashir on March 4, 2009. It was delivered to the Sudanese government which, naturally, did not execute it. However, the precedent was set for al-Bashir's being the first sitting leader of a nation-state indicted by the new ICC. Al-Bashir ran for reelection as president in 2010.

# Idi Amin (1923/1925–2003)

Amin served in the military beginning in 1946 and in 1961 was made a lieutenant by the British. In 1962, Uganda received independence from the United Kingdom. By 1964, Amin was made a colonel by the new government and deputy commander of the army and the air force. After a coup in 1966, Amin was made a major general and the commander of the military forces. In 1971, Amin staged a coup and was declared president and chief of the armed forces. To secure his seizure of power, Amin ordered the execution of his tribal enemies, murdering between 100,000 and 300,000. Entire villages were wiped out and the civilian leadership, including doctors, teachers, clergy, bankers, business leaders, and journalists, were targeted and murdered. He created death squads, consisting of members of his presidential guard. Tyranny reigned across Uganda. In 1975, Amin promoted himself to field marshall and in 1976 named himself president for life. In 1979, Amin was forced out of power by invading Tanzanian military forces and settled in Saudi Arabia. Amin died in a Saudi hospital in 2003.

# Ion Antonescu (1882–1946)

Born in a small village north of Bucharest, Romania, Antonescu attended French military schools, and by 1907 was an officer in the Romanian army. When World War I began in 1914, the nation remained neutral, but in 1916 declared war on Austria-Hungary. At war's end, because of the treaties dictated by the victorious Allies, Romania doubled its size, bringing into the nation new ethnic groups. This led to the rise of the strident nationalist party in the nation, which was strongly anti-Semitic. Antonescu remained in the military and during the between-wars era was military attaché in Paris and then London. Although an anti-Semite, he married a Jewish-French woman and had a son. In 1934, he became a general and was appointed chief of the Romanian general staff. During the 1930s the Iron Guard, an anti-Communist, anti-Semitic organization was formed in Romania. During the period before the Second World War began, the Nazis funded the Iron Guard so that it could continue its brutal repression of Communists and the Jews. By the start of the Second World

War, there were almost 800,000 Jews living in Romania, the third-largest Jewish population, following Russia and Poland. Shortly after the beginning of the war, the prime minister declared Romanian neutrality. However, he was assassinated and very quickly the king agreed to Nazi demands. In 1940, Antonescu became prime minister and immediately demanded the resignation of the king. In this move, he had the support of the Iron Guard. He then established a new government, called the National Legionary Government and became its leader. Antonescu allowed the Nazi army to occupy the nation and introduced harsh anti-Semitic laws as well as restrictions on Greek and Armenian businessmen. In 1941, after a failed coup by the Iron Guard, Antonescu became dictator, army marshall, chief of state, and president. Further anti-Jewish measures were introduced with the intent of removing Jews from Romania. After attacking Russia alongside the Nazi armies in 1941, Antonescu issued an order to the army: "Be merciless. . . . I am not disturbed if the world considers us barbarians. You can use your machine-guns if it is necessary. And I can tell you that the law does not exist. So let us give up all the formalities and use this complete freedom. I assume all responsibility and claim that the law does not exist." In all, more than 300,000 Jews were exterminated under his orders. In all, by war's end, more than 420,000 Jews of Romania's prewar Jewish population of 760,000 died. In 1944, the government-in-exile returned, and Romania switched sides and supported the Allies, especially the Russian armies. After capture by the Russians, Antonescu was returned to his country to face trial as a war criminal. In May 1946, he was convicted for war crimes and was executed by firing squad on June 1, 1946.

# Col. Theoneste Bagosora (1941–)

Col. Theoneste Bagosora attended military academies in Rwanda and France. Bagosora was a colonel in Rwanda's army. He was a Hutu and was a senior cabinet director in Rwanda's defense ministry in 1994 when the genocide began against the Tutsi and moderate Hutus in that nation. He was part of the inner circle of extremist Hutus who planned and carried out the three-month extermination of 800,000 in his nation. The Hutu planning for the genocide began in 1990 and was implemented in April 1994. Colonel Bagosora convened a meeting of senior Hutu military officers, and after it ended, the extermination of the Tutsi began. Hutu militias, called the *Interahamwe*, set up roadblocks across the nation, and all Tutsis were killed on the spot—often with garden tools or machetes. Bagosora was the person responsible for distributing the guns and machetes used by the militias to kill the Tutsis. Bagosora was the first official of the Hutu military coup brought before the International Criminal Tribunal, Rwanda (ICTR) to face charges of genocide and war crimes. He was charged with genocide. At the 2002 trial in Tanzania, the United Nations (UN) military officer in charge of the UN peacekeepers, Canadian general Romeo Dallaire, called Bagosora the "kingpin" behind the genocide who "controlled—as well as anyone could—the genocidal militia." The tribunal sentenced Bagosora to life imprisonment for his central role in the murders of the Tutsi in 1994. He and two other leading members of the militia, Maj. Aloys Ntabakuze and Col. Anatole Nsengiyumva, were convicted for committing genocide, crimes against humanity, and war crimes. The trial lasted six years, ending in 2008, and the court heard from 242 witnesses.

# Ismail Enver (1881–1922)

Enver was born in 1881 to a wealthy family in Constantinople. He was sent to Germany for studies and became a passionate follower of German military leaders. He became one of the young radical Turks and a chief organizer of the 1908 Young Turk Revolution. In 1913, he led the coup that overturned the government and installed the Committee of Union and Progress (CUP) in power. In 1914, he became minister of war and, given his love of Germany, convinced his colleagues to enter the war on the side of the Central Powers (Germany and Austria). He played a major role in the Armenian massacres that began in 1915. In his ministry Enver had a secret group of radical militants known as the Special Organization (SO). The sole task of the SO, led by a medical doctor, was the extermination of the Armenian population in the empire. The SO used mobile killing units and systematically killed the Armenians while the victims were marched to the desert. (During World War II, the Nazis replicated the SO with their own mobile detachments whose task was to hunt down and murder Jews.) At the war's end, Enver fled to Germany where he was associated with German Communists. In the postwar trials in Turkey, he was sentenced to death in absentia for his leadership role in the massacre of the Armenians. In 1920, he offered his services to the newly created Soviet government. The Soviet military sent Enver to Central Asia to stop the Muslims there from rebelling against Soviet rule. Instead, Enver joined the Muslim revolutionaries. He was killed in action by Soviet military forces in Turkestan.

## Gen. Romeo Lucas Garcia (1924–2006)

General Garcia was always associated with the military and right-wing dictators in Guatemala. He graduated from the military academy in 1949 and was always associated with military leaders and dictators after the democratic government of Jacobo Arbenz was overthrown in 1954. In 1975, Garcia was appointed defense minister and head of the army general staff. From 1978 to 1982, Garcia was the dictatorial president of Guatemala. During his four years in power an average of 200 murders and "disappearances" took place every month. His targets were social democrats, trade unionist leaders, and the indigenous Mayan peasantry. In two years, 1980–1982, nongovernmental organizations (NGOs) uncovered no less than 344 massacres of Garcia's enemies. His chosen successor in 1982 never took office because of a coup by a military junta, led by General Rios Montt.

In 2000, Guatemala's Association for Justice and Reconciliation sought to bring Garcia to justice in the national court system. Garcia and his close associates were charged with war crimes and genocide. The evidence was produced by forensic anthropologists who worked at identifying the "disappeared" at newly discovered massacre sites in the country. However, by this time, Garcia was very ill and suffered from Alzheimer's disease. He died in 2006.

## Adolf Hitler (1889–1945)

Adolf Hitler, the killer of over six million Jews between 1939 and 1945 and millions of other civilians across Europe, was born in Austria, the son of an officious customs official. He left school in 1905 and wandered aimlessly until the First World War began in 1914. He was living in Vienna and came into contact with the ultranationalist, anti-Semitic Christian Socialist Party. Between 1907 and the outbreak of war in 1914, Hitler developed his extreme anti-Semitism and racial mythology/ideology of the perfect and pure Aryan man. Joining the German army while he was in Munich, Germany, Hitler fought on the Western front where he was wounded twice and won a number of awards for bravery, including the Iron Cross, First Class.

When the war ended, Hitler, like so many other war veterans, joined in the fighting that took place in Munich between rival movements. In 1919, he became a political officer in the army in Munich. He attended a meeting of the nationalistic, socialistic, and Jew-hating German Workers' Party. Hitler found his home in the Party, and by 1921 he became *der Führer* of the renamed organization, the National Socialist German Workers Party (NSDAP), known as the Nazi Party. His leadership led to the growth of the party and by 1923, there were nearly 60,000 members of the Nazi Party, primarily located in Munich. In early November 1923, Hitler staged the Beer Hall Putsch to try to force the Bavarian government to join him in his march to Berlin. He failed and was tried for treason and sentenced to a year in the old fortress in Landsberg. While in prison, he wrote *Mein Kampf*, a book that contained his political ideas and his strategy for coming to power in Germany. Laced throughout the book were his thoughts about the threat of the Jews to the German race and the need to exterminate the Jewish race because they were parasites and vermin who, if not exterminated, would destroy the Aryan race. Hitler's Nazi Party reemerged because of the worldwide depression.

In the 1930 elections, the Nazi Party garnered almost 6.5 million votes and became a popular alternative to the German Communist Party. In 1932, President Hindenburg called on Hitler to head a coalition government of Nazis, German Nationalists, and a handful of independent politicians. By the time Hindenburg died, in 1934, Hitler had brutally terminated the coalition and had brought the German government under his control. He became der Führer, head of state, and commander in chief of the military forces. He immediately developed a propaganda machine that used the radio, the movies, and the press to rally the German masses behind his plans for a new Germany. Alongside the propaganda machinery, run by Joseph Goebbels, Hitler created the necessary ingredient for maintaining total control of the nation. Heinrich Himmler was appointed the leader of the Nazi police system, which included the feared secret police, the Gestapo.

Beginning in 1934, there was a series of laws passed that stripped the German Jewish population of *all* rights—civil, political, economic, and social. Jewish shops and factories were either destroyed or Aryanized by the Nazis. With his total control of the Nation, Hitler turned to development of plans to grab "living space" for the Aryan race of Germans—in central and eastern Europe: Poland, the Balkans, and Russia. He built up the Germany military, especially the air force and the army. He challenged the Western powers, the United Kingdom and France, with his rearmament plans, his taking back the Ruhr territory, the joining of Austria to Germany in 1938, and the dismemberment of Czechoslovakia in 1938 and 1939. He entered into a nonaggression pact with the Soviet Union in 1939. Hitler was ready for war with the West. Allied with Italy and Japan, the Axis powers, in September 1939 Hitler attacked Poland and World War II began in Europe. With the start of the war, Hitler and his surrogates developed the Final Solution to the Jewish problem in Germany and across Europe: the Holocaust. Across Europe, Jews in the nations occupied by Germany were deported to Polish and German killing centers where most were murdered within hours of their arrival at these concentration camps. More than 6 million Jews were slaughtered by the Nazis from 1939 to 1945. Until the very end of the war in May 1945, Hitler demanded that all the Jews be exterminated. With the Russians a few miles from Berlin, Germany, Hitler committed suicide on April 30, 1945.

# Saddam Hussein (1937–2006)

Saddam Hussein, a Sunni Muslim, was dictator of Iraq from 1979 until 2003, when his regime was overthrown by a U.S.-led invasion. By the age of 20, Hussein had joined the revolutionary Baath Party while he was a university student. He launched his political career in 1958 by assassinating a supporter of Iraqi ruler Abdul-Karim Qassim. Saddam rose in the ranks after a Baath coup in 1963 (he had been in exile in Egypt from 1959 until his return in 1963), and by 1979 he was Iraq's president and de facto dictator. He led Iraq through a decade-long war with Iran, and in August 1990 his forces invaded the neighboring country of Kuwait. A U.S.-led alliance organized by the first President Bush ran Hussein's forces out of Kuwait in the Gulf War, which ended in February 1991. However, Saddam still remained in power. In addition to his Iranian enemies, Hussein hated the Kurds living in Iraq as well as Shiite Muslims. The *Anfal* campaign against the Kurds was the bloodiest slaughter during Hussein's regime. Between 1986 and

1989, Hussein's orders led to the extermination of 182,000 Kurdish men, women, and children—and all animals. Many of the Kurds were killed by deadly chemical gas. Hussein blamed the Iranians for the murders, which was untrue. Hussein came under renewed pressure in 2002 from the son of the first President Bush. Hussein's regime was overthrown by an invasion of U.S. and British forces in March of 2003. Hussein disappeared, but U.S. forces captured him on December 13, 2003, after finding him hiding in a small underground pit on a farm near the town of Tikrit. Late in 2005 he went on trial in Iraq for the 1982 deaths of over 140 Shiite Muslim men in the town of Dujail. On November 5, 2006, he was convicted and sentenced to death by hanging. The sentence was upheld after appeal, and Hussein was executed in Baghdad by hanging on the morning of December 30, 2006.

# Shiro Ishii (1892–1959)

Shiro Ishii studied medicine and in 1920 became a doctor in the Japan Medical Corps. He left the army and received a Ph.D. but rejoined the army in 1927. His task was to learn about biological and chemical weapons. In 1930, Ishii established a center for bacteriological research at the Tokyo Army Medical College. After Japan annexed Manchuria, Ishii, who was promoted to Colonel, in 1940, was placed in command of the Epidemic Prevention and Water Purification Department of the Army located near Harbin, Manchuria, later designated as Unit 731. His task was to develop and test biological and chemical weapons for use in war. Toward that end, Japan's captives, mainly Chinese but including some prisoners of war, were used as guinea pigs to test the viability of these weapons. They were injected with pathogens—anthrax, typhoid, gas, gangrene, botulism, meningitis, and yellow fever, among others—and then were left to die. While some were still alive, autopsies were performed on these conscious prisoners. Furthermore, Ishii's Unit 731 provided the army with typhoid and other killer bacteria to "field test" on Chinese civilians. By the war's end, more than 200,000 were killed because of the actions of Unit 731, including 3,000 killed in the autopsy rooms. At the end of the war, Ishii went into hiding to escape punishment for war crimes. In 1946, he was captured by American forces. However, he was never indicted and received immunity from prosecution from the Americans because he gave them all the data Unit 731 collected from its experiments during the war. Unit 731 was not mentioned at the Tokyo war crimes tribunal; none of its leaders, including Ishii faced the bar of justice for their crimes. Unit 731's activities disappeared from history until the early 1980s, when stories were published describing its nefarious activities during the war. Ishii died of cancer in 1959.

# Radovan Karadzic (1945–)

Karadzic was born in Montenegro. During the Second World War, his father was a Chetnik who fought the Nazis and the Communists. In 1960, he moved to Sarajevo, the capital city of Bosnia and Herzegovina (BiH) to study medicine. He graduated as a physician and psychiatrist. Until the demise of Yugoslavia in 1990, he worked in a number of medical facilities in the country. In 1990, he helped create the Serbian Democratic Party (SDP) and became its president. He was supported by Slobodan Milosevic, the president of Serbia. Elections were held that year in BiH, with the votes split between Muslim Party of Democratic Action (86 seats), the SDP (72 seats), and the Croatian Democratic Union of BiH (44 seats). In 1992, after a number of states in the former Yugoslavia chose independence (Croatia and Slovenia), a referendum was held in BiH on whether to secede from Yugoslavia. The Muslims and Croats voted in favor; the Bosnian Serbs did not. And after that, the war began between BiH and the Bosnian Serbs (supported by Serbian troops and supplies). Sarajevo, surrounded on three sides by Bosnian Serb troops, was constantly bombarded for three years. Karadzic, the SDP leader, proclaimed the formation of a Bosnian Serb Republic in BiH— Republika Srpska. As the war continued, with the Bosnian Serbs winning, there was a concerted effort to expel the Muslims and Croats from Serb-held territory. This largely successful effort had a name soon to be known by the world: "ethnic cleansing." Women were placed in rape camps, and about 100,000 men and young men were exterminated by the Bosnian Serb army and the militias. After the war ended in 1995, both men were indicted for numerous crimes by the ICTY, which wrote: Karadzic and Gen. Ratko Mladic were "Criminally responsible for the unlawful confinement, murder, rape, sexual assault, torture, beating, robbery and inhumane treatment of civilians." Thirteen years after the end of the war, in 2008, Karadzic was captured and turned over to the International Criminal Tribunal, Yugoslavia (ICTY) to answer the many charges against him. His trial has continued to the present time (2010). General Mladic is still a free man.

# Haile Mariam Mengistu (1937–)

Haile Mengistu was born in 1937 in Kefa province, Ethiopia, and was an army officer and head of state (1974–1991). In 1974 Mengistu headed a group of rebel soldiers that overthrew Emperor Haile Selassi. After assassinating his rivals, Mengistu became the new regime's acknowledged strongman. Elected as one of its representatives to the military council (or *Derg*) that seized power in September 1974, he soon became one of its most outspoken radical nationalist members. He became vice chairman in November 1974 and chairman in February 1977, after a shoot-out in which his predecessor and hundreds of military officers in the coup were killed. He ruthlessly eliminated his civilian opponents—especially the "counter revolutionaries," students, and people associated with the Ethiopian People's Revolutionary Party—in the Red Terror of 1976–1978. He sought an alliance with the Soviet Union. He was able to defeat the Somali invasion of 1977–1978, with massive Soviet and Cuban military aid, and sought to build a powerful and centralized Ethiopian state on Marxist-Leninist principles. By 1978 he had crushed a major rebellion in Eritrea, and, with Soviet and Cuban help, beat down an invasion of the nation by the Somalis. In the 1980s he faced new rebellions in Eritrea and Tigray, and devastating droughts and famines drew attention to his failed agricultural policies.

The culminating point of this process, the formation of the Workers' Party of Ethiopia in September 1984, coincided with a terrible famine that cost hundreds of thousands of lives. Mengistu's centralizing dictatorship aroused increasing opposition, especially from the northern regions of Eritrea, where effective guerrilla insurgencies contested his rule. In May 1991, with guerrilla armies closing on the Ethiopian capital, Addis Ababa, the Dergue was overthrown, and he fled to exile in Zimbabwe. In 1999, he went to South Africa for medical treatment. However, he immediately returned to his safe haven in Zimbabwe. Mengistu's trial in absentia began in Ethiopia in 1994 and ended in 2006. Mengistu's charge sheet and evidence list was 8,000 pages long. The evidence against him included signed execution orders, videos of torture sessions, and personal testimonies. Mengistu was found guilty as charged on December 12, 2006, and was sentenced to life in prison in January 2007. In addition to the genocide conviction, he was also found guilty of imprisonment, illegal homicide, and illegal confiscation of property.

# Slobodan Milosevic (1941–2006)

The first European head of state to be prosecuted for genocide and war crimes, Slobodan Milosevic emerged to embody the dark side of European leadership. In short, he became Europe's chief menace, the most dangerous figure in post–Cold War Europe. From 1991 to 1999, he presided over mayhem and mass murder in southeastern Europe. In a long list of villains, he was the central figure. To the civilian victims of Srebrenica and Vukovar, Sarajevo and Dubrovnik, Pristina and Banja Luka, he personified the evil men can do. However, although a brilliant tactician who ran rings around his peers and rivals in Croatia, Bosnia and Kosovo, confounded the Serbian opposition, and outwitted an endless array of international mediators, Milosevic was a lousy strategist. With no ultimate aim except short-term gain, he won most of the battles and lost all the wars. In the process, he left a legacy of more than 200,000 dead in Bosnia and 2 million people (half the population) homeless. He ethnically cleansed more than 800,000 Albanians from their homes in Kosovo. He had political opponents and former friends and colleagues in Belgrade murdered. In Bosnia, he triggered the worst crisis in transatlantic relations before the Iraq War and left the UN and the European Union looking spineless and humiliated, their foreign policy making and peacekeeping credibility in tatters. Milosevic was first indicted for war crimes in Kosovo in March 1999 by Louise Arbour, the Canadian chief prosecutor for the ICTY in The Hague. Arbour's successor, the Swiss jurist Carla Del Ponte, extended the charge sheet to include indictments on Croatia and Bosnia, in the latter case accusing him of genocide for his alleged collusion in the massacre of more than 7,000 Muslim males at Srebrenica in July 1995. Specifically, on November 23, 2001, Milosevic was charged with the following crimes: "(1) Genocide and complicity in Genocide; (2) Crimes against humanity involving persecution, extermination, murder, imprisonment, torture, deportation and inhumane acts (forcible transfers); (3) Grave breaches of the Geneva Conventions of 1949 involving willful killing, unlawful confinement, willfully causing great suffering, unlawful deportation or transfer, and extensive destruction and appropriation of property; (4) Violations of the laws or customs of war involving inter alia attacks on civilians, unlawful destruction, plunder of property and cruel treatment." That he ended up in the dock in The Hague at all surprised many who have studied the man through the 1990s. Given his predisposition for violence, his apparent lack of remorse for the pain and suffering he caused, and a troubled family history of suicides and death, it was always thought that Milosevic would go down in a bloodbath in Belgrade or opt to kill himself rather than be turned over to the ICTY and die while on trial in The Hague.

# Gen. Ratko Mladic (1943–)

Ratko Mladic was born in BiH. His father was killed in the Second World War by the Ustase (the Croatian allies of the Nazis). He entered the Yugoslav military and reached a command position in the 1970s. In 1991, he was appointed commander of the 9th Corps of the Yugoslavian army in Croatia. In 1992, he took command of the 80,000 soldiers stationed in the BiH. They became the military backbone of the Bosnian Serb forces battling the Muslims and Croats. This force was joined by the notorious Bosnian-Serb militias and, in less than two months, under the leadership of Radovan Karadzic and Mladic, seized control of two-thirds of the country. The UN, in 1993, tried to form six safe areas where non-Bosnian Serbs would be protected by the UN peacekeepers. These areas included Srebrenica, Bihac, Tuzla, Zepa, Sarajevo, and Gorazde. However, near the end of the war, Bosnian Serbs captured the safe areas of Srebrenica and Zepa. More than 40,000 Muslims were expelled, and another 8,000 were exterminated by the Bosnian Serb militias, on the orders of General Mladic. In 1995, the siege of Sarajevo was lifted as part of a peace treaty. In three years, more than 10,000 persons were killed, including 1,500 children. More than 200,000 lost their lives during the war, and more than three million lost their homes and property. In July 1995, Karadzic and Mladic were indicted by the ICTY on 16 counts, including genocide, war crimes, crimes against civilians, the taking of UN peacekeepers as hostages, and the destruction of places of worship. Both men avoided capture until Karadzic's arrest. However, as of 2010, Mladic is still free, allegedly living openly in Serbia and being protected by the Serbian government and military.

# Jose Efrain Rios Montt (1926–)

Montt began his military career in the Guatemalan army in 1946 and by 1972 was a general. He is a born-again evangelical Protestant with ties to Christian fundamentalists in the United States. Beginning in 1962, a 34-year civil war broke out between leftist guerilla groups and the government for control of the nation. The military forces increased troops in uniform and developed a sophisticated intelligence network to deal with the rebel groups—assisted by the United States. In the 1960s, "death squads" were organized to exterminate the rebels—but also indigenous Mayans. Gen. Jose Efrain Rios Montt headed the Guatemala military government from 1982 to 1983, succeeding Gen. Romeo Lucas Garcia through a military coup in 1982. He headed the three-person junta and immediately annulled the constitution and dissolved parliament. Political parties were banned, and the election law was cancelled. His leadership came in a period during which the government carried out extensive human rights violations. In June 1982, he disbanded the junta and assumed the presidency. His 14 months in power was seen by many as the bloodiest reign in more than 400 years. While he was dictator, 100,000 Guatemalans were killed or disappeared, and between 500,000 and 1.5 million others were forced to flee from the death squads. He remains an influential and powerful politician and currently holds a seat in the Guatemalan Congress after being elected in September 2007. Rios Montt's brief presidency was probably the most violent period of the 36-year internal conflict in Guatemala, which resulted in thousands of deaths of mostly unarmed indigenous civilians. A UN-sponsored truth commission concluded that acts of genocide had been committed "through methods whose cruelty has outraged the moral conscience of the civilized world." Led by Nobel Prize laureate Rigoberta Menchú, survivors frustrated by severe delays, obstruction, and harassment in Guatemalan courts petitioned Spain's National Court to hear a case charging Rios Montt and other former officials with serious crimes under international law, using the principle of *universal jurisdiction*. In July 2006, Spain's National Court (SNC) charged Rios Montt and the other former senior officials with genocide, terrorism, torture and illegal detention. The SNC subsequently issued warrants for their arrest, and Guatemalan authorities took some of the accused into custody to ensure that they would not flee the country. In December 2007, however, the Guatemalan Constitutional Court granted the appeal of two of the suspects wanted by the Spanish court, ruling that they were not extraditable to Spain for trial. Although the appeal was brought forward by only two of the suspects, the decision makes it unlikely that the Guatemalan court will move to extradite Rios Montt to Spain to face the charges against him. The case in Spain will continue. In the winter and spring of 2008, courageous witnesses gave testimony to courts in both Guatemala City and Madrid despite grave personal risk. The court in Guatemala was acting on behalf of the Spanish court. In short, the international warrants for the arrest of Rios Montt and the other high level officials wanted by the SNC won't go away. However, experts have observed that unless one of the defendants leaves Guatemala and is arrested, the case in Spain will not come to trial because Spain does not recognize a trial in which the defendant is not present for court proceedings.

# Anton Pavelic (1889–1959)

Pavelic was born a short distance south of Sarajevo, BiH. After attending a Jesuit seminary for secondary school, he studied law at the University of Zagreb, located in the capital of Croatia. After graduation from law school, Pavelic opened a law office in Zagreb. He became a member of an extreme right-wing nationalist party that advocated freedom for Croatia. In 1919, he was made interim secretary of a nationalist organization. For Pavelic, the only reality was, as he wrote: "a free and independent Croat state comprising the entire historical and ethnic territory of the Croat people." He said that Croatia's enemies were the Serbian government, international Freemasonry, Jews, and Communists. After the end of the First World War, the Allies created Yugoslavia, which consisted of Serbs, Croats, Bosnians, Macedonians, and Slovenes. In the 1920s he was an active member of the Croat nationalist party and won a seat in the Parliament. In 1929, the king dissolved the legislature and created a "Royal Dictatorship."

All civil liberties were denied, political parties were banned, and self-government was abolished. Pavelic fled to Vienna where he took control of the Croat Youth Movement. He came into contact with the new Italian dictator, Benito Mussolini, and by

1932, relocated to Rome and then turned the Youth Movement into what would become the dreaded Ustase, a terrorist organization known for its hatred of Serbs and Bosnians. In 1934, the Yugoslavian king was assassinated in France by Ustase terrorists. Pavelic, who was still in Italy, was tried in absentia and sentenced to death by a French court. Italy refused to send Pavelic to France for his punishment. In 1939, the Second World War began and by 1941 Germany coerced Yugoslavia to sign the Tripartite Pact, joining that nation (and other eastern European nations) to the Axis powers, Germany, Italy, and Japan.

However, anti-Fascist air force pilots mutinied against the Pact and Pavelic, from Italy, called on Croat soldiers to "use your weapons against the Serbian soldiers and officers. We are fighting shoulder to shoulder with our German and Italian allies." In April 1941, the victorious German army marched into Zagreb, and Pavelic's deputy (the Ustase leader in Croatia) proclaimed the Independent State of Croatia. A few days later Pavelic returned to Zagreb after more than a decade away from his homeland. Soon after his return, the Nazis, at the urging of Mussolini, made Pavelic chieftain of the Croat government. His first speech set the tone for the rest of the war in Yugoslavia. The primary task of his government was to "purify" Croatia and to bring about the "elimination of alien elements." His major weapon was the Ustase, which was used to torture, deport, and exterminate the two million alien elements then living in Croatia: Jews, Gypsies, and Serbs. South of Zagreb, Pavelic established the Jasenovac concentration camp to hold and then murder these elements. Joining the Ustase terrorists in this killing task were some Croatian Catholic clergy. By the war's end, the Ustase, under Pavelic's leadership, exterminated 30,000 Jews, about 29,000 gypsies, and between 300,000 and 600,000 Serbs. Pavelic once again left Croatia in 1945 for Rome, Italy, where he was protected by the Vatican. In 1948, he moved to a monastery near Rome, disguised as a Catholic priest. Later that year, Vatican agents smuggled him out of harm's way to Argentina, where he revived the Ustase movement and served as an advisor to Argentinian president Juan Peron. Between 1946 and 1948, nearly 8,000 Ustase arrived in Argentina under Peron's protection. In 1957, the Yugoslavian secret police finally located Pavelic and planned his assassination. He was seriously wounded in the attempt and fled to fascist Spain, led by military dictator Fransisco Franco. In 1959, Pavelic died from his wounds while living in Madrid.

# Gen. Augusto Pinochet (1915–2006)

Pinochet was a Chilean army general who became a dictatorial president of Chile. From 1973 to 1998, he was commander in chief of the army, president of the Chilean Junta from 1973 to 1981, and president of the Republic of Chile from 1974 until 1990, when the country went back to democratic rule. In 1973, he led the junta (including the army, navy, air force, and the Carabineros leaders) that overthrew democratically elected president Salvadore Allende, banned all leftist and communist parties, and established a military dictatorship. All other political parties were subsequently banned from functioning in Chile. His regime murdered thousands of political opponents, almost 100,000 Chilean civilians were interned, and more than 30,000 tortured. Others "disappeared" because of their political views. More than 200,000 other Chileans went into exile because of fears for their lives. After he retired as commander in chief in 1998, he became senator for life. During that year, he visited the United Kingdom for medical treatment and was arrested on a Spanish provisional warrant for the murders and disappearances of hundreds of Spanish citizens living in Chile while Pinochet was president. A second provisional arrest warrant was issued by a Spanish judge Baltasar Garzon charging the former dictator with systematic torture, murder, illegal detention, and forced disappearances. These 1998 warrants were the first ones ever issued to a former head of state arrested on the principle of universal jurisdiction. He was eventually released in March 2000 on medical grounds and returned to Chile. In December 2000, he was indicted by Chile for the disappearances or kidnapping of 75 political opponents. In 2002, the Chilean Supreme Court dismissed all charges for medical reasons. In 2004, the Chilean Supreme Court overturned its earlier decision; it concluded that Pinochet was medically fit to stand trial and placed him under house arrest. He was indicted again in 2006 for murder and disappearances. However, he died in December 2006 without ever being convicted of the many charges against him.

# Pol Pot (1928–1998)

Pol Pot was born Saloth Sar on May 19, 1928, near Anlong Veng, Cambodia. He was educated by Buddhists and at a private Catholic institution in Phnom Penh and then enrolled at a technical school in the town of Kompong Cham to learn carpentry. He later obtained a government scholarship to study radio and electrical technology in Paris. However, in France Pol Pot began to spend less time studying and more time becoming involved with the Communist Party. After returning to Cambodia in 1953, Pol Pot drifted into the Vietnamese-influenced United Khmer Issarak (Freedom) Front of Cambodian Communists. The Front was one of many Cambodian groups that opposed French control of Cambodia as well as the government of Prince Norodom Sihanouk. After Cambodia won its independence from the French in 1954, Pol Pot became involved with the Khmer People's Revolutionary Party (KPRP), the first Cambodian Communist Party. Pol Pot and his army, called the Khmer Rouge, came to power in Cambodia (Kampuchea) in 1975. He was named prime minister of the new communist government in 1976 and began a program of violent reform. The Khmer Rouge abolished currency, religion, and private property and evacuated cities in the hopes of creating an agrarian society that emulated the Chinese Communist experiment, free of Western influence. Under his regime, forced labor, executions, and famine killed between 1.5 and 2 million Cambodians (more than 20 percent of the population). When Vietnam invaded Cambodia in 1979, Pol Pot—called Brother Number One by followers—was ousted from the capital, Phnom Penh, but continued to lead the Khmer Rouge army in exile. He resigned as leader of the army in 1985, and by the late 1990s a split in the Khmer Rouge caused his former comrades to turn on him and imprison him for murder. He died unrepentant in 1998; the cause of death is still a mystery: some say he had a heart attack, some say he was murdered, and some say he killed himself.

# Joseph Stalin (1879–1953)

Stalin was born in 1879 to a poor family in Georgia. Scarred by smallpox and with a somewhat deformed arm, these maladies led to a life-long distrust of others in society, especially when he was around intellectuals. His mother sent Stalin to the capital, Tiflis, to study for the priesthood. He never finished his religious studies. Instead, he joined the young revolutionaries in the city and helped them by organizing workers, delivering revolutionary leaflets, and engaging in robberies to help fund the revolutionaries. After the start of the Russian Revolution in 1917, he was appointed by Vladimir Lenin to a number of positions in the new Soviet government. In 1922, Stalin was appointed as general secretary of the Communist Party's Central Committee. He used this bureaucratic position to gain enormous power through his appointment of men and women to fill positions in the new government. Lenin died in 1924, and Stalin went about consolidating his power by having his Communist Party rivals executed. He capped his rise to absolute power when he had his last remaining enemies brought before show trials and charged with being "enemies of the people." His last enemy, Leon Trotsky, was killed in 1940 in Mexico City with an ice pick wielded by one of Stalin's men. Stalin's major task after consolidating his power was to have backward Russia become a major industrial power in the world. In his effort to achieve this goal, he nationalized agriculture into collective farms and created Five-Year Plans to coordinate these efforts toward industrialization. This effort came at a tremendous human cost. Millions of Kulaks starved to death, and millions more were brought into the Gulag system where they worked for the state until they died. In 1939, Stalin negotiated a nonaggression pact with Hitler's Germany. In 1941, Hitler attacked the Soviet Union. Stalin was totally unprepared for war; during the 1930s, he had decimated the military officer class with his purge trials. The Nazi armies quickly seized the Ukraine and Belarus. Leningrad was under constant siege by Nazi artillery, and the Nazi armies were just a few miles from the Kremlin in Moscow. The tide turned after the Soviet armies broke the siege at Stalingrad in 1943. The Germans suffered a disastrous defeat in the winter of 1943 and began their long retreat back to the West with the Soviet army following them and liberating the captive eastern European nations. After the war, at a number of conferences with his Western allies, the United Kingdom, the United States, and France, at Teheran and Yalta, and Potsdam, Stalin succeeded in maintaining the Soviet Union as a major world power. Stalin was able to bring these Eastern European nations under his sphere of influence, thus beginning the Cold War with the West. He continued to purge his enemies after the war, calling them traitors, sending them to the Gulag or having them murdered. In 1953, Stalin died, and the purges generally ended with his death.

# Haji Suharto (1921–2008)

Born June 8, 1921, in Kemusu Argamulja, Java, Dutch East Indies, Haji Suharto was the second president of Indonesia (1967–1998). Suharto initially served in the Dutch colonial army, but after the Japanese conquest (1942) he joined a Japanese-sponsored defense corps. After Japan's surrender he joined the guerrilla forces seeking independence from the Dutch. When Indonesia became independent (1950), he was a lieutenant colonel. A strong anticommunist, he crushed what was purported to be an attempted communist coup d'état in 1965 with a ruthless purge of communists and leftists throughout the country that left as many as 1,000,000 dead. That moment came on September 30, 1965, when the PKI (Communist Party) leader, Dipa Nusantara Aidit (apparently acting on his own), and a small group of leftwing officers launched a botched coup in which six senior generals were killed. Suharto, who mysteriously survived, quickly suppressed the uprising. Over the next six months, army units and local vigilante groups launched a nationwide purge of so-called communists, a catch-all label that included labor and civic leaders and thousands of others who would never have even heard of Karl Marx. Most were shot, stabbed, beaten to death, or thrown down wells in acts of horrifying violence. Suharto deposed the sitting president, Sukarno, and appointed himself president in 1967. He established authoritarian rule and was repeatedly elected without opposition. Vast numbers of political opponents were killed, jailed, or sent to labor camps during three decades of Suharto's rule, with tens of thousands dying in East Timor alone following its illegal annexation in 1975. A severe economic downturn focused public attention on his government's corruption, and this led to massive demonstrations that prompted his resignation in 1998, after 31 years in power.

# Pasha Mehmat Talat (1874–1921)

Talat was one of the leaders of the new Turkish government, the Committee of Union and Progress (CUP or the Young Turk Movement), that reigned during the First World War. Along with two other leaders of the CUP, Enver Pasha and Djemal Pasha, the trio, known as the Three Pashas, ran the government until nearly the end of the war. As interior minister, Talat, in April 1915, ordered the arrest of 235 Armenian leaders in Constantinople (present-day Istanbul). One month later, Talat was responsible for passage of the Tehcir Law of May 1915. This law began the massacre of ethnic Armenians living in the Ottoman Empire. As minister of the interior, the deportation of Turkey's Armenian population fell under his jurisdiction. On September 16, 1915, Talat sent the following message to the Prefecture of Aleppo: "you have already been advised that the Government . . . has decided to destroy completely all the indicated persons [Armenians] living in Turkey. . . . Their existence must come to an end, however tragic the means may be; and no regard must be paid to either age or sex, or to conscientious scruples. Minister of the Interior, Talat."

In 1917, Talat became the Grand Vizier, but he was unsuccessful in turning the tide of the war. Between 1917 and his hurried departure on a German submarine in early November 1918, the Turkish armies were defeated in Jerusalem and in Baghdad by British forces. After the war ended, there were Turkish trials against the leading CUP leaders for having ordered and implemented the Armenian Massacre. In July 1919, Talat and other CUP leaders were condemned to death in absentia. (At this time, Talat was living in Berlin.) German officials were very reluctant to return Talat to the new government. He was assassinated by an Armenian revolutionary in Berlin, Germany, on March 15, 1921.

# Father Joseph Tiso (1887–1947)

Joseph Tiso was a Catholic priest in Slovakia. After World War I ended, there was the geographic and political destruction of the Austro-Hungarian Empire and the creation of Czechoslovakia. Tiso, who had been on an upward trajectory in the Catholic Church, immediately dropped his church affiliation and declared himself to be a Slovak nationalist and entered politics in the newly created nation.

Although anti-Semitic, during the interwar period he became minister of health and kept his views about the Jews secret. By 1938, however, Jews in Slovakia came under harsh attacks; they saw their civil rights destroyed by the government, which supported Hitler's efforts on the continent. By now, Tiso had become president of Slovakia and was in support of Hitler's plans for exterminating Jews. Jewish property was taken by the government. With the beginning of the war, Hitler invaded Czechoslovakia and offered the Slovaks an independent state in exchange for an alliance with Germany. In 1940, Tiso's government began deporting Jews at the request of the Nazi government. Although the Vatican and Jewish groups tried to persuade Tiso not to follow the Nazi requests, he continued the deportations with the full knowledge that the Jews were being sent to their deaths. In 1944, *Time* magazine described Tiso as a "canny bulletheaded nationalist. With political craft and German aid, Tiso has fed his countrymen relatively well, provided state jobs, promoted Slovaks in government service, and suppressed pro-Czechs by deporting them or threatening to" (*Time*, April 17, 1944, Foreign News: Pride and a Priest, at www.time.com). After a 1944 civilian anti-Fascist revolt in Slovakia, Tiso lost domestic support and, because the German army occupied the country, he became a puppet leader for the Nazis and continued to deport Jews to the death camps. Slovakia was the only nation to pay the Nazis 500 marks to "cover the expenses" of relocating Slovakian Jews to the death camps. Almost 70,000 of Slovakia's 90,000 Jews were exterminated by the Nazis. In 1947, Tiso was tried by the new government for his actions against the Jews, found guilty, and executed.

# Mao Tse-Tung (1893–1976)

Mao Tse-Tung (Zedung) was a child of farmers in Hunan province. As a young man, he came into contact with Chinese revolutionaries and the ideas of Karl Marx and Lenin. By 1921, he was a member of the Chinese Communist Party. By 1925, fleeing from the Nationalist Party of Chiang Kai-Shek, he returned to Hunan. After studying the plight of the farmers in the province, Zedung was convinced that the Chinese Communist revolution would begin with the farmers and other rural workers, not in the cities. Constantly hounded by the Nationalist Party, between 1934 and 1935, he led the Long March to Yan'du, where they built their party headquarters and Mao became chairman of the Chinese Communist Party. During the late 1930s both the Communists and the Nationalists joined against their common enemy, Japan. After the war, with the help of the Soviet Union, Mao's armies won decisive battles against the Nationalists and took control of the nation in 1949. Like Stalin, Mao wanted to modernize as quickly as possible through Land Reform and Five-Year Plans and what he termed The Great Leap Forward in 1958. The Great Leap led to a horrendous famine that took 20 million lives between 1959 and 1962. The next innovation Mao introduced was the Cultural Revolution of 1966–1976. This led, until Mao's death in 1976, to the Red Guards, groups of young adults who set up tribunals across China to try and to punish the bourgeois segments in the nation. During this decade, millions of these Chinese were prosecuted and ultimately killed. The killing ended with Mao's death in 1976.

# Gen. Jorge Raphael Videla (1925–)

Jorge Rafael Videla Redondo was the 43rd president of Argentina from 1976 to 1981. He was named commander in chief by President Isabel Perón in 1975. Perón, former vice president to her husband, Juan Peron, succeeded to the presidency following his death. Her authoritarian administration was unpopular and ineffectual. Videla headed a military coup that deposed her on March 24, 1976. A military junta made up of himself, representing the army, Adm. Emilio Massera (navy), and Brig. Gen. Orlando Ramon Agosti (air force). Two days after the coup, Videla formally assumed the presidency, and the newly installed military government arrested, detained, tortured, and killed suspected terrorists and political opponents. Human rights violations became commonplace. According to estimates, at least 9,000 and up to about 30,000 Argentinians were subject to forced disappearance (*desaparecidos*) and most probably were killed; many were illegally detained and tortured, and others fled the country. Politically, all legislative power was concentrated in the hands of Videla's nine-man junta, and every single important position in the national government was filled with loyal military officers. The junta banned prohibited labor unions and strikes by workers, abolished the nation's judiciary, and suspended civil liberties. Despite these cruel abuses, Videla's regime continued to have the backing of the Argentine Roman Catholic Church and the local media. Democracy was restored in 1983, and Videla was put on trial and found guilty. He was sentenced to life imprisonment and was discharged from the military in 1985. The tribunal found Videla guilty of homicide, disappearances, torture, and many other crimes. Videla was imprisoned for only five years.

In 1990, President Carlos Menem pardoned Videla together with many other former members of the military regime. Menem cited the need to get over past conflicts as his main reason. Videla briefly returned to prison in 1998 when a judge found him guilty of the kidnapping of babies during the Dirty Wars. Videla spent 38 days in prison, and was later put under house arrest because of his declining health. Since 2003, the new government has not recognized Videla as having been a legal president of the country, and his portrait has been removed from the military school. There have also been many legal prosecutions of officials associated with the crimes of the regime. Although pardoned in 2006, in April 25, 2007, a federal court struck down his presidential pardon and restored his human rights abuse convictions. In 2008, he was once again placed under house arrest.

# Lothar Von Trotha (1848–1920)

Von Trotha was the German military commander responsible for the slaughter of the Herreros in 1906–1908. Born in Magdeburg, he joined the Prussian Army in 1865 and fought in a number of wars for which he was awarded the Iron Cross 2nd Class. In 1894, Trotha was appointed commander of the colonial force in German East Africa. In 1904, he was appointed commander in chief of German South West Africa. It was at the beginning of the Herrero wars, and the German troops were having great difficulty with the native tribesmen. Trotha devised a military plan to chase the Herrero into the western portion of the Kalahari Desert. He ordered his troops to poison the wells and to shoot any Herrero on sight, whether man, woman, or child. He then issued an Extermination Order, which read: "Within the German borders, every Herrero, whether armed or unarmed, with or without cattle, will be shot. I shall not accept any more women or children. I shall drive them back to their people—otherwise I shall order shots to be fired at them." The outcry in Germany was so great that the Kaiser removed Trotha from his command. He returned to Germany in November 1905 and was made general of infantry in 1910. He died in 1920 of typhoid fever.

# 6

# Documents

## Documents

### General Orders No. 100: Instructions for the Government of Armies of the United States in the Field by Francis Lieber: April 24, 1863

*This Military Order established limitations on Union forces regarding their treatment of captured Confederate soldiers. It was adopted by General Lee for use in the Confederate army. Subsequently, many nations adopted these rules for their own armies.*

SECTION III

**Prisoners of War, Hostages, Booty on the Battlefield.**

**Article 49**
A prisoner of war is a public enemy armed or attached to the hostile army for active aid, who has fallen into the hands of the captor, either fighting or wounded, on the field or in the hospital, by individual surrender or by capitulation.

All soldiers, of whatever species of arms; all men who belong to the rising en masse of the hostile country; all those who are attached to the army for its efficiency and promote directly the object of the war, except such as are hereinafter provided for; all disabled men or officers on the field or elsewhere, if captured; all enemies who have thrown away their arms and ask for quarter, are prisoners of war, and as such exposed to the inconveniences as well as entitled to the privileges of a prisoner of war.

. . .

### Article 56
A prisoner of war is subject to no punishment for being a public enemy, nor is any revenge wreaked upon him by the intentional infliction of any suffering, or disgrace, by cruel imprisonment, want of food, by mutilation, death, or any other barbarity.

### Article 60
It is against the usage of modern war to resolve, in hatred and revenge, to give no quarter. No body of troops has the right to declare that it will not give, and therefore will not expect, quarter; but a commander is permitted to direct his troops to give no quarter, in great straits, when his own salvation makes it impossible to cumber himself with prisoners.

### Article 61
Troops that give no quarter have no right to kill enemies already disabled on the ground, or prisoners captured by other troops.

### Article 62
All troops of the enemy known or discovered to give no quarter in general, or to any portion of the army, receive none.

. . .

### Article 68
Modern wars are not internecine wars, in which the killing of the enemy is the object. The destruction of the enemy in modern war, and, indeed, modern war itself, are means to obtain that object of the belligerent which lies beyond the war. Unnecessary or revengeful destruction of life is not lawful.

### Article 70
The use of poison in any manner, be it to poison wells, or food, or arms, is wholly excluded from modern warfare. He that uses it puts himself out of the pale of the law and usages of war.

### Article 71
Whoever intentionally inflicts additional wounds on an enemy already wholly disabled, or kills such an enemy, or who orders or encourages soldiers to do so, shall suffer death, if duly convicted, whether he belongs to the Army of the United States, or is an enemy captured after having committed his misdeed.

. . .

**Article 75**
Prisoners of war are subject to confinement or imprisonment such as may be deemed necessary on account of safety, but they are to be subjected to no other intentional suffering or indignity. The confinement and mode of treating a prisoner may be varied during his captivity according to the demands of safety.

**Article 76**
Prisoners of war shall be fed upon plain and wholesome food, whenever practicable, and treated with humanity.

. . .

**Article 80**
Honorable men, when captured, will abstain from giving to the enemy information concerning their own army, and the modern law of war permits no longer the use of any violence against prisoners in order to extort the desired information or to punish them for having given false information.

# The Hague Peace Conference, 1899

*This conference, one of a number convened in the last decade of the 19th century and the first decade of the 20th century, was an international effort to proscribe certain acts of war that were cruel and/or unnecessary.*

## Final Act of the International Peace Conference; July 29, 1899

. . . In a series of meetings, between the May 18 and the July 29, 1899, in which the constant desire of the above-mentioned Delegates has been to realize, in the fullest manner possible, the generous views of the August Initiator of the Conference and the intentions of their Governments, the Conference has agreed, for submission for signature by the Plenipotentiaries, on the text of the Conventions and Declarations enumerated below and annexed to the present Act:

   I.   Convention for the peaceful adjustment of international differences.
   II.  Convention regarding the laws and customs of war by land.
   III. Convention for the adaptation to maritime warfare of the principles of the Geneva Convention of the August, 22, 1864.
   IV.  Three Declarations:
        1. To prohibit the launching of projectiles and explosives from balloons or by other similar new methods.

2. To prohibit the use of projectiles the only object of which is the diffusion of asphyxiating or deleterious gases.
3. To prohibit the use of bullets which expand or flatten easily in the human body, such as bullets with a hard envelope, of which the envelope does not entirely cover the core, or is pierced with incisions.

. . . Guided by the same sentiments, the Conference has adopted unanimously the following Resolution:

"The Conference is of opinion that the restriction of military charges, which are at present a heavy burden on the world, is extremely desirable for the increase of the material and moral welfare of mankind."

It has, besides, formulated the following wishes:

. . .

4. The Conference expresses the wish that the questions with regard to rifles and naval guns, as considered by it, may be studied by the Governments with the object of coming to an agreement respecting the employment of new types and calibers.
5. The Conference expresses the wish that the Governments, taking into consideration the proposals made at the Conference, may examine the possibility of an agreement as to the limitation of armed forces by land and sea, and of war budgets.

. . .

6. The Conference expresses the wish that the proposal to settle the question of the bombardment of posts, towns, and villages by a naval force may be referred to a subsequent Conference for consideration.

# The Kellogg-Briand Pact, 1928, Excerpts

*This was an international effort to try to end all wars in the future by rejecting warfare as an instrument of national policy. Shortly after it was signed, in 1931, Japan began its war against China.*

*This treaty between the United States and other Powers providing for the renunciation of war as an instrument of national policy. Signed at Paris,*

*August 27, 1928; ratification advised by the Senate, January 16, 1929; ratified by the President, January 17, 1929; instruments of ratification deposited at Washington by the United States of America, Australia, Dominion of Canada, Czechoslovakia, Germany, Great Britain, India, Irish Free State, Italy, New Zealand, and Union of South Africa, March 2, 1929: by Poland, March 26, 1929; by Belgium, March 27 1929; by France, April 22, 1929; by Japan, July 24, 1929; proclaimed, July 24, 1929.*

### ARTICLE I
The High Contracting Parties solemnly declare in the names of their respective peoples that they condemn recourse to war for the solution of international controversies, and renounce it, as an instrument of national policy in their relations with one another.

### ARTICLE II
The High Contracting Parties agree that the settlement or solution of all disputes or conflicts of whatever nature or of whatever origin they may be, which may arise among them, shall never be sought except by pacific means.

### ARTICLE III
The present Treaty shall be ratified by the High Contracting Parties named in the Preamble in accordance with their respective constitutional requirements, and shall take effect as between them as soon as all their several instruments of ratification shall have been deposited at Washington.

This Treaty shall, when it has come into effect as prescribed in the preceding paragraph, remain open as long as may be necessary for adherence by all the other Powers of the world. Every instrument evidencing the adherence of a Power shall be deposited at Washington and the Treaty shall immediately upon such deposit become effective.

# Raphael Lemkin, *Axis Rule in Occupied Europe: Laws of Occupation, Analysis of Government, and Proposals for Redress,* 1944

*Raphael Lemkin coined the new word "genocide" in 1943 (see the book's preface, dated November 15, 1943) both as a continuation of his 1933 Madrid Proposal and as part of his analysis of German occupation policies in Europe. In this 670-page book, Axis Rule, Lemkin introduced and directly addressed the question of genocide in 16 pages of Chapter IX entitled "Genocide."*

## Chapter IX. Genocide—A New Term and New Conception for Destruction of Nations, Excerpts

New conceptions require new terms. By "genocide" we mean the destruction of a nation or of an ethnic group. This new word, coined by the author to denote an old practice in its modern development, is made from the ancient Greek word *genos* (race, tribe) and the Latin *cide* (killing), thus corresponding in its formation to such words as tyrannicide, homicide, infanticide, etc. Generally speaking, genocide does not necessarily mean the immediate destruction of a nation, except when accomplished by mass killings of all members of a nation. It is intended rather to signify a coordinated plan of different actions aiming at the destruction of essential foundations of the life of national groups, with the aim of annihilating the groups themselves. The objectives of such a plan would be disintegration of the political and social institutions, of culture, language, national feelings, religion, and the economic existence of national groups and the destruction of the personal security, liberty, health, dignity, and even the lives of the individuals belonging to such groups. Genocide is directed against the national group as an entity, and the actions involved are directed against individuals, not in their individual capacity, but as members of the national group.

. . . It required a long period of evolution in civilized society to mark the way from wars of extermination . . . to the conception of wars as being essentially limited to activities against armies and states. In the present war, . . . the Germans prepared, waged, and continued a war not merely against states and their armies but against peoples. For the German occupying authorities war thus appears to offer the most appropriate occasion for carrying out their policy of genocide. . . . Because the imposition of this policy of genocide is more destructive for a people than injuries suffered in the actual fighting, the German people will be stronger than the subjugated peoples after the war even if the German army is defeated. In this respect genocide is a new technique of occupation aimed at winning the peace even though the war itself is lost.

. . . Even before the war Hitler envisaged genocide as a means of changing the biological interrelations in Europe in favor of Germany. Hitler's conception of genocide is based not upon cultural but biological patterns. He believes that "*Germanization* can only be carried out with the *soil* and never with *men*."

. . . The plan of genocide had to be adapted to political considerations in different countries. It could not be implemented in full force in all the conquered states, and hence the plan varies as to subject, modalities, and degree of intensity in each occupied country. Some groups—such as the Jews—are to be destroyed completely. A distinction is made between peoples considered to be related by blood to the German people (such as Dutchmen, Norwegians, Flemings, Luxembourgers) and peoples not thus related by blood (such as the Poles, Slovenes, Serbs). The populations of the first group are deemed worthy of being Germanized. . . .

# Constitution of the International Military Tribunal (The Nuremberg Charter), 1945, Excerpts

*In the course of World War II the Allied governments issued several declarations concerning the punishment of war criminals. On October 7, 1942, it was announced that a United Nations War Crimes Commission would be set up for the investigation of war crimes. It was not, however, until October 20, 1943, that the actual establishment of the Commission took place. In the Moscow Declaration of October 30, 1943, the three main Allied powers (United Kingdom, United States, USSR) issued a joint statement that the German war criminals should be judged and punished in the countries in which their crimes were committed, but that, "the major criminals, whose offences have no particular geographical localization," would be punished "by the joint decision of the Governments of the Allies." The Agreement was drafted at a conference held in London from June 26 to August 8, 1945.*

ARTICLE 1
In pursuance of the Agreement signed on the 8th day of August 1945 by the Government of the United States of America, the Provisional Government of the French Republic, the Government of the United Kingdom of Great Britain and Northern Ireland and the Government of the Union of Soviet Socialist Republics, there shall be established an International Military Tribunal (hereinafter called "the Tribunal") for the just and prompt trial and punishment of the major war criminals of the European Axis.

ARTICLE 2
The Tribunal shall consist of four members, each with an alternate. One member and one alternate shall be appointed by each of the Signatories. . . .

. . .

## ARTICLE 6

The Tribunal established by the Agreement referred to Article 1 hereof for the trial and punishment of the major war criminals of the European Axis countries shall have the power to try and punish persons who, acting in the interests of the European Axis countries, whether as individuals or as members of organizations, committed any of the following crimes.

The following acts, or any of them, are crimes coming within the jurisdiction of the Tribunal for which there shall be individual responsibility:

(a) **CRIMES AGAINST PEACE**: namely, planning, preparation, initiation or waging of a war of aggression, or a war in violation of international treaties, agreements or assurances, or participation in a common plan or conspiracy for the accomplishment of any of the foregoing;

(b) **WAR CRIMES**: namely, violations of the laws or customs of war. Such violations shall include, but not be limited to, murder, ill-treatment, or deportation to slave labor or for any other purpose of civilian population of or in occupied territory, murder or ill-treatment of prisoners of war or persons on the seas, killing of hostages, plunder of public or private property, wanton destruction of cities, towns or villages, or devastation not justified by military necessity;

(c) **CRIMES AGAINST HUMANITY**: namely, murder, extermination, enslavement, deportation, and other inhumane acts committed against any civilian population, before or during the war; or persecutions on political, racial, or religious grounds in execution of or in connection with any crime within the jurisdiction of the Tribunal, whether or not in violation of the domestic law of the country where perpetrated.

Leaders, organizers, instigators, and accomplices participating in the formulation or execution of a common plan or conspiracy to commit any of the foregoing crimes are responsible for all acts performed by any persons in execution of such plan.

## ARTICLE 7
The official position of defendants, whether as Heads of State or responsible officials in Government Departments, shall not be considered as freeing them from responsibility or mitigating punishment.

## ARTICLE 8
The fact that the Defendant acted pursuant to orders of his Government or of a superior shall not free him from responsibility, but may be

considered in mitigation of punishment if the Tribunal determines that justice so requires.

. . .

## ARTICLE 14

Each Signatory shall appoint a Chief Prosecutor for the investigation of the charges against and the prosecution of major war criminals. The Chief Prosecutors shall act as a committee for the following purposes:

    (a) to agree upon a plan of the individual work of each of the Chief Prosecutors and his staff,

    (b) to settle the final designation of major war criminals to be tried by the Tribunal,

    (c) to approve the Indictment and the documents to be submitted therewith,

    (d) to lodge the Indictment and the accompany documents with the Tribunal,

    (e) to draw up and recommend to the Tribunal for its approval draft rules of procedure, contemplated by Article 13 of this Charter. The Tribunal shall have the power to accept, with or without amendments, or to reject, the rules so recommended.

The Committee shall act in all the above matters by a majority vote and shall appoint a Chairman as may be convenient and in accordance with the principle of rotation: provided that if there is an equal division of vote concerning the designation of a Defendant to be tried by the Tribunal, or the crimes with which he shall be charged, that proposal will be adopted which was made by the party which proposed that the particular Defendant be tried, or the particular charges be preferred against him.

. . .

## ARTICLE 16

In order to ensure fair trial for the Defendants, the following procedure shall be followed:

    (a) The Indictment shall include full particulars specifying in detail the charges against the Defendants. A copy of the Indictment and of all the documents lodged with the Indictment, translated into a language which he

understands, shall be furnished to the Defendant at
reasonable time before the Trial.

(b) During any preliminary examination or trial of
a Defendant he will have the right to give any explanation relevant to the charges made
against him.

(c) A preliminary examination of a Defendant and his Trial
shall be conducted in, or translated into, a language
which the Defendant understands.

(d) A Defendant shall have the right to conduct his own
defense before the Tribunal or to have the assistance
of Counsel.

(e) A Defendant shall have the right through himself or
through his Counsel to present evidence at the Trial in
support of his defense, and to cross-examine any witness
called by the Prosecution.

**ARTICLE 17**

The Tribunal shall have the power

(a) to summon witnesses to the Trial and to require
their attendance and testimony and to put questions
to them

(b) to interrogate any Defendant,

(c) to require the production of documents and other eviden-
tiary material,

(d) to administer oaths to witnesses,

(e) to appoint officers for the carrying out of any task
designated by the Tribunal including the power to have
evidence taken on commission.

. . .

**ARTICLE 19**

The Tribunal shall not be bound by technical rules of evidence. It shall
adopt and apply to the greatest possible extent expeditious and non-
technical procedure, and shall admit any evidence which it deems to be
of probative value.

**ARTICLE 22**

The permanent seat of the Tribunal shall be in Berlin. . . . The first trial
shall be held at Nuremberg, and any subsequent trials shall be held at
such places as the Tribunal may decide.

**ARTICLE 24**

The proceedings at the Trial shall take the following course:

(a)   The Indictment shall be read in court.

(b)   The Tribunal shall ask each Defendant whether he pleads "guilty" or "not guilty."

(c)   The prosecution shall make an opening statement.

(d)   The Tribunal shall ask the prosecution and the defense what evidence (if any) they wish to submit to the Tribunal, and the Tribunal shall rule upon the admissibility of any such evidence.

(e)   The witnesses for the Prosecution shall be examined and after that the witnesses for the Defense. Thereafter such rebutting evidence as may be held by the Tribunal to be admissible shall be called by either the Prosecution or the Defense.

(f)   The Tribunal may put any question to any witness and to any defendant, at any time.

(g)   The Prosecution and the Defense shall interrogate and may cross-examine any witnesses and any Defendant who gives testimony.

(h)   The Defense shall address the court.

(i)   The Prosecution shall address the court.

(j)   Each Defendant may make a statement to the Tribunal.

(k)   The Tribunal shall deliver judgment and pronounce sentence.

. . .

**ARTICLE 26**

The judgment of the Tribunal as to the guilt or the innocence of any Defendant shall give the reasons on which it is based, and shall be final and not subject to review.

**ARTICLE 27**

The Tribunal shall have the right to impose upon a Defendant, on conviction, death or such other punishment as shall be determined by it to be just.

Source: United Nations, *Charter of the International Military Tribunal — Agreement for the Prosecution and Punishment of the Major War Criminals of the European Axis*, August 8, 1945. Reproduced with permission of the United Nations Publication Board.

# Universal Declaration of Human Rights, December 10, 1948

*On December 10, 1948, the General Assembly of the United Nations adopted and proclaimed the Universal Declaration of Human Rights the full text of which appears below. Following this historic act the Assembly called upon all*

*Member countries to publicize the text of the Declaration and "to cause it to be disseminated, displayed, read, and expounded principally in schools and other educational institutions, without distinction based on the political status of countries or territories."*

## PREAMBLE

Whereas recognition of the inherent dignity and of the equal and inalienable rights of all members of the human family is the foundation of freedom, justice and peace in the world,

Whereas disregard and contempt for human rights have resulted in barbarous acts which have outraged the conscience of mankind, and the advent of a world in which human beings shall enjoy freedom of speech and belief and freedom from fear and want has been proclaimed as the highest aspiration of the common people,

Whereas it is essential, if man is not to be compelled to have recourse, as a last resort, to rebellion against tyranny and oppression, that human rights should be protected by the rule of law,

Whereas it is essential to promote the development of friendly relations between nations,

Whereas the peoples of the United Nations have in the Charter reaffirmed their faith in fundamental human rights, in the dignity and worth of the human person and in the equal rights of men and women and have determined to promote social progress and better standards of life in larger freedom,

Whereas Member States have pledged themselves to achieve, in co-operation with the United Nations, the promotion of universal respect for and observance of human rights and fundamental freedoms,

Whereas a common understanding of these rights and freedoms is of the greatest importance for the full realization of this pledge,

Now, Therefore THE GENERAL ASSEMBLY proclaims THIS UNIVERSAL DECLARATION OF HUMAN RIGHTS as a common standard of achievement for all peoples and all nations, to the end that every individual and every organ of society, keeping this Declaration constantly in mind, shall strive by teaching and education to promote respect for these rights and freedoms and by progressive measures, national and international, to secure their universal and effective recognition and observance, both among the peoples of Member States themselves and among the peoples of territories under their jurisdiction.

### Article 1

- All human beings are born free and equal in dignity and rights. They are endowed with reason and

conscience and should act towards one another in a
spirit of brotherhood.

**Article 2**

- Everyone is entitled to all the rights and freedoms set forth
  in this Declaration, without distinction of any kind, such
  as race, colour, sex, language, religion, political or other
  opinion, national or social origin, property, birth or other
  status. Furthermore, no distinction shall be made on the
  basis of the political, jurisdictional or international status of
  the country or territory to which a person belongs, whether
  it be independent, trust, non-self-governing or under any
  other limitation of sovereignty.

**Article 3**

- Everyone has the right to life, liberty, and security of
  person.

**Article 4**

- No one shall be held in slavery or servitude; slavery and
  the slave trade shall be prohibited in all their forms.

**Article 5**

- No one shall be subjected to torture or to cruel, inhuman or
  degrading treatment or punishment.

**Article 6**

- Everyone has the right to recognition everywhere as a
  person before the law.

**Article 7**

- All are equal before the law and are entitled without
  any discrimination to equal protection of the law. All are
  entitled to equal protection against any discrimination in
  violation of this Declaration and against any incitement to
  such discrimination.

**Article 8**

- Everyone has the right to an effective remedy by the competent national tribunals for acts violating the fundamental
  rights granted him by the constitution or by law.

**Article 9**

- No one shall be subjected to arbitrary arrest,
  detention or exile.

### Article 10

- Everyone is entitled in full equality to a fair and public hearing by an independent and impartial tribunal, in the determination of his rights and obligations and of any criminal charge against him.

### Article 11

1. Everyone charged with a penal offence has the right to be presumed innocent until proved guilty according to law in a public trial at which he has had all the guarantees necessary for his defence.
2. No one shall be held guilty of any penal offence on account of any act or omission which did not constitute a penal offence, under national or international law, at the time when it was committed. Nor shall a heavier penalty be imposed than the one that was applicable at the time the penal offence was committed.

### Article 12

- No one shall be subjected to arbitrary interference with his privacy, family, home or correspondence, nor to attacks upon his honour and reputation. Everyone has the right to the protection of the law against such interference or attacks.

### Article 13

1. Everyone has the right to freedom of movement and residence within the borders of each state.
2. Everyone has the right to leave any country, including his own, and to return to his country.

### Article 14

1. Everyone has the right to seek and to enjoy in other countries asylum from persecution.
2. This right may not be invoked in the case of prosecutions genuinely arising from non-political crimes or from acts contrary to the purposes and principles of the United Nations.

### Article 15

1. Everyone has the right to a nationality.
2. No one shall be arbitrarily deprived of his nationality nor denied the right to change his nationality.

### Article 16

1. Men and women of full age, without any limitation due to race, nationality or religion, have the right to marry and to found a family. They are entitled to equal rights as to marriage, during marriage and at its dissolution.
2. Marriage shall be entered into only with the free and full consent of the intending spouses.
3. The family is the natural and fundamental group unit of society and is entitled to protection by society and the State.

### Article 17

1. Everyone has the right to own property alone as well as in association with others.
2. No one shall be arbitrarily deprived of his property.

### Article 18

- Everyone has the right to freedom of thought, conscience and religion; this right includes freedom to change his religion or belief, and freedom, either alone or in community with others and in public or private, to manifest his religion or belief in teaching, practice, worship and observance.

### Article 19

- Everyone has the right to freedom of opinion and expression; this right includes freedom to hold opinions without interference and to seek, receive and impart information and ideas through any media and regardless of frontiers.

### Article 20

1. Everyone has the right to freedom of peaceful assembly and association.
2. No one may be compelled to belong to an association.

### Article 21

1. Everyone has the right to take part in the government of his country, directly or through freely chosen representatives.
2. Everyone has the right of equal access to public service in his country.
3. The will of the people shall be the basis of the authority of government; this will shall be expressed in periodic and genuine elections which shall be by universal and equal

suffrage and shall be held by secret vote or by equivalent free voting procedures.

**Article 22**

- Everyone, as a member of society, has the right to social security and is entitled to realization, through national effort and international co-operation and in accordance with the organization and resources of each State, of the economic, social and cultural rights indispensable for his dignity and the free development of his personality.

**Article 23**

1. Everyone has the right to work, to free choice of employment, to just and favourable conditions of work and to protection against unemployment.
2. Everyone, without any discrimination, has the right to equal pay for equal work.
3. Everyone who works has the right to just and favourable remuneration ensuring for himself and his family an existence worthy of human dignity, and supplemented, if necessary, by other means of social protection.
4. Everyone has the right to form and to join trade unions for the protection of his interests.

**Article 24**

- Everyone has the right to rest and leisure, including reasonable limitation of working hours and periodic holidays with pay.

**Article 25**

1. Everyone has the right to a standard of living adequate for the health and well-being of himself and of his family, including food, clothing, housing and medical care and necessary social services, and the right to security in the event of unemployment, sickness, disability, widowhood, old age or other lack of livelihood in circumstances beyond his control.
2. Motherhood and childhood are entitled to special care and assistance. All children, whether born in or out of wedlock, shall enjoy the same social protection.

**Article 26**

1. Everyone has the right to education. Education shall be free, at least in the elementary and fundamental

stages. Elementary education shall be
compulsory. Technical and professional education shall be
made generally available and higher education shall be
equally accessible to all on the basis of merit.

2. Education shall be directed to the full development of the
human personality and to the strengthening of respect for
human rights and fundamental freedoms. It shall promote understanding, tolerance and friendship among all
nations, racial or religious groups, and shall further the
activities of the United Nations for the maintenance of
peace.

3. Parents have a prior right to choose the kind of education
that shall be given to their children.

### Article 27

1. Everyone has the right freely to participate in the cultural
life of the community, to enjoy the arts
and to share in scientific advancement and its benefits.

2. Everyone has the right to the protection of the moral and
material interests resulting from any scientific, literary or
artistic production of which he is the author.

### Article 28

- Everyone is entitled to a social and international order in
which the rights and freedoms set forth in this Declaration
can be fully realized.

### Article 29

1. Everyone has duties to the community in which alone the
free and full development of his personality is possible.

2. In the exercise of his rights and freedoms, everyone shall
be subject only to such limitations as are determined by
law solely for the purpose of securing due recognition and
respect for the rights and freedoms of others and of meeting the just requirements of morality, public order and the
general welfare in a democratic society.

3. These rights and freedoms may in no case be exercised contrary to the purposes and principles of the United Nations.

### Article 30

- Nothing in this Declaration may be interpreted as implying
for any State, group or person any right to engage in any
activity or to perform any act aimed at the destruction of
any of the rights and freedoms set forth herein.

## Convention on the Prevention and Punishment of the Crime of Genocide, December 9, 1948

*The Convention on Genocide was among the first United Nations conventions addressing humanitarian issues. It was adopted in 1948 in response to the atrocities committed during World War II and followed G.A. Res. 180(II) of December 21, 1947, in which the UN recognized that "genocide is an international crime, which entails the national and international responsibility of individual persons and states." The Convention has since then been widely accepted by the international community and ratified by the overwhelming majority of States.*

*Noteworthy, the Convention provides for a precise definition of the crime of genocide, in particular in terms of the required intent and the prohibited acts (Article II). It also specifies that the crime of genocide may be committed in time of peace or in time of war.*

The Contracting Parties,

Having considered the declaration made by the General Assembly of the United Nations in its resolution 96 (I) dated December 11, 1946, that genocide is a crime under international law, contrary to the spirit and aims of the United Nations and condemned by the civilized world

Recognizing that at all periods of history genocide has inflicted great losses on humanity, and

Being convinced that, in order to liberate mankind from such an odious scourge, international co-operation is required,

Hereby agree as hereinafter provided:

**Article 1**
The Contracting Parties confirm that genocide, whether committed in time of peace or in time of war, is a crime under international law which they undertake to prevent and to punish.

**Article 2**
In the present Convention, genocide means any of the following acts committed with intent to destroy, in whole or in part, a national, ethnical, racial or religious group, as such:

  (a)  Killing members of the group;

(b) Causing serious bodily or mental harm to members of the group;
(c) Deliberately inflicting on the group conditions of life calculated to bring about its physical destruction in whole or in part;
(d) Imposing measures intended to prevent births within the group;
(e) Forcibly transferring children of the group to another group.

**Article 3**
The following acts shall be punishable:

(a) Genocide;
(b) Conspiracy to commit genocide;
(c) Direct and public incitement to commit genocide;
(d) Attempt to commit genocide;
(e) Complicity in genocide.

**Article 4**
Persons committing genocide or any of the other acts enumerated in article III shall be punished, whether they are constitutionally responsible rulers, public officials or private individuals.

. . .

**Article 6**
Persons charged with genocide or any of the other acts enumerated in article III shall be tried by a competent tribunal of the State in the territory of which the act was committed, or by such international penal tribunal as may have jurisdiction with respect to those Contracting Parties which shall have accepted its jurisdiction.

. . .

*Source*: Convention on the Prevention and Punishment of the Crime of Genocide, adopted by Resolution 260 (III) A of the United Nations General Assembly on December 9, 1948. http://www.hrweb.org/legal/genocide.html. Reprinted with permission of the United Nations Publications Board.

# Summary of Geneva Conventions, 1949

*The Geneva Conventions and their Additional Protocols are at the core of international humanitarian law, the body of international law that regulates the conduct of armed conflict and seeks to limit its effects. They specifically protect people who are not taking part in the hostilities (civilians, health workers, and aid workers) and those who are no longer participating in the hostilities, such as wounded, sick, and shipwrecked soldiers and prisoners of war. The Conventions and their Protocols call for measures to be taken to prevent or put an end to all breaches. They contain stringent rules to deal with what are known as "grave breaches." Those responsible for grave breaches must be sought, tried, or extradited, whatever nationality they may hold.*

### The first Geneva Convention protects wounded and sick soldiers on land during war.

This Convention represents the fourth updated version of the Geneva Convention on the wounded and sick following those adopted in 1864, 1906, and 1929. It contains 64 articles. These provide protection for the wounded and sick, but also for medical and religious personnel, medical units, and medical transports. The Convention also recognizes the distinctive emblems. It has two annexes containing a draft agreement relating to hospital zones and a model identity card for medical and religious personnel.

### The second Geneva Convention protects wounded, sick, and shipwrecked military personnel at sea during war.

This Convention replaced Hague Convention of 1907 for the Adaptation to Maritime Warfare of the Principles of the Geneva Convention. It closely follows the provisions of the first Geneva Convention in structure and content. It has 63 articles specifically applicable to war at sea. For example, it protects hospital ships. It has one annex containing a model identity card for medical and religious personnel.

### The third Geneva Convention applies to prisoners of war.

This Convention replaced the Prisoners of War Convention of 1929. It contains 143 articles whereas the 1929 Convention had only 97. The categories of persons entitled to prisoner of war status were broadened in accordance with Conventions I and II. The conditions and places of captivity were more precisely defined, particularly with regard to the labor of prisoners of war, their financial resources, the relief they receive, and the judicial proceedings instituted against them. The Convention establishes the principle that prisoners of war shall be released and repatriated without delay after the cessation of active hostilities. The Convention has five annexes containing various model regulations and identity and other cards.

**The fourth Geneva Convention affords protection to civilians, including those in occupied territory.**

The Geneva Conventions, which were adopted before 1949, were concerned with combatants only, not with civilians. The events of World War II showed the disastrous consequences of the absence of a convention for the protection of civilians in wartime. The Convention adopted in 1949 takes account of the experiences of World War II. It is composed of 159 articles. It contains a short section concerning the general protection of populations against certain consequences of war, without addressing the conduct of hostilities, as such, which was later examined in the Additional Protocols of 1977. The bulk of the Convention deals with the status and treatment of protected persons, distinguishing between the situation of foreigners on the territory of one of the parties to the conflict and that of civilians in occupied territory. It spells out the obligations of the Occupying Power vis-à-vis the civilian population and contains detailed provisions on humanitarian relief for populations in occupied territory. It also contains a specific regime for the treatment of civilian internees. It has three annexes containing a model agreement on hospital and safety zones, model regulations on humanitarian relief and model cards.

**Common Article 3**
Article 3, common to the four Geneva Conventions, marked a breakthrough, as it covered, for the first time, situations of non-international armed conflicts. These types of conflicts vary greatly. They include traditional civil wars, internal armed conflicts that spill over into other States, or internal conflicts in which third States or a multinational force intervenes alongside the government. Common Article 3 establishes fundamental rules from which no derogation is permitted. It is like a mini-Convention within the Conventions as it contains the essential rules of the Geneva Conventions in a condensed format and makes them applicable to conflicts not of an international character:

- It requires humane treatment for all persons in enemy hands, without any adverse distinction. It specifically prohibits murder, mutilation, torture, cruel, humiliating and degrading treatment, the taking of hostages and unfair trial.
- It requires that the wounded, sick and shipwrecked be collected and cared for.
- It grants the ICRC the right to offer its services to the parties to the conflict.

- It calls on the parties to the conflict to bring all or parts of the Geneva Conventions into force through so-called special agreements.
- It recognizes that the application of these rules does not affect the legal status of the parties to the conflict.

Given that most armed conflicts today are non-international, applying Common Article 3 is of the utmost importance. Its full respect is required.

# Statute of the International Tribunal for the Former Yugoslavia, May 1993, Amended May 1998, 2000, Excerpts

*Having been established by the Security Council acting under Chapter VII of the Charter of the United Nations, the International Tribunal for the Prosecution of Persons Responsible for Serious Violations of International Humanitarian Law Committed in the Territory of the Former Yugoslavia since 1991 (hereinafter referred to as "the International Tribunal") shall function in accordance with the provisions of the present Statute.*

### Article 1
### Competence of the International Tribunal

The International Tribunal shall have the power to prosecute persons responsible for serious violations of international humanitarian law committed in the territory of the former Yugoslavia since 1991 in accordance with the provisions of the present Statute.

### Article 2
### Grave breaches of the Geneva Conventions of 1949

The International Tribunal shall have the power to prosecute persons committing or ordering to be committed grave breaches of the Geneva Conventions of 12 August 1949, namely the following acts against persons or property protected under the provisions of the relevant Geneva Convention:

(a) willful killing;
(b) torture or inhuman treatment, including biological experiments;
(c) wilfully causing great suffering or serious injury to body or health;
(d) extensive destruction and appropriation of property, not justified by military necessity and carried out unlawfully and wantonly;

(e)  compelling a prisoner of war or a civilian to serve in the forces of a hostile power;

(f)  wilfully depriving a prisoner of war or a civilian of the rights of fair and regular trial;

(g)  unlawful deportation or transfer or unlawful confinement of a civilian;

(h)  taking civilians as hostages.

## Article 3
## Violations of the laws or customs of war

The International Tribunal shall have the power to prosecute persons violating the laws or customs of war. Such violations shall include, but not be limited to:

(a)  employment of poisonous weapons or other weapons calculated to cause unnecessary suffering;

(b)  wanton destruction of cities, towns or villages, or devastation not justified by military necessity;

(c)  attack, or bombardment, by whatever means, of unde-fended towns, villages, dwellings, or buildings;

(d)  seizure of, destruction or wilful damage done to institu-tions dedicated to religion, charity and education, the arts and sciences, historic monuments and works of art and science;

(e)  plunder of public or private property.

## Article 4
## Genocide

1.  The International Tribunal shall have the power to prose-cute persons committing genocide as defined in paragraph 2 of this article or of committing any of the other acts enumer-ated in paragraph 3 of this article.

2.  Genocide means any of the following acts committed with intent to destroy, in whole or in part, a national, ethnical, racial or religious group, as such:

   (a)  killing members of the group;

   (b)  causing serious bodily or mental harm to members of the group;

(c) deliberately inflicting on the group conditions of life calculated to bring about its physical destruction in whole or in part;

(d) imposing measures intended to prevent births within the group;

(e) forcibly transferring children of the group to another group.

. . .

## Article 5
### Crimes against humanity

The International Tribunal shall have the power to prosecute persons responsible for the following crimes when . . . directed against any civilian population:

(a) murder;
(b) extermination;
(c) enslavement;
(d) deportation;
(e) imprisonment;
(f) torture;
(g) rape;
(h) persecutions on political, racial and religious grounds;
(i) other inhumane acts.

. . .

## Article 9
### Concurrent jurisdiction

1. The International Tribunal and national courts shall have concurrent jurisdiction to prosecute persons for serious violations of international humanitarian law committed in the territory of the former Yugoslavia since January 1, 1991.

2. The International Tribunal shall have primacy over national courts. At any stage of the procedure, the International Tribunal may formally request national courts to defer to the competence of the International Tribunal in accordance with the present Statute and the Rules of Procedure and Evidence of the International Tribunal.

### Organization of the International Tribunal
The International Tribunal shall consist of the following organs:

(a)  the Chambers, comprising three Trial Chambers and an Appeals Chamber;
(b)  the Prosecutor; and
(c)  a Registry, servicing both the Chambers and the Prosecutor.

. . .

### Article 18
### Investigation and preparation of indictment

1.  The Prosecutor shall initiate investigations *ex officio* or on the basis of information obtained from any source, particularly from Governments, United Nations organs, intergovernmental and non-governmental organisations. The Prosecutor shall assess the information received or obtained and decide whether there is sufficient basis to proceed.
2.  The Prosecutor shall have the power to question suspects, victims and witnesses, to collect evidence and to conduct on-site investigations. In carrying out these tasks, the Prosecutor may, as appropriate, seek the assistance of the State authorities concerned.
3.  If questioned, the suspect shall be entitled to be assisted by counsel of his own choice, including the right to have legal assistance assigned to him without payment by him in any such case if he does not have sufficient means to pay for it, as well as to necessary translation into and from a language he speaks and understands.
4.  Upon a determination that a prima facie case exists, the Prosecutor shall prepare an indictment containing a concise statement of the facts and the crime or crimes with which the accused is charged under the Statute. The indictment shall be transmitted to a judge of the Trial Chamber.

### Article 19
### Review of the indictment

1.  The judge of the Trial Chamber to whom the indictment has been transmitted shall review it. If satisfied that a prima facie case has been established by the Prosecutor, he shall confirm the indictment.
    If not so satisfied, the indictment shall be dismissed.

2. Upon confirmation of an indictment, the judge may, at the request of the Prosecutor, issue such orders and warrants for the arrest, detention, surrender or transfer of persons, and any other orders as may be required for the conduct of the trial.

## Article 20
## Commencement and conduct of trial proceedings

1. The Trial Chambers shall ensure that a trial is fair and expeditious and that proceedings are conducted in accordance with the rules of procedure and evidence, with full respect for the rights of the accused and due regard for the protection of victims and witnesses.

. . .

## Article 21
## Rights of the accused

1. All persons shall be equal before the International Tribunal.
2. In the determination of charges against him, the accused shall be entitled to a fair and public hearing, subject to article 22 of the Statute.
3. The accused shall be presumed innocent until proved guilty according to the provisions of the present Statute.
4. In the determination of any charge against the accused pursuant to the present Statute, the accused shall be entitled to the following minimum guarantees, in full equality:
   (a) to be informed promptly and in detail in a language which he understands of the nature and cause of the charge against him;
   (b) to have adequate time and facilities for the preparation of his defence and to communicate with counsel of his own choosing;
   (c) to be tried without undue delay;
   (d) to be tried in his presence, and to defend himself in person or through legal assistance of his own choosing; to be informed, if he does not have legal assistance, of this right; and to have legal assistance assigned to him, in any case where the interests of justice so require, and without payment by him in any such case if he does not have sufficient means to pay for it;
   (e) to examine, or have examined, the witnesses against him and to obtain the attendance

and examination of witnesses on his behalf under the
same conditions as witnesses against him;

(f)  to have the free assistance of an interpreter if he cannot understand or speak the language used in the
International Tribunal;

(g)  not to be compelled to testify against himself or to confess guilt.

### Article 22
### Protection of victims and witnesses

The International Tribunal shall provide in its rules of
procedure and evidence for the protection of victims and
witnesses. Such protection measures shall include, but shall
not be limited to, the conduct of in camera proceedings and
the protection of the victim's identity.

### Article 23
### Judgement

1.  The Trial Chambers shall pronounce judgements
and impose sentences and penalties on persons
convicted of serious violations of international
humanitarian law.

2.  The judgement shall be rendered by a majority of
the judges of the Trial Chamber, and shall be delivered
by the Trial Chamber in public. It shall be accompanied
by a reasoned opinion in writing, to which separate
or dissenting opinions may be appended.

### Article 24
### Penalties

1.  The penalty imposed by the Trial Chamber shall be
limited to imprisonment. In determining the terms of
imprisonment, the Trial Chambers shall have recourse
to the general practice regarding prison sentences in the
courts of the former Yugoslavia.

2.  In imposing the sentences, the Trial Chambers should
take into account such factors as the gravity of the
offence and the individual circumstances of the
convicted person.

3.  In addition to imprisonment, the Trial Chambers may
order the return of any property and proceeds acquired
by criminal conduct, including by means of duress, to
their rightful owners.

Article 25
## Appellate proceedings

1. The Appeals Chamber shall hear appeals from persons convicted by the Trial Chambers or from the Prosecutor on the following grounds:
   (a) an error on a question of law invalidating the decision; or
   (b) an error of fact which has occasioned a miscarriage of justice.
2  The Appeals Chamber may affirm, reverse or revise the decisions taken by the Trial Chambers.

. . .

Article 27
## Enforcement of sentences

Imprisonment shall be served in a State designated by the International Tribunal from a list of States which have indicated to the Security Council their willingness to accept convicted persons. Such imprisonment shall be in accordance with the applicable law of the State concerned, subject to the supervision of the International Tribunal.

. . .

*Source*: Updated Statute of the International Criminal Tribunal for the Former Yugoslavia, at http://www.icty.org/sid/135. Reproduced with permission from the United Nations Publication Board.

# Statute of the International Criminal Tribunal for the Prosecution of Persons Responsible for Genocide and Other Serious Violations of International Humanitarian Law Committed in the Territory of Rwanda and Rwandan Citizens Responsible for Genocide and Other Such Violations Committed in the Territory of Neighbouring States, between January 1, 1994 and December 31, 1994

ICTR, Excerpts

*Having been established by the Security Council acting under Chapter VII of the Charter of the United Nations, the International Criminal Tribunal for the Prosecution of Persons Responsible for Genocide and Other Serious*

*Violations of International Humanitarian Law Committed in the Territory of Rwanda and Rwandan citizens responsible for genocide and other such violations committed in the territory of neighbouring States, between January 1, 1994 and December 31, 1994 (hereinafter referred to as "the International Tribunal for Rwanda") shall function in accordance with the provisions of the present Statute.*

**Article 1**

The International Tribunal for Rwanda shall have the power to prosecute persons responsible for serious violations of international humanitarian law committed in the territory of Rwanda and Rwandan citizens responsible for such violations committed in the territory of neighbouring States, between January 1, 1994 and December 31, 1994, in accordance with the provisions of the present Statute.

**Article 2**

Genocide

. . .

**Article 3**

Crimes against humanity

. . .

**Article 6**

Individual criminal responsibility. . . .

. . .

**Article 10**

The International Tribunal for Rwanda shall consist of the following organs:

(a)  The Chambers, comprising two Trial Chambers and an Appeals Chamber;
(b)  The Prosecutor; and
(c)  A Registry.

. . .

# Preamble and Selected Articles, Rome Statute of the International Criminal Court, July 17, 1998

*The United Nations has been considering the establishment of a permanent international criminal court since its creation. After years of negotiations, a Diplomatic Conference was held from June 15 to July 17, 1998, in Rome which finalized and adopted the statute for the International Criminal Court (ICC). The statute was finally adopted by a vote where 120 were in favor, 7 against, and 21 abstained. The establishment of an ICC represents a major progress for better implementation of international humanitarian law and a clear step forward in the battle against impunity. The ICC will be established in The Hague and will have jurisdiction over suspected perpetrators of genocide, crimes against humanity, war crimes or aggression, including superiors or military commanders. The court may exercise its jurisdiction, if the State on the territory of which the act or omission occurred or the State of nationality of the suspect is Party to the statute or has accepted the jurisdiction of the court. The Prosecutor can refer cases proprio motu (on his/her own initiative). The court has not a retroactive effect. The ICC is not intended to take over jurisdiction exercised by national courts: the ICC is intended to exercise its jurisdiction only when the state is unwilling or genuinely unable to prosecute. States continue to have the primary duty to prosecute suspected war criminals before their own courts.*

## PREAMBLE
*The States Parties to this Statute,*

Conscious that all peoples are united by common bonds, their cultures pieced together in a shared heritage, and concerned that this delicate mosaic may be shattered at any time,

Mindful that during this century millions of children, women and men have been victims of unimaginable atrocities that deeply shock the conscience of humanity,

Recognizing that such grave crimes threaten the peace, security and well-being of the world,

Affirming that the most serious crimes of concern to the international community as a whole must not go unpunished and that their effective prosecution must be ensured by taking measures at the national level and by enhancing international cooperation,

Determined to put an end to impunity for the perpetrators of these crimes and thus to contribute to the prevention of such crimes,

Recalling that it is the duty of every State to exercise its criminal jurisdiction over those responsible for international crimes,

Reaffirming the Purposes and Principles of the Charter of the United Nations, and in particular that all States shall refrain from the

threat or use of force against the territorial integrity or political independence of any State, or in any other manner inconsistent with the
Purposes of the United Nations,

Emphasizing in this connection that nothing in this Statute shall be
taken as authorizing any State Party to intervene in an armed conflict or
in the internal affairs of any State,

Determined to these ends and for the sake of present and future
generations, to establish an independent permanent International
Criminal Court in relationship with the United Nations system, with
jurisdiction over the most serious crimes of concern to the international
community as a whole,

Emphasizing that the International Criminal Court established
under this Statute shall be complementary to national criminal
jurisdictions,

Resolved to guarantee lasting respect for and the enforcement of
international justice,

Have agreed as follows . . .

## PART 1. ESTABLISHMENT OF THE COURT

### Article 1
### The Court

An International Criminal Court ("the Court") is hereby established. It shall be a permanent institution and shall have the power to
exercise its jurisdiction over persons for the most serious crimes of international concern, as referred to in this Statute, and shall be complementary to national criminal jurisdictions. The jurisdiction and functioning
of the Court shall be governed by the provisions of this Statute.

. . .

### Article 3
### Seat of the Court

1. The seat of the Court shall be established at The Hague in
   the Netherlands ("the host State").

. . .

### Article 4
### Legal status and powers of the Court

1. The Court shall have international legal personality. It shall
   also have such legal capacity as may be necessary for the
   exercise of its functions and the fulfilment of its purposes.

2.  The Court may exercise its functions and powers, as provided in this Statute, on the territory of any State Party and, by special agreement, on the territory of any other State.

**Article 5**
**Crimes within the jurisdiction of the Court**

1.  The jurisdiction of the Court shall be limited to the most serious crimes of concern to the international community as a whole. The Court has jurisdiction in accordance with this Statute with respect to the following crimes:
    (a)  The crime of genocide;
    (b)  Crimes against humanity;
    (c)  War crimes;
    (d)  The crime of aggression.
2.  The Court shall exercise jurisdiction over the crime of aggression once a provision is adopted in accordance with articles 121 and 123 defining the crime and setting out the conditions under which the Court shall exercise jurisdiction with respect to this crime. Such a provision shall be consistent with the relevant provisions of the Charter of the United Nations.

. . .

**Article 13**
**Exercise of jurisdiction**

The Court may exercise its jurisdiction with respect to a crime referred to in Article 5 in accordance with the provisions of this Statute if:

(a)  A situation in which one or more of such crimes appears to have been committed is referred to the Prosecutor by a State Party in accordance with article 14;
(b)  A situation in which one or more of such crimes appears to have been committed is referred to the Prosecutor by the Security Council acting under Chapter VII of the Charter of the United Nations; or
(c)  The Prosecutor has initiated an investigation in respect of such a crime in accordance with article 15.

## Article 14
## Referral of a situation by a State Party

1. A State Party may refer to the Prosecutor a situation in which one or more crimes within the jurisdiction of the Court appear to have been committed requesting the Prosecutor to investigate the situation for the purpose of determining whether one or more specific persons should be charged with the commission of such crimes.

2. As far as possible, a referral shall specify the relevant circumstances and be accompanied by such supporting documentation as is available to the State referring the situation.

## Article 15
## Prosecutor

1. The Prosecutor may initiate investigations proprio motu on the basis of information on crimes within the jurisdiction of the Court.

. . .

## Article 17
## Issues of admissibility

1. Having regard to paragraph 10 of the Preamble and article 1, the Court shall determine that a case is inadmissible where:

    (a) The case is being investigated or prosecuted by a State which has jurisdiction over it, unless the State is unwilling or unable genuinely to carry out the investigation or prosecution;

    (b) The case has been investigated by a State which has jurisdiction over it and the State has decided not to prosecute the person concerned, unless the decision resulted from the unwillingness or inability of the State genuinely to prosecute;

    (c) The person concerned has already been tried for conduct which is the subject of the complaint, and a trial by the Court is not permitted under article 20, paragraph 3;

(d) The case is not of sufficient gravity to justify further action by the Court.

2. In order to determine unwillingness in a particular case, the Court shall consider, having regard to the principles of due process recognized by international law, whether one or more of the following exist, as applicable:

(a) The proceedings were or are being undertaken or the national decision was made for the purpose of shielding the person concerned from criminal responsibility for crimes within the jurisdiction of the Court referred to in article 5;

(b) There has been an unjustified delay in the proceedings which in the circumstances is inconsistent with an intent to bring the person concerned to justice;

(c). The proceedings were not or are not being conducted independently or impartially, and they were or are being conducted in a manner which, in the circumstances, is inconsistent with an intent to bring the person concerned to justice.

3. In order to determine inability in a particular case, the Court shall consider whether, due to a total or substantial collapse or unavailability of its national judicial system, the State is unable to obtain the accused or the necessary evidence and testimony or otherwise unable to carry out its proceedings.

### Article 18
### Preliminary rulings regarding admissibility

1. When a situation has been referred to the Court pursuant to article 13 (a) and the Prosecutor has determined that there would be a reasonable basis to commence an investigation, or the Prosecutor initiates an investigation pursuant to articles 13 (c) and 15, the Prosecutor shall notify all States Parties and those States which, taking into account the information available, would normally exercise jurisdiction over the crimes concerned. The Prosecutor may notify such States on a confidential basis and, where the Prosecutor believes it necessary to protect persons, prevent destruction of evidence or prevent the absconding of persons, may limit the scope of the information provided to States.

. . .

3. The Prosecutor's deferral to a State's investigation shall be open to review by the Prosecutor six months after the date of deferral or at any time when there has been a significant change of circumstances based on the State's unwillingness or inability genuinely to carry out the investigation.

. . .

5. When the Prosecutor has deferred an investigation in accordance with paragraph 2, the Prosecutor may request that the State concerned periodically inform the Prosecutor of the progress of its investigations and any subsequent prosecutions. States Parties shall respond to such requests without undue delay.

6. Pending a ruling by the Pre-Trial Chamber, or at any time when the Prosecutor has deferred an investigation under this article, the Prosecutor may, on an exceptional basis, seek authority from the Pre-Trial Chamber to pursue necessary investigative steps for the purpose of preserving evidence where there is a unique opportunity to obtain important evidence or there is a significant risk that such evidence may not be subsequently available.

. . .

## Article 21
## Applicable law

1. The Court shall apply:
   (a) In the first place, this Statute, Elements of Crimes and its Rules of Procedure and Evidence;
   (b) In the second place, where appropriate, applicable treaties and the principles and rules of international law, including the established principles of the international law of armed conflict;
   (c) Failing that, general principles of law derived by the Court from national laws of legal systems of the world including, as appropriate, the national laws of States that would normally exercise jurisdiction over the crime, provided that those principles are not inconsistent with this Statute and with international law and internationally recognized norms and standards.

. . .

3. The application and interpretation of law pursuant to this article must be consistent with internationally recognized human rights, and be without any adverse distinction founded on grounds such as gender as defined in article 7, paragraph 3, age, race, colour, language, religion or belief, political or other opinion, national, ethnic or social origin, wealth, birth or other status.

## Article 22
### Nullum crimen sine lege

1. A person shall not be criminally responsible under this Statute unless the conduct in question constitutes, at the time it takes place, a crime within the jurisdiction of the Court.

. . .

## Article 24
### Non-retroactivity ratione personae

1. No person shall be criminally responsible under this Statute for conduct prior to the entry into force of the Statute.

. . .

## Article 25
### Individual criminal responsibility

1. The Court shall have jurisdiction over natural persons pursuant to this Statute.
2. A person who commits a crime within the jurisdiction of the Court shall be individually responsible and liable for punishment in accordance with this Statute.

. . .

## Article 27
### Irrelevance of official capacity

1. This Statute shall apply equally to all persons without any distinction based on official capacity. In particular, official

capacity as a Head of State or Government, a member of a Government or parliament, an elected representative or a government official shall in no case exempt a person from criminal responsibility under this Statute, nor shall it, in and of itself, constitute a ground for reduction of sentence.

. . .

**Article 28**

. . .

(a)   A military commander or person effectively acting as a military commander shall be criminally responsible for crimes within the jurisdiction of the Court committed by forces under his or her effective command and control, or effective authority and control as the case may be, as a result of his or her failure to exercise control properly over such forces, where:

   (i)   That military commander or person either knew or, owing to the circumstances at the time, should have known that the forces were committing or about to commit such crimes; and

  (ii)   That military commander or person failed to take all necessary and reasonable measures within his or her power to prevent or repress their commission or to submit the matter to the competent authorities for investigation and prosecution.

(b)   With respect to superior and subordinate relationships not described in paragraph (a), a superior shall be criminally responsible for crimes within the jurisdiction of the Court committed by subordinates under his or her effective authority and control, as a result of his or her failure to exercise control properly over such subordinates, where:

   (i)   The superior either knew, or consciously disregarded information which clearly indicated, that the subordinates were committing or about to commit such crimes;

  (ii)   The crimes concerned activities that were within the effective responsibility and control of the superior; and

 (iii)   The superior failed to take all necessary and reasonable measures within his or her power to prevent or repress their commission or to submit the matter to the competent authorities for investigation and prosecution.

### Article 29
### Non-applicability of statute of limitations

The crimes within the jurisdiction of the Court shall not be subject to any statute of limitations.

### Article 30
### Mental element

1. Unless otherwise provided, a person shall be criminally responsible and liable for punishment for a crime within the jurisdiction of the Court only if the material elements are committed with intent and knowledge.

. . .

### Article 33
### Superior orders and prescription of law

1. The fact that a crime within the jurisdiction of the Court has been committed by a person pursuant to an order of a Government or of a superior, whether military or civilian, shall not relieve that person of criminal responsibility unless:
   (a) The person was under a legal obligation to obey orders of the Government or the superior in question;
   (b) The person did not know that the order was unlawful; and
   (c) The order was not manifestly unlawful.

. . .

### Article 34
### Organs of the Court

The Court shall be composed of the following organs:

(a) The Presidency;
(b) An Appeals Division, a Trial Division and a Pre-Trial Division;
(c) The Office of the Prosecutor;
(d) The Registry.

. . .

## Article 36
## Qualifications, nomination and election of judges

1. Subject to the provisions of paragraph 2, there shall be 18 judges of the Court.

. . .

3. (a) The judges shall be chosen from among persons of high moral character, impartiality and integrity who possess the qualifications required in their respective States for appointment to the highest judicial offices.

. . .

## Article 38
## The Presidency

1. The President and the First and Second Vice-Presidents shall be elected by an absolute majority of the judges. They shall each serve for a term of three years or until the end of their respective terms of office as judges, whichever expires earlier. They shall be eligible for re-election once.

. . .

3. The President, together with the First and Second Vice-Presidents, shall constitute the Presidency, which shall be responsible for:
   (a) The proper administration of the Court, with the exception of the Office of the Prosecutor;. . . .

## Article 39
## Chambers

1. As soon as possible after the election of the judges, the Court shall organize itself into the divisions specified in article 34, paragraph (b). The Appeals Division shall be composed of the President and four other judges, the Trial Division of not less than six judges and the Pre-Trial Division of not less than six judges. The assignment of judges to divisions shall be based on the nature of the functions to be performed by each division and the qualifications and experience of the judges elected to the Court, in such a way

that each division shall contain an appropriate combination of expertise in criminal law and procedure and in international law. The Trial and Pre-Trial Divisions shall be composed predominantly of judges with criminal trial experience.

. . .

## Article 40
## Independence of the judges

1. The judges shall be independent in the performance of their functions.
2. Judges shall not engage in any activity which is likely to interfere with their judicial functions or to affect confidence in their independence.
3. Judges required to serve on a full-time basis at the seat of the Court shall not engage in any other occupation of a professional nature.

. . .

## Article 42
## The Office of the Prosecutor

1. The Office of the Prosecutor shall act independently as a separate organ of the Court. It shall be responsible for receiving referrals and any substantiated information on crimes within the jurisdiction of the Court, for examining them and for conducting investigations and prosecutions before the Court. A member of the Office shall not seek or act on instructions from any external source.
2. The Office shall be headed by the Prosecutor. The Prosecutor shall have full authority over the management and administration of the Office, including the staff, facilities and other resources thereof. The Prosecutor shall be assisted by one or more Deputy Prosecutors, who shall be entitled to carry out any of the acts required of the Prosecutor under this Statute. The Prosecutor and the Deputy Prosecutors shall be of different nationalities. They shall serve on a full-time basis.
3. The Prosecutor and the Deputy Prosecutors shall be persons of high moral character, be highly competent in and have extensive practical experience in the

prosecution or trial of criminal cases. They shall have an excellent knowledge of and be fluent in at least one of the working languages of the Court.

4. The Prosecutor shall be elected by secret ballot by an absolute majority of the members of the Assembly of States Parties. The Deputy Prosecutors shall be elected in the same way from a list of candidates provided by the Prosecutor. The Prosecutor shall nominate three candidates for each position of Deputy Prosecutor to be filled. Unless a shorter term is decided upon at the time of their election, the Prosecutor and the Deputy Prosecutors shall hold office for a term of nine years and shall not be eligible for re-election.

. . .

7. Neither the Prosecutor nor a Deputy Prosecutor shall participate in any matter in which their impartiality might reasonably be doubted on any ground. They shall be disqualified from a case in accordance with this paragraph if, inter alia, they have previously been involved in any capacity in that case before the Court or in a related criminal case at the national level involving the person being investigated or prosecuted.

. . .

## Article 43
## The Registry

1. The Registry shall be responsible for the non-judicial aspects of the administration and servicing of the Court, without prejudice to the functions and powers of the Prosecutor in accordance with article 42.

. . .

## Article 44
## Staff

1. The Prosecutor and the Registrar shall appoint such qualified staff as may be required to their respective offices. In the case of the Prosecutor, this shall include the appointment of investigators.

. . .

## Article 48
## Privileges and immunities

1. The Court shall enjoy in the territory of each State Party such privileges and immunities as are necessary for the fulfilment of its purposes.
2. The judges, the Prosecutor, the Deputy Prosecutors and the Registrar shall, when engaged on or with respect to the business of the Court, enjoy the same privileges and immunities as are accorded to heads of diplomatic missions and shall, after the expiry of their terms of office, continue to be accorded immunity from legal process of every kind in respect of words spoken or written and acts performed by them in their official capacity.
3. The Deputy Registrar, the staff of the Office of the Prosecutor and the staff of the Registry shall enjoy the privileges and immunities and facilities necessary for the performance of their functions, in accordance with the agreement on the privileges and immunities of the Court.
4. Counsel, experts, witnesses or any other person required to be present at the seat of the Court shall be accorded such treatment as is necessary for the proper functioning of the Court, in accordance with the agreement on the privileges and immunities of the Court.

## Article 51
## Rules of Procedure and Evidence

1. The Rules of Procedure and Evidence shall enter into force upon adoption by a two-thirds majority of the members of the Assembly of States Parties.

. . .

## Article 53
## Initiation of an investigation

1. The Prosecutor shall, having evaluated the information made available to him or her, initiate an investigation unless he or she determines that there is no reasonable basis to proceed under this Statute.

. . .

(b) In addition, the Pre-Trial Chamber may, on its own initiative, review a decision of the Prosecutor not to proceed if it is based solely on paragraph 1 (c) or 2 (c). In such a case, the decision of the Prosecutor shall be effective only if confirmed by the Pre-Trial Chamber.

. . .

4. The Prosecutor may, at any time, reconsider a decision whether to initiate an investigation or prosecution based on new facts or information.

## Article 54
## Duties and powers of the Prosecutor with respect to investigations

1. The Prosecutor shall:
   (a) In order to establish the truth, extend the investigation to cover all facts and evidence relevant to an assessment of whether there is criminal responsibility under this Statute, and, in doing so, investigate incriminating and exonerating circumstances equally;
   (b) Take appropriate measures to ensure the effective investigation and prosecution of crimes within the jurisdiction of the Court, and in doing so, respect the interests and personal circumstances of victims and witnesses, including age, gender as defined in article 7, paragraph 3, and health, and take into account the nature of the crime, in particular where it involves sexual violence, gender violence or violence against children; and
   (c) Fully respect the rights of persons arising under this Statute.

. . .

3. The Prosecutor may:
   (a) Collect and examine evidence;
   (b) Request the presence of and question persons being investigated, victims and witnesses;
   (c) Seek the cooperation of any State or intergovernmental organization or arrangement in accordance with its respective competence and/or mandate;
   (d) Enter into such arrangements or agreements, not inconsistent with this Statute, as may be necessary to facilitate the cooperation of a State, intergovernmental organization or person;

    (e)  Agree not to disclose, at any stage of the proceedings, documents or information that the Prosecutor obtains on the condition of confidentiality and solely for the purpose of generating new evidence, unless the provider of the information consents; and

    (f)  Take necessary measures, or request that necessary measures be taken, to ensure the confidentiality of information, the protection of any person or the preservation of evidence.

**Article 55**
**Rights of persons during an investigation**

1.  In respect of an investigation under this Statute, a person:

    (a)  Shall not be compelled to incriminate himself or herself or to confess guilt;

    (b)  Shall not be subjected to any form of coercion, duress or threat, to torture or to any other form of cruel, inhuman or degrading treatment or punishment;

    (c)  Shall, if questioned in a language other than a language the person fully understands and speaks, have, free of any cost, the assistance of a competent interpreter and such translations as are necessary to meet the requirements of fairness; and

    (d)  Shall not be subjected to arbitrary arrest or detention, and shall not be deprived of his or her liberty except on such grounds and in accordance with such procedures as are established in this Statute.

2.  Where there are grounds to believe that a person has committed a crime within the jurisdiction of the Court and that person is about to be questioned either by the Prosecutor, or by national authorities pursuant to a request made under Part 9, that person shall also have the following rights of which he or she shall be informed prior to being questioned:

    (a)  To be informed, prior to being questioned, that there are grounds to believe that he or she has committed a crime within the jurisdiction of the Court;

    (b)  To remain silent, without such silence being a consideration in the determination of guilt or innocence;

    (c)  To have legal assistance of the person's choosing, or, if the person does not have legal assistance, to have legal assistance assigned to him or her, in any case where the interests of justice so require, and without payment by the person in any such case if the person does not have sufficient means to pay for it; and

(d) To be questioned in the presence of counsel unless the person has voluntarily waived his or her right to counsel.

. . .

## Article 57
### Functions and powers of the Pre-Trial Chamber

1. Unless otherwise provided in this Statute, the Pre-Trial Chamber shall exercise its functions in accordance with the provisions of this article.

. . .

3. In addition to its other functions under this Statute, the Pre-Trial Chamber may:

(a) At the request of the Prosecutor, issue such orders and warrants as may be required for the purposes of an investigation;

(b) Upon the request of a person who has been arrested or has appeared pursuant to a summons under article 58, issue such orders, including measures such as those described in article 56, or seek such cooperation pursuant to Part 9 as may be necessary to assist the person in the preparation of his or her defence;

(c) Where necessary, provide for the protection and privacy of victims and witnesses, the preservation of evidence, the protection of persons who have been arrested or appeared in response to a summons, and the protection of national security information;

(d) Authorize the Prosecutor to take specific investigative steps within the territory of a State Party without having secured the cooperation of that State under Part 9 if, whenever possible having regard to the views of the State concerned, the Pre-Trial Chamber has determined in that case that the State is clearly unable to execute a request for cooperation due to the unavailability of any authority or any component of its judicial system competent to execute the request for cooperation under Part 9.

(e) Where a warrant of arrest or a summons has been issued under article 58, and having due regard to the strength of the evidence and the rights of the parties concerned, as provided for in this Statute and the Rules of Procedure and Evidence, seek the cooperation of States pursuant to article 93, paragraph 1 (k), to take protective measures for the purpose of forfeiture, in particular for the ultimate benefit of victims.

**Article 58**
**Issuance by the Pre-Trial Chamber of a warrant of arrest or a summons to appear**

1. At any time after the initiation of an investigation, the Pre-Trial Chamber shall, on the application of the Prosecutor, issue a warrant of arrest of a person if, having examined the application and the evidence or other information submitted by the Prosecutor, it is satisfied that:
   (a) There are reasonable grounds to believe that the person has committed a crime within the jurisdiction of the Court; and
   (b) The arrest of the person appears necessary:
       (i) To ensure the person's appearance at trial,
       (ii) To ensure that the person does not obstruct or endanger the investigation or the court proceedings, or
       (iii) Where applicable, to prevent the person from continuing with the commission of that crime or a related crime which is within the jurisdiction of the Court and which arises out of the same circumstances.

. . .

4. The warrant of arrest shall remain in effect until otherwise ordered by the Court.

. . .

7. As an alternative to seeking a warrant of arrest, the Prosecutor may submit an application requesting that the Pre-Trial Chamber issue a summons for the person to

appear. If the Pre-Trial Chamber is satisfied that there are reasonable grounds to believe that the person committed the crime alleged and that a summons is sufficient to ensure the person's appearance, it shall issue the summons, with or without conditions restricting liberty (other than detention) if provided for by national law, for the person to appear.

. . .

### Article 59
### Arrest proceedings in the custodial State

1. A State Party which has received a request for provisional arrest or for arrest and surrender shall immediately take steps to arrest the person in question in accordance with its laws and the provisions of Part 9.

. . .

3. The person arrested shall have the right to apply to the competent authority in the custodial State for interim release pending surrender.

. . .

7. Once ordered to be surrendered by the custodial State, the person shall be delivered to the Court as soon as possible.

### Article 60
### Initial proceedings before the Court

1. Upon the surrender of the person to the Court, or the person's appearance before the Court voluntarily or pursuant to a summons, the Pre-Trial Chamber shall satisfy itself that the person has been informed of the crimes which he or she is alleged to have committed, and of his or her rights under this Statute, including the right to apply for interim release pending trial.
2. A person subject to a warrant of arrest may apply for interim release pending trial. If the Pre-Trial Chamber is satisfied that the conditions set forth in article 58,

paragraph 1, are met, the person shall continue to be
detained. If it is not so satisfied, the Pre-Trial Chamber
shall release the person, with or without conditions.

. . .

11. Once the charges have been confirmed in accordance with
this article, the Presidency shall constitute a Trial Chamber
which, subject to paragraph 9 and to article 64, paragraph
4, shall be responsible for the conduct of subsequent
proceedings and may exercise any function of the Pre-Trial
Chamber that is relevant and capable of application in
those proceedings.

## PART 6. THE TRIAL

. . .

### Article 63
### Trial in the presence of the accused

1. The accused shall be present during the trial.
2. If the accused, being present before the Court, continues
to disrupt the trial, the Trial Chamber may remove the
accused and shall make provision for him or her to observe
the trial and instruct counsel from outside the courtroom, through the use of communications technology, if
required. Such measures shall be taken only in exceptional
circumstances after other reasonable alternatives have
proved inadequate, and only for such duration as is strictly
required.

### Article 64
### Functions and powers of the Trial Chamber

. . .

2. The Trial Chamber shall ensure that a trial is fair and expeditious and is conducted with full respect for the rights of
the accused and due regard for the protection of victims
and witnesses.

. . .

7. The trial shall be held in public. The Trial Chamber may, however, determine that special circumstances require that certain proceedings be in closed session for the purposes set forth in article 68, or to protect confidential or sensitive information to be given in evidence.

8. (a) At the commencement of the trial, the Trial Chamber shall have read to the accused the charges previously confirmed by the Pre-Trial Chamber. The Trial Chamber shall satisfy itself that the accused understands the nature of the charges. It shall afford him or her the opportunity to make an admission of guilt in accordance with article 65 or to plead not guilty.

   (b) At the trial, the presiding judge may give directions for the conduct of proceedings, including to ensure that they are conducted in a fair and impartial manner. Subject to any directions of the presiding judge, the parties may submit evidence in accordance with the provisions of this Statute.

9. The Trial Chamber shall have, inter alia, the power on application of a party or on its own motion to:

   (a)    Rule on the admissibility or relevance of evidence; and

   (b)    Take all necessary steps to maintain order in the course of a hearing.

10. The Trial Chamber shall ensure that a complete record of the trial, which accurately reflects the proceedings, is made and that it is maintained and preserved by the Registrar.

. . .

## Article 66
## Presumption of innocence

1. Everyone shall be presumed innocent until proved guilty before the Court in accordance with the applicable law.

2. The onus is on the Prosecutor to prove the guilt of the accused.

3. In order to convict the accused, the Court must be convinced of the guilt of the accused beyond reasonable doubt.

## Article 67
## Rights of the accused

1. In the determination of any charge, the accused shall be entitled to a public hearing, having regard to the

provisions of this Statute, to a fair hearing conducted impartially, and to the following minimum guarantees, in full equality:

(a) To be informed promptly and in detail of the nature, cause and content of the charge, in a language which the accused fully understands and speaks;

(b) To have adequate time and facilities for the preparation of the defence and to communicate freely with counsel of the accused's choosing in confidence;

(c) To be tried without undue delay;

(d) Subject to article 63, paragraph 2, to be present at the trial, to conduct the defence in person or through legal assistance of the accused's choosing, to be informed, if the accused does not have legal assistance, of this right and to have legal assistance assigned by the Court in any case where the interests of justice so require, and without payment if the accused lacks sufficient means to pay for it;

(e) To examine, or have examined, the witnesses against him or her and to obtain the attendance and examination of witnesses on his or her behalf under the same conditions as witnesses against him or her. The accused shall also be entitled to raise defences and to present other evidence admissible under this Statute;

(f) To have, free of any cost, the assistance of a competent interpreter and such translations as are necessary to meet the requirements of fairness, if any of the proceedings of or documents presented to the Court are not in a language which the accused fully understands and speaks;

(g) Not to be compelled to testify or to confess guilt and to remain silent, without such silence being a consideration in the determination of guilt or innocence;

(h) To make an unsworn oral or written statement in his or her defence; and

(i) Not to have imposed on him or her any reversal of the burden of proof or any onus of rebuttal.

. . .

## Article 68
## Protection of the victims and witnesses and their participation in the proceedings

1. The Court shall take appropriate measures to protect the safety, physical and psychological well-being, dignity and privacy of victims and witnesses.

. . .

## Article 69
## Evidence

1. Before testifying, each witness shall, in accordance with the Rules of Procedure and Evidence, give an undertaking as to the truthfulness of the evidence to be given by that witness.

. . .

4. The Court may rule on the relevance or admissibility of any evidence, taking into account, inter alia, the probative value of the evidence and any prejudice that such evidence may cause to a fair trial or to a fair evaluation of the testimony of a witness, in accordance with the Rules of Procedure and Evidence.

. . .

## Article 73
## Third-party information or documents

If a State Party is requested by the Court to provide a document or information in its custody, possession or control, which was disclosed to it in confidence by a State, intergovernmental organization or international organization, it shall seek the consent of the originator to disclose that document or information. If the originator is a State Party, it shall either consent to disclosure of the information or document or undertake to resolve the issue of disclosure with the Court, subject to the provisions of article 72. If the originator is not a State Party and refuses to consent to disclosure, the requested State shall inform the Court that it is unable to provide the document or information because of a pre-existing obligation of confidentiality to the originator.

### Article 74
### Requirements for the decision

1. All the judges of the Trial Chamber shall be present at each stage of the trial and throughout their deliberations. The Presidency may, on a case-by-case basis, designate, as available, one or more alternate judges to be present at each stage of the trial and to replace a member of the Trial Chamber if that member is unable to continue attending.
2. The Trial Chamber's decision shall be based on its evaluation of the evidence and the entire proceedings. The decision shall not exceed the facts and circumstances described in the charges and any amendments to the charges. The Court may base its decision only on evidence submitted and discussed before it at the trial.
3. The judges shall attempt to achieve unanimity in their decision, failing which the decision shall be taken by a majority of the judges.
4. The deliberations of the Trial Chamber shall remain secret.

. . .

### Article 75
### Reparations to victims

1. The Court shall establish principles relating to reparations to, or in respect of, victims, including restitution, compensation and rehabilitation. On this basis, in its decision the Court may, either upon request or on its own motion in exceptional circumstances, determine the scope and extent of any damage, loss and injury to, or in respect of, victims and will state the principles on which it is acting.

. . .

### Article 76
### Sentencing

1. In the event of a conviction, the Trial Chamber shall consider the appropriate sentence to be imposed and shall

take into account the evidence presented and submissions made during the trial that are relevant to the sentence.

. . .

4. The sentence shall be pronounced in public and, wherever possible, in the presence of the accused.

. . .

### Article 77
### Applicable penalties

1. Subject to Article 110, the Court may impose one of the following penalties on a person convicted of a crime referred to in Article 5 of this Statute:
   (a) Imprisonment for a specified number of years, which may not exceed a maximum of 30 years; or
   (b) A term of life imprisonment when justified by the extreme gravity of the crime and the individual circumstances of the convicted person.
2. In addition to imprisonment, the Court may order:
   (a) A fine under the criteria provided for in the Rules of Procedure and Evidence;
   (b) A forfeiture of proceeds, property and assets derived directly or indirectly from that crime, without prejudice to the rights of bona fide third parties.

. . .

### Article 81
### Appeal against decision of acquittal or conviction or against sentence

1. A decision under article 74 may be appealed in accordance with the Rules of Procedure and Evidence as follows:
   (a) The Prosecutor may make an appeal on any of the following grounds:
      (i) Procedural error,
      (ii) Error of fact, or
      (iii) Error of law;

(b). The convicted person, or the Prosecutor on that person's behalf, may make an appeal on any of the following grounds:
  (i)  Procedural error,
  (ii) Error of fact,
  (iii) Error of law, or
  (iv) Any other ground that affects the fairness or reliability of the proceedings or decision.

. . .

### Article 82
### Appeal against other decisions

1. Either party may appeal any of the following decisions in accordance with the Rules of Procedure and Evidence:
   (a) A decision with respect to jurisdiction or admissibility;
   (b) A decision granting or denying release of the person being investigated or prosecuted;
   (c) A decision of the Pre-Trial Chamber to act on its own initiative under article 56, paragraph 3;
   (d) A decision that involves an issue that would significantly affect the fair and expeditious conduct of the proceedings or the outcome of the trial, and for which, in the opinion of the Pre-Trial or Trial Chamber, an immediate resolution by the Appeals Chamber may materially advance the proceedings.

### Article 83
### Proceedings on appeal

1. For the purposes of proceedings under article 81 and this article, the Appeals Chamber shall have all the powers of the Trial Chamber.
2. If the Appeals Chamber finds that the proceedings appealed from were unfair in a way that affected the reliability of the decision or sentence, or that the decision or sentence appealed from was materially affected by error of fact or law or procedural error, it may:
   (a) Reverse or amend the decision or sentence; or
   (b) Order a new trial before a different Trial Chamber.
5. The Appeals Chamber may deliver its judgement in the absence of the person acquitted or convicted.

. . .

### Article 86
### General obligation to cooperate

States Parties shall, in accordance with the provisions of this Statute, cooperate fully with the Court in its investigation and prosecution of crimes within the jurisdiction of the Court.

### Article 87
### Requests for cooperation: general provisions

. . .

5. (a) The Court may invite any State not party to this Statute to provide assistance under this Part on the basis of an ad hoc arrangement, an agreement with such State or any other appropriate basis.

. . .

### Article 89
### Surrender of persons to the Court

1. The Court may transmit a request for the arrest and surrender of a person, together with the material supporting the request outlined in article 91, to any State on the territory of which that person may be found and shall request the cooperation of that State in the arrest and surrender of such a person. States Parties shall, in accordance with the provisions of this Part and the procedure under their national law, comply with requests for arrest and surrender.

. . .

### Article 93
### Other forms of cooperation

1. States Parties shall, in accordance with the provisions of this Part and under procedures of national law, comply with requests by the Court to provide the following assistance in relation to investigations or prosecutions:
   (a) The identification and whereabouts of persons or the location of items;
   (b) The taking of evidence, including testimony under oath, and the production of evidence, including expert opinions and reports necessary to the Court;

(c) The questioning of any person being investigated or prosecuted;

(d) The service of documents, including judicial documents;

(e) Facilitating the voluntary appearance of persons as witnesses or experts before the Court;

(f) The temporary transfer of persons as provided in paragraph 7;

(g) The examination of places or sites, including the exhumation and examination of grave sites;

(h) The execution of searches and seizures;

(i) The provision of records and documents, including official records and documents;

(j) The protection of victims and witnesses and the preservation of evidence;

(k) The identification, tracing and freezing or seizure of proceeds, property and assets and instrumentalities of crimes for the purpose of eventual forfeiture, without prejudice to the rights of bona fide third parties; and

(l) Any other type of assistance which is not prohibited by the law of the requested State, with a view to facilitating the investigation and prosecution of crimes within the jurisdiction of the Court.

. . .

### Article 103
### Role of States in enforcement of sentences of imprisonment

1.  (a) A sentence of imprisonment shall be served in a State designated by the Court from a list of States which have indicated to the Court their willingness to accept sentenced persons.

    (b) At the time of declaring its willingness to accept sentenced persons, a State may attach conditions to its acceptance as agreed by the Court and in accordance with this Article

    (c) A State designated in a particular case shall promptly inform the Court whether it accepts the Court's designation.

. . .

## Article 104
## Change in designation of State of enforcement

1. The Court may, at any time, decide to transfer a sentenced person to a prison of another State.
2. A sentenced person may, at any time, apply to the Court to be transferred from the State of enforcement.

## Article 105
## Enforcement of the sentence

1. Subject to conditions which a State may have specified in accordance with article 103, paragraph 1 (b), the sentence of imprisonment shall be binding on the States Parties, which shall in no case modify it.

. . .

## Article 106
## Supervision of enforcement of sentences and conditions of imprisonment

1. The enforcement of a sentence of imprisonment shall be subject to the supervision of the Court and shall be consistent with widely accepted international treaty standards governing treatment of prisoners.

. . .

## Article 107
## Transfer of the person upon completion of sentence

1. Following completion of the sentence, a person who is not a national of the State of enforcement may, in accordance with the law of the State of enforcement, be transferred to a State which is obliged to receive him or her, or to another State which agrees to receive him or her, taking into account any wishes of the person to be transferred to that State, unless the State of enforcement authorizes the person to remain in its territory.

. . .

### Article 112
### Assembly of States Parties

1. An Assembly of States Parties to this Statute is hereby established. Each State Party shall have one representative in the Assembly who may be accompanied by alternates and advisers. Other States which have signed this Statute or the Final Act may be observers in the Assembly.
2. The Assembly shall:
   (a) Consider and adopt, as appropriate, recommendations of the Preparatory Commission;
   (b) Provide management oversight to the Presidency, the Prosecutor and the Registrar regarding the administration of the Court;
   (c) Consider the reports and activities of the Bureau established under paragraph 3 and take appropriate action in regard thereto;
   (d) Consider and decide the budget for the Court;
   (e) Decide whether to alter, in accordance with article 36, the number of judges;
   (f) Consider pursuant to article 87, paragraphs 5 and 7, any question relating to non-cooperation;
   (g) Perform any other function consistent with this Statute or the Rules of Procedure and Evidence.
3. (a) The Assembly shall have a Bureau consisting of a President, two Vice-Presidents and 18 members elected by the Assembly for three-year terms.
   (b) The Bureau shall have a representative character, taking into account, in particular, equitable geographical distribution and the adequate representation of the principal legal systems of the world.

. . .

### Article 113
### Financial Regulations

Except as otherwise specifically provided, all financial matters related to the Court and the meetings of the Assembly of States Parties, including its Bureau and subsidiary bodies, shall be governed by this Statute and the Financial Regulations and Rules adopted by the Assembly of States Parties.

. . .

## Article 119
## Settlement of disputes

1. Any dispute concerning the judicial functions of the Court shall be settled by the decision of the Court.
2. Any other dispute between two or more States Parties relating to the interpretation or application of this Statute which is not settled through negotiations within three months of their commencement shall be referred to the Assembly of States Parties. The Assembly may itself seek to settle the dispute or may make recommendations on further means of settlement of the dispute, including referral to the International Court of Justice in conformity with the Statute of that Court.

. . .

## Article 125
## Signature, ratification, acceptance, approval or accession

1. This Statute shall be open for signature by all States in Rome, at the headquarters of the Food and Agriculture Organization of the United Nations, on July 17, 1998. Thereafter, it shall remain open for signature in Rome at the Ministry of Foreign Affairs of Italy until October 17, 1998. After that date, the Statute shall remain open for signature in New York, at United Nations Headquarters, until December 31, 2000.
2. This Statute is subject to ratification, acceptance or approval by signatory States. Instruments of ratification, acceptance or approval shall be deposited with the Secretary-General of the United Nations.
3. This Statute shall be open to accession by all States. Instruments of accession shall be deposited with the Secretary-General of the United Nations.

## Article 126
## Entry into force

1. This Statute shall enter into force on the first day of the month after the 60th day following the date of the deposit of the 60th instrument of ratification, acceptance, approval

or accession with the Secretary-General of the United Nations.

2. For each State ratifying, accepting, approving or acceding to this Statute after the deposit of the 60th instrument of ratification, acceptance, approval or accession, the Statute shall enter into force on the first day of the month after the 60th day following the deposit by such State of its instrument of ratification, acceptance, approval or accession.

**Article 127**
**Withdrawal**

1. A State Party may, by written notification addressed to the Secretary-General of the United Nations, withdraw from this Statute. The withdrawal shall take effect one year after the date of receipt of the notification, unless the notification specifies a later date.

. . .

*Source*: Rome Statute of the International Criminal Court, http:// untreaty.un.org/cod/icc/index.html. Reproduced with permission from the United Nations Publications Board.

# Proposed Text of Article 98 Agreements with the United States, July 2002

*In an effort to bypass the jurisdiction of the ICC, the United States, beginning in 2001, entered into bilateral agreements with other nations. A sample BIA follows.*

A Reaffirming the importance of bringing to justice those who commit genocide, crimes against humanity and war crimes,

B Recalling that the Rome Statute of the International Criminal Court done at Rome on July 17, 1998 by the United Nations Diplomatic Conference of Plenipotentiaries on the Establishment of an International Criminal Court is intended to complement and not supplant national criminal jurisdiction,

C Considering that the Government of the United States of America has expressed its intention to investigate and to prosecute where appropriate acts within the jurisdiction of the International Criminal Court alleged to have been committed by its officials, employees, military personnel, or other nationals,

D  Bearing in mind Article 98 of the Rome Statute,
E  Hereby agree as follows:
  1.  For purposes of this agreement, "persons" are current or former Government officials, employees (including contractors), or military personnel or nationals of one Party.
  2.  Persons of one Party present in the territory of the other shall not, absent the expressed consent of the first Party,
     (a)  be surrendered or transferred by any means to the International Criminal Court for any purpose, or
     (b)  be surrendered or transferred by any means to any other entity or third country, or expelled to a third country, for the purpose of surrender to or transfer to the International Criminal Court.
  3.  When the United States extradites, surrenders, or otherwise transfers a person of the other Party to a third country, the United States will not agree to the surrender or transfer of that person to the International Criminal Court by the third country, absent the expressed consent of the Government of X.
  4.  When the Government of X extradites, surrenders, or otherwise transfers a person of the United States of America to a third country, the Government of X will not agree to the surrender or transfer of that person to the International Criminal Court by a third country, absent the expressed consent of the Government of the United States.
  5.  This Agreement shall enter into force upon an exchange of notes confirming that each Party has completed the necessary domestic legal requirements to bring the Agreement into force. It will remain in force until one year after the date on which one Party notifies the other of its intent to terminate this Agreement. The provisions of this Agreement shall continue to apply with respect to any act occurring, or any allegation arising, before the effective date of termination.

# Article 98 Waivers Signed by the United States and a Second Nation-State, 2002–2008

*The Rome Statute includes Article 98, which states: Article 98(2) Cooperation with respect to waiver of immunity and consent to surrender: The Court may not proceed with a request for surrender which would require the requested State to act inconsistently with its obligations under international agreements pursuant to which the consent of a sending State is required to surrender a person of that State to the Court, unless the Court can first obtain the cooperation of the sending State for the giving of consent for the surrender. Starting in 2002, the United States began negotiating these agreements with individual countries, and has concluded at least one hundred such agreements. Countries that sign these agreements with the United States agree not to surrender Americans to the jurisdiction.*

*Source*: www.georgetown.edu/guides/article_98.cfm.

### Countries That Have Signed Article 98 Agreements with the United States

Afghanistan; entered into force August 23, 2003.
Albania; entered into force July 7, 2003.
Algeria; entered into force April 13, 2004.
Angola; entered into force October 6, 2005.
Antigua and Barbuda; entered into force September 29, 2003.
Armenia; entered into force March 17, 2005.
Azerbaijan; entered into force August 28, 2003.
Bangladesh; entered into force March 29, 2004.
Belize; entered into force December 8, 2003.
Benin; entered into force August 25, 2005.
Bhutan; entered into force August 16, 2004.
Bosnia-Herzegovina; entered into force July 7, 2003.
Botswana; entered into force September 28, 2003.
Brunei; entered into force March 3, 2004.
Burkina Faso; entered into force October 14, 2003.
Burundi; entered into force July 24, 2003.
Cambodia; entered into force June 29, 2005.
Cameroon; entered into force December 1, 2003.
Cape Verde; entered into force November 19, 2004.
Central African Republic; entered into force January 19, 2004.
Chad; entered into force June 30, 2003.
Colombia; entered into force September 17, 2003.
Comoros; entered into force June 30, 2004.
Congo; entered into force June 2, 2004.
Congo, Democratic Republic of the; entered into force July 22, 2003.
Cote D'Ivoire; entered into force October 16, 2003.
Djibouti; entered into force July 2, 2003.
Dominica; entered into force May 10, 2004.
Dominican Republic; entered into force August 12, 2004.
East Timor; entered into force October 30, 2003.
Egypt; entered into force March 5, 2003. There is also an extension agreement.
Equatorial Guinea; entered into force May 6, 2004.
Eritrea; entered into force July 8, 2004.
Fiji; entered into force December 17, 2003.

Gabon; entered into force April 15, 2003.
Gambia; entered into force June 27, 2003.
Georgia; entered into force June 26, 2003.
Ghana; entered into force October 31, 2003.
Grenada; entered into force March 11, 2004.
Guinea; entered into force March 25, 2004.
Guinea Bissau; entered into force February 8, 2005.
Guyana; entered into force May 18, 2004.
Haiti; entered into force January 12, 2004.
Honduras; entered into force June 30, 2003.
India; entered into force December 3, 2003.
Israel; entered into force November 27, 2003.
Kazakhstan; entered into force October 10, 2004.
Kiribati; entered into force March 4, 2004.
Laos; entered into force December 24, 2003.
Lesotho; entered into force June 21, 2006.
Liberia; entered into force November 3, 2003.
Macedonia; entered into force November 12, 2003.
Madagascar; entered into force August 4, 2003.
Malawi; entered into force September 23, 2003.
Maldives; entered into force July 8, 2003.
Marshall Islands; entered into force June 26, 2003.
Mauritania; entered into force July 6, 2003.
Mauritius; entered into force June 30, 2003.
Micronesia; entered into force June 30, 2003.
Mongolia; entered into force June 27, 2003.
Montenegro; entered into force April 19, 2007.
Morocco; entered into force November 19, 2003.
Mozambique; entered into force March 2, 2004.
Nauru; entered into force December 4, 2003.
Nepal; entered into force July 22, 2003.
Nicaragua; entered into force September 12, 2003.
Nigeria; entered into force October 6, 2003.
Oman; entered into force August 1, 2004.
Pakistan; entered into force November 6, 2003.
Palau; entered into force July 7, 2003.
Panama; entered into force November 6, 2003.
Papua New Guinea; entered into force September 30, 2004.
Philippines; entered into force May 13, 2003.
Rwanda; entered into force July 11, 2003.
Saint Kitts and Nevis; entered into force January 31, 2005.
Sao Tome and Principe; entered into force November 12, 2003.
Senegal; entered into force June 27, 2003.
Seychelles; entered into force July 17, 2003.
Sierra Leone; entered into force May 20, 2003.
Singapore; entered into force October 17, 2003.

Solomon Islands; entered into force March 17, 2004.
Sri Lanka; entered into force July 4, 2003.
Swaziland; entered into force September 20, 2006.
Tajikistan; entered into force June 23, 2003.
Thailand; entered into for June 3, 2003.
Togo; entered into force January 15, 2004.
Tonga; entered into force March 24, 2004.
Tunisia; entered into force December 22, 2003.
Turkmenistan; entered into force January 30, 2004.
Tuvalu; entered into force February 3, 2003.
Uganda; entered into force October 23, 2003.
United Arab Emirates; entered into force February 15, 2004.
Uzbekistan; entered into force January 7, 2003.
Yemen; entered into force December 17, 2003.
Zambia; entered into force July 2, 2003.

# Nongovernmental Organization Coalition Letter to Congress Regarding Bilateral Immunity Agreements, May 30, 2008

*Hundreds of nongovernmental organizations (NGOs) participated in the drafting of the ICC and lobbied successfully for its ratification. All were opposed to American efforts to circumvent the ICC through the mechanism of the bilateral immunity agreements (BIA). The following is a memo regarding the legitimacy of these bilateral agreements.*

Dear Member of Congress,

As Congress begins the FY09 appropriations process, we, the undersigned organizations, would like to bring to your attention an important policy matter tied to the State/Foreign Operations appropriations bill. Since the summer of 2002, the Bush administration has aggressively sought to conclude bilateral immunity agreements (BIAs) with almost all countries, including every country in the world that has ratified the International Criminal Court (ICC) treaty. Many nations have refused to sign a BIA because they believe that doing so would breach their legal obligations under the Rome Statute, the treaty that established the Court. Countries, including those not party to the Court, have also refused in order to protect their sovereignty and out of respect for the ICC's values and purposes.

BIA agreements are of dubious benefit and the quest to secure them is a source of considerable friction between the U.S. and its allies in Europe, Africa, and Latin America. In the meantime the ICC has opened cases in Sudan, Uganda, and the Democratic Republic of Congo in an attempt to bring to justice some of the world's most heinous criminals. Rather than continue to support a policy that empowers non-cooperation with the Court, we urge Congress instead to include text in this year's appropriations bill that has been suggested by Representative Betty McCollum (D-Minn.), stipulating that "none of the funds made available in this Act under the heading 'Economic Support Fund' shall be restricted based on the relationship between any government and the International Criminal Court."

The ICC treaty known as the Rome Statute, respects the Status of Forces (SOFA) and Status of Mission (SOMA) agreements that protect U.S. service personnel and civilian officials. Unfortunately, BIAs go much further by shielding private citizens and foreign U.S. contractors from the ICC. This makes BIAs especially offensive to other countries by forcing them to give up their sovereign right to apply their own legal procedures—in this case making use of the ICC—to persons who commit crimes on their territory.

Moreover, because they are bilateral in nature, BIAs can also shield foreign war criminals from the Court's jurisdiction, even if they are in U.S. custody. We strongly believe the current Congress should not continue to support this failed Bush administration initiative.

In 2004, Congress passed the Nethercutt Amendment, which threatened to cut off vital Economic Support Funds (ESF) to countries unwilling to sign BIA agreements. Former Rep. Jim Kolbe, then Republican chair of the Appropriations Subcommittee, spoke strongly against this amendment when it came to the House floor: "At a time when we are fighting the war on terrorism, reducing this tool of diplomatic influence is not a good idea. If we accept [this amendment], the U.S. will be hamstringing itself, placing a straitjacket on its diplomatic tools . . ." Although the Nethercutt language was not included in the FY07 Foreign Operations appropriations bill, it was unfortunately included, at the request of House appropriators, in the Consolidated Appropriations Act, 2008 (H.R. 2764, Section 671).

Congress has already recognized the negative impact of the BIA campaign and wisely voted to repeal two similar BIA related sanctions which were signed into law by the president: on Foreign Military Financing (FMF) and International Military Education and Training (IMET). House appropriators should bring a complete end to this counterproductive policy by adopting the McCollum language as part of the FY09 State/Foreign Operations appropriations bill.

One of our staff members will be in contact with your staff to answer any questions or respond to any concerns. We look forward to thanking you for your support on this important matter.
Sincerely,
Americans for Democratic Action
Amnesty International USA
Better World Campaign
Center for American Progress
Church Women United

Citizens for Global Solutions
Council for a Livable World
Evangelical Lutheran Church in America
Friends' Committee on National Legislation
Genocide Intervention Network
Human Rights First
Human Rights Watch
Maryknoll Office for Global Concerns
National Association of Social Workers
National Education Association
National Association of Evangelicals
Open Society Policy Center
Peace Action and Peace Action Education Fund
Presbyterian Church USA
United Church of Christ, Justice and Witness Ministries
United Methodist Church, General Board of Church and Society
United Nations Association—USA
Universal Human Rights Network
Unitarian Universalist Association of Congregations
World Organization for Human Rights, USA

# Chapter 7, UN Charter, 1945: Action with Respect to Threats to the Peace, Breaches of the Peace, and Acts of Aggression

### Article 39
The Security Council shall determine the existence of any threat to the peace, breach of the peace, or act of aggression and shall make recommendations, or decide what measures shall be taken in accordance with Articles 41 and 42, to maintain or restore international peace and security.

. . .

### Article 41
The Security Council may decide what measures not involving the use of armed force are to be employed to give effect to its decisions, and it may call upon the Members of the United Nations to apply such measures. These may include complete or partial interruption of economic relations and of rail, sea, air, postal, telegraphic, radio, and other means of communication, and the severance of diplomatic relations.

Article 42

Should the Security Council consider that measures provided for in Article 41 would be inadequate or have proved to be inadequate, it may take such action by air, sea, or land forces as may be necessary to maintain or restore international peace and security. Such action may include demonstrations, blockade, and other operations by air, sea, or land forces of Members of the United Nations.

Article 43

All Members of the United Nations, in order to contribute to the maintenance of international peace and security, undertake to make available to the Security Council, on its call and in accordance with a special agreement or agreements, armed forces, assistance, and facilities, including rights of passage, necessary for the purpose of maintaining international peace and security.

. . .

Article 45

In order to enable the United Nations to take urgent military measures Members shall hold immediately available national air-force contingents for combined international enforcement action.

. . .

Article 46

Plans for the application of armed force shall be made by the Security Council with the assistance of the Military Staff Committee.

Article 47

1. There shall be established a Military Staff Committee to advise and assist the Security Council on all questions relating to the Security Council's military requirements for the maintenance of international peace and security, the employment and command of forces placed at its disposal, the regulation of armaments, and possible disarmament.
2. The Military Staff Committee shall consist of the Chiefs of Staff of the permanent members of the Security Council or their representatives. Any Member of the United Nations not permanently represented on the Committee shall be invited by the Committee to be associated with it when

the efficient discharge of the Committee's responsibilities requires the participation of that Member in its work.

. . .

### Article 49

The Members of the United Nations shall join in affording mutual assistance in carrying out the measures decided upon by the Security Council.

. . .

### Article 51

Nothing in the present Charter shall impair the inherent right of individual or collective self-defense if an armed attack occurs against a Member of the United Nations, until the Security Council has taken measures necessary to maintain international peace and security. Measures taken by Members in the exercise of this right of self-defense shall be immediately reported to the Security Council and shall not in any way affect the authority and responsibility of the Security Council under the present Charter to take at any time such action as it deems necessary in order to maintain or restore international peace and security.

# 7

# Directory of Organizations

This chapter presents the reader and researcher with links to nongovernmental organizations (NGOs) and government organizations whose work addresses the need to prevent, stop, or punish perpetrators of genocide across the world. The directory that follows lists but a small number of such organizations. The Internet provides the reader/researcher with *all* Web sites that deal with these important legal and political issues.

## NGOs Working on Genocide and Human Rights Issues

There are many hundreds of private NGOs, many of which are international in scope, that deal with genocide and Holocaust issues. The amount of information on NGOs on the Internet is enormous, so locating NGO information by subject or geography can be time-consuming. However, the following links can help you get started. The University of California, Berkeley libraries also obtain print publications from NGOs, which can be located by searching in the Pathfinder or Melvyl directories.

There is also an NGO Code of Ethics and Conduct that these NGOs follow in their national and international activities. Some of the more important of these shared fundamental principles follow:

A. **Responsibility, Service, and Public Mindedness:**
Responsibly maintaining itself, an NGO should

conduct its activities for the sake of others, whether for the public at large or a particular segment of the public. . . .

B. **Cooperation Beyond Boundaries:** Significant progress toward world peace and global well-being can be fostered through interreligious, intercultural, and interracial work and across artificial barriers of politics and ethnicity that tend to separate people and their institutions. NGOs should maintain ethical, cooperative relationships with other NGOs and should partner where possible and appropriate for the sake of the greater public good. An NGO should be willing to work beyond borders of politics, religion, culture, race, and ethnicity, within the limits of the organizing documents and with organizations and individuals that share common values and objectives.

C. **Human Rights and Dignity:** As the Universal Declaration of Human Rights states, "All human beings are born free and equal in dignity and rights, are endowed with reason and conscience, and should act towards one another in a spirit of brotherhood" (Universal Declaration of Human Rights, Article 1). The family is the fundamental natural group unit of society promoting human rights and human dignity (Universal Declaration of Human Rights, Article 16). An NGO should not violate any person's fundamental human rights, with which each person is endowed. An NGO should recognize that all people are born free and equal in dignity. . . .

D. **Religious Freedom:** "Everyone has the right of freedom of thought, conscience and religion; this right includes freedom to change his religion or belief, and freedom, either alone or in community with others and in public or private, to manifest his religion or belief in teaching, practice, worship and observance" (Universal Declaration of Human Rights, Article 18). An NGO should respect religious freedom. . . .

E. **Truthfulness and Legality:** An NGO should be honest and truthful in its dealings with its donors, project beneficiaries, staff, membership, partner organizations, government, and the public in general, and should respect the laws of any jurisdiction in which it is active. An NGO should give out accurate information, whether regarding itself and its projects, or regarding any individual, organization, project, or legislation it opposes or is discussing (see World Association of Nongovernmental Organizations for the Full Code of NGO Ethics, at www .wango.org.).

## The NGO Directory

Some of the major NGOs, along with their e-mail addresses, are listed below.

### Adalah

http://www.adalah.org

Adalah ("justice" in Arabic) is an independent human rights organization and legal center. It was established in November 1996 to promote and defend the rights of Palestinian Arab citizens of Israel (close to 20 percent of the population, or about 1.2 million people) and Palestinians living in the Occupied Palestinian Territory.

### Advocacy Project

http://www.advocacynet.org

The goal of the Advocacy Project is to produce social change by helping marginalized communities claim their rights. They believe that change is best achieved by those who are most directly affected and partner with advocates to represent those communities.

### African Rights

http://www.afrights@gn.apc.org

This organization is dedicated to working on issues of grave human rights abuses, conflict, famine, and civil reconstruction in Africa, recognizing the limitations upon existing human rights, humanitarian, and conflict resolution approaches to Africa's most pressing problems.

## Al-Haq

http://www.al-haq.org

Al-Haq works in the Occupied Palestinian Territory to uphold the rule of law and respect for human rights. Al-Haq is an independent Palestinian nongovernmental human rights organization that focuses on monitoring, documenting, and advocating against the violations of the individual and collective rights of Palestinians under international law, irrespective of the identity of the perpetrator, using both national and international mechanisms. This Web site provides the reader with the NGO's policies, programs, and strategies for realizing its mission.

## American Association of Jurists (AAJ)

http://www.aaj.org

The AAJ's fundamental principles and objectives are the struggle for self-determination of peoples: full economic independence as well as sovereignty of the State over its wealth and natural resources; the struggle against imperialism, fascism, and colonialism and the discrimination against women, the indigenous people, and national minorities; the defense of real peace based on the principle of peaceful coexistence between States of different social and economic systems; and the defense and promotion of human rights and the realization of better and more effective guarantees to their protection.

## Amnesty International

http://www.amnesty.org

Amnesty International conducts research and generates action to prevent and end grave abuses of human rights and to demand justice for those whose rights have been violated. It exerts influence on governments, political bodies, companies, and intergovernmental groups. Activists conduct mass demonstrations, vigils, and direct lobbying as well as online and offline campaigning.

## Armenian National Institute, Washington, D.C.

http://www.armenian-genocide.org

This site provides information about the Armenian genocide (statements, resolutions, proclamations, trial extracts), educational resources (how to teach about genocide, resource guides, curricula, and information on video documentaries), and genocide research (chronology, sample documents, photos, survey to press coverage, and guide to bibliographies).

### Australian Institute for Holocaust and Genocide Studies

http://www.aihgs.com

This site contains lists of courses, staff, center publications, a very brief genocide bibliography (A–Z), a list of other genocide Web sites, and a special "Pontian Genocide and Asia Minor Holocaust Research Unit," which collects and translates archives and eyewitness testimonies.

### Cambodian Genocide Project, Yale University, New Haven, Connecticut

http://www.yale.edu/cgp

This is a data-based Web site contains thousands of files of records of Khmer Rouge genocide; most are bilingual, with summaries in both Khmer and English.

### Campaign against Genocide

http://www.campaignagainstgenocide.org

Campaign against Genocide is a coalition of NGOs, led by Genocide Watch. Its goal is to use past history of genocides in order to build a better future. The coalition seeks to educate people about what genocide is and why it must be stopped. This campaign is a single, grassroots "spark designed to ignite a wildfire across the consciousness of the developed world" until every person knows genocide as a part of world history and is determined that it will never again be a part of the future. The Web site provides the reader/researcher with data regarding past and ongoing genocidal actions across the world.

### Center for Constitutional Rights (CCR)

http://www.ccrjustice.org

The Center for Constitutional Rights (CCR) was founded in 1966 by attorneys who represented civil rights movements in the

South. CCR is a nonprofit legal and educational organization dedicated to advancing and protecting the rights guaranteed by the U.S. Constitution and the Universal Declaration of Human Rights. CCR supports the creative use of law as a positive force for social change. Its work began on behalf of civil rights activists, and over the last four decades CCR has lent its expertise and support to virtually every popular movement for social justice.

### Center for Human Rights & Constitutional Law

**http://www.centerforhumanrights.org**

The Center for Human Rights & Constitutional Law is a nonprofit, public interest legal foundation dedicated to furthering and protecting the civil, constitutional, and human rights of immigrants, refugees, children, and the poor.

### Citizens for Global Solutions

**http://www.globalsolutions.org**

This organization focuses on getting the U.S. government to adopt specific measures to stop genocide from happening in the first place. Citizens for Global Solutions promotes international law and the corresponding international institutions such as the UN and the International Criminal Court.

### Coalition for International Justice (CIJ)

**http://www.haguejusticeportal.net**

The Coalition for International Justice (CIJ) supports the international war crimes tribunals for Rwanda and the former Yugoslavia and criminal and transitional justice initiatives for East Timor, Sierra Leone, Cambodia, and Sudan. CIJ, an international, nonprofit organization, initiates and conducts advocacy and public education campaigns, targeting decision makers in Washington and other capitals, media, and the public. In conjunction with other NGOs around the world, CIJ helps focus and maximize the impact of individual and collective advocacy with regard to international and hybrid tribunals. In the field, CIJ provides practical assistance on legal, technical, and outreach matters to the tribunals and other justice initiatives. Its Web site provides information to the reader regarding the status of these judicial initiatives as well as giving viewers its advocacy arguments for international justice.

### The Committee on Conscience of the U.S. Holocaust Memorial Museum

http://www.ushm.org/conscience

This Web site publishes "genocide watch" and "genocide warning" notices for particular countries and situations with brief overviews.

### Concordia University, Montreal, Montreal Institute for Genocide and Human Rights Studies (MIGS)

http://migs.concordia.ca

This site reviews human rights NGOs and related sites, specialized sites by country or region, and general news sources that relate to genocide and human rights issues.

### Crimes of War

http://www.crimesofwar.org

This site discusses the rules of war and gives definitions and case studies of crimes of war, crimes against humanity, and genocide. It also examines contemporary conflict situations and trials, showing the range of legal opinions. It contains good Web links to legal and human rights sources.

### Danish Center for Holocaust and Genocide Studies

http://www.dchf.dk

This site presents information in Danish and English including material on Danish Jews during the Holocaust.

### Derechos

http://www.derechos.org

This NGO was the first group formed on the Internet in order to address human rights and their violation by governments across the world. Its Web site contains up-to-date information about human rights violations occurring across the world, with a special emphasis on the dilemmas associated with the "disappeared" in Central and South America.

### Genocide Watch

http://www.genocidewatch.org

This Web site is the coordinator of the International Campaign to End Genocide, founded at The Hague Appeal for Peace Conference.

### Human Rights First

http://www.humanrightsfirst.org

Human Rights First, formerly The Lawyer's Committee for Human Rights, works particularly on the legal side of human rights protection, promoting respect for the legal protections promised in the Universal Declaration of Human Rights and subsequent international or multipartite human rights legal documents.

### Human Rights Watch (HRW)

http://www.hrw.org

HRW is one of the world's leading independent organizations dedicated to defending and protecting human rights. By focusing international attention where human rights are violated, the NGO gives voice to the oppressed and hold oppressors accountable for their crimes. Their researchers engage in rigorous, objective investigations wherever human rights have been violated by governments. The organization also develops strategic, targeted advocacy in order to build intense pressure for action and raise the cost of human rights abuse. Since its founding in 1978 (then called Helsinki Watch), Human Rights Watch has worked tenaciously to lay the legal and moral groundwork for deep-rooted change and has fought to bring greater justice and security to people around the world.

### Institute for the Study of Genocide (ISG)

http://www.instituteforthestudyofgenocide.org

The Institute for the Study of Genocide (ISG), located at John Jay College of Criminal Justice of the City University of New York, is an independent nonprofit organization chartered by the University of the State of New York. The ISG promotes and disseminates scholarship and policy analyses on the causes, consequences, and prevention of genocide. It was founded in 1982 to fill a gap in the academic and the human rights communities, which did not recognize the continued prevalence of genocide.

### International Association of Genocide Scholars

http://www.genocidescholars.org

This NGO's focus is the *prevention* of genocide, but it also covers the full spectrum of scholarship of genocide.

### International Committee of Jurists (ICJ)

http://www.icj.org

The International Commission of Jurists (ICJ) is dedicated to the primacy, coherence, and implementation of international law and principles that advance human rights. The ICJ supports an impartial, objective, and authoritative legal approach to the protection and promotion of human rights through the rule of law. The ICJ provides legal expertise at international and national levels to ensure that developments in international law adhere to human rights principles and that international standards are implemented at the national level.

### International Committee of the Red Cross (ICRC)

http://www.icrc.org

The mission of the International Committee of the Red Cross (ICRC) is to protect the lives and dignity of victims of armed conflict and other situations of violence and to provide them with assistance. The ICRC also endeavors to prevent suffering by promoting and strengthening humanitarian law and universal humanitarian principles. Established in 1863, the ICRC is at the origin of the Geneva Conventions and the International Red Cross and Red Crescent Movement. It directs and coordinates the international activities conducted by the Movement in armed conflicts and other situations of violence.

### International Human Rights Law Group (IHRG)

http://www.ihrg.org

The IHRG is dedicated to the belief that religious freedom is the first, most important, freedom given to all persons. Its goal is to work with various government and ministry leaders to assure that this first freedom is protected and even encouraged throughout the World. The NGO believes that democracy thrives where religious freedom thrives. Whether it is the right to share ones' religious beliefs in a public area, the right to determine the educational choices of ones own children, or the right to exist as a recognized religious organization, it is important to those who believe and to those who do not believe that these rights are protected.

## Kurdish Human Rights Protect (KHRP)

http://www.khrp.org

KHRP's expert fact-finding and trial observation delegations to the Middle East's conflict regions continue to lend a sense of international solidarity to the most disadvantaged living there, while warning perpetrators that their contravention of international human rights norms will not go unchecked. Through independent investigations of allegations and concerns, fact-finding and trial observation missions play an essential part in monitoring human rights abuses. The missions also help maintain vital links with victims and survivors of human rights abuse and their defenders, who are frequently also the subject of human rights abuse.

## Lawyers against the War (LAW)

http://www.lawyersagainstthewar.org

Lawyers against the War (LAW) is an international group of lawyers and others who support the use of national and international law to settle disputes, prosecute offenders, and protect human rights; oppose the illegal use of force between states, in particular the illegal U.S.-led use of force against Afghanistan and Iraq; and, support the rule of law and adherence to international law.

## Montreal Institute for the Study of Genocide and Human Rights Studies

http://www.instituteforthestudyofgenocide.org

The Institute seeks to understand the underlying reasons for genocide and other crimes against humanity. It also presents concrete policy recommendations to resolve conflicts before they intensify and spiral into mass atrocity crimes.

Oxfam

http://www.oxfam.org

Oxfam works to reduce the number of people who become ill, are displaced, or are killed in armed conflicts. This NGO tries to ensure that children, who are innocent victims of any conflict, are protected. Preventing conflict starts at the local level, and Oxfam helps communities identify the root causes of conflict and find creative ways to build peace. Oxfam's peace and security initiatives are built on a central tenet: conflict violates the inherent rights of all people. Its work is designed to build local capacity for peace, to confront those who profit from conflict, and to advocate for peace. Its Web site provides the researcher with accurate data regarding armed conflicts, including genocidal actions by governments.

**Prevent Genocide International**

http://www.preventgenocide.org

This site is a global education and action network working to prevent the crime of genocide. This Web site is available in multiple languages. It includes genocide law in the criminal codes of 70 nations, the Genocide Convention in 35 languages, the word "genocide" in 70 languages, and a collection of the writings of Raphael Lemkin, who coined the word genocide in 1943.

**Refugees International**

http://www.refugeesinternational.org

Refugees International was started in 1979 as a citizens' movement to protect Indochinese refugees. Since then, it has expanded to become the leading advocacy organization that provokes action from global leaders to resolve refugee crises. It does not accept government or UN funding. Its expert recommendations are highly valued by the very people whose decisions bring immediate relief and lifesaving solutions to refugees: senior officials of the U.S. administration, the UN, and governments around the world, and members of the U.S. Congress. Each year, Refugees International conducts 20 to 25 field missions to identify displaced people's needs for basic services such as food, water, health care, housing, access to education, and protection from harm. Because of its on-site knowledge of humanitarian emergencies, the NGO successfully challenges policy makers and aid agencies to improve the lives of displaced people around the world.

### The Sikh Genocide Project

http://www.sikhgenocide.org

The Sikh Genocide Project Web site focuses on the 20th anniversary of state-sponsored extermination of Sikhs in India. It also presents "Third Sikh Holocaust," a four-part QuickTime movie.

### Silent Voices Speak

http://www.silentvoicesspeak.org

This site has a mixed-media art exhibition, based primarily on artist Barbara Shilo's archival photographs of the Holocaust, with an accompanying text that uses art to "enhance public understanding of the Holocaust and its relation to present day social injustice." It sponsors a lecture series on contemporary genocide, ethnic cleansing, racism, and anti-Semitism.

### Society for Threatened People (STP)

http://www.gfbv.de

The Society for Threatened Peoples (STP) is an independent international human rights organization. It encourages ethnic, linguistic, and cultural diversity and is an independent voice for minorities and indigenous peoples worldwide. The NGO's most important activities involve the protection of minorities and threatened peoples, the promotion of human rights, and the fight against human rights violations. This Web site informs, through publicity and campaigns, the world's public about the situations impacting threatened peoples. With these activities the group aims to create an awareness of its concerns and their efforts in the community. It also provides an extensive documentation on various issues for any people interested in its work and human rights in general.

### Sudan Organization against Torture (SOAT)

http://www.soatsudan.org

This NGO is a human rights organization established in 1993 working in Sudan and the UK and has members worldwide. SOAT's primary objective is preventing torture and challenging impunity. SOAT works to rehabilitate Sudanese survivors of torture; to provide legal assistance to survivors and individuals

threatened with inhumane and degrading punishments; to provide human rights education; and to research, document, and
campaign against human rights abuses in Sudan on both national
and international levels.

**University of Minnesota, Center for Holocaust and Genocide
Studies**

http://www.chgs.umn.edu/

The site includes a "Virtual Museum of Holocaust and Genocide
Art"; historical narratives and documents; and links, bibliographies,
and educational resources. The section on the Armenian Genocide
features a collection of editorial cartoons about the genocide at the
time it occurred.

**World Federalist Association's (WFA) "Campaign to End
Genocide"**

http://www.endgenocide.org

This site has information about the policy goals supported by the
WFA, which they believe are necessary to end genocide.

# Intergovernmental Organizations (IGOs) Working on Genocide Issues

Since 1945, the UN system, including their specialized agencies,
has been the major IGO in the modern world. This section enumerates the goals and purposes of those UN agencies dedicated
to human rights, security for innocent persons caught in civil
war, and resolving issues that touch on crimes against humanity
and genocide.

**AccessUN**

http://www.libraries.iub.edu/scripts/countResources.php?
resourceId=6

The site indexes and makes available UN documents from 1946
to date. Most documents are included in the microfiche collection

from 1984. Hard copy is located in the Public Documents and Maps Department, Indiana University, Bloomington.

### International Criminal Tribunal for the Former Yugoslavia (ICTY)

**http://www.icty.org**

The International Criminal Tribunal for the former Yugoslavia (ICTY) is a UN court of law dealing with war crimes that took place during the conflicts in the Balkans in the 1990s. Since its establishment in 1993 it has irreversibly changed the landscape of international humanitarian law and provided victims an opportunity to voice the horrors they witnessed and experienced. In its precedent-setting decisions on genocide, war crimes, and crimes against humanity, the Tribunal has shown that an individual's senior position can no longer protect from prosecution. It has now shown that those suspected of bearing the greatest responsibility for atrocities committed can be called to account, as well as that guilt should be individualized, to protect entire communities from being identified as "collectively responsible." Its Web site contains all documents, including trial transcripts, of the cases heard and decided by this court.

### International Criminal Tribunal for Rwanda (ICTR)

**http://www.ictr.org**

Recognizing that serious violations of humanitarian law were committed in Rwanda, and acting under Chapter VII of the UN Charter, the Security Council created the International Criminal Tribunal for Rwanda (ICTR) by Resolution 955 of November 8, 1994. The purpose of this measure is to contribute to the process of national reconciliation in Rwanda and to the maintenance of peace in the region. The ICTR was established for the prosecution of persons responsible for genocide and other serious violations of international humanitarian law committed in the territory of Rwanda between January 1, 1994, and December 31, 1994. It may also deal with the prosecution of Rwandan citizens responsible for genocide and other such violations of international law committed in the territory of neighboring States during the same period. This official Web site of the ICTR contains all documents and trial transcripts of those who were charged with committing acts of genocide, crimes against humanity, and war crimes.

## The UN System

### UN Children's Fund (UNICEF)

http://www.unicef.org

This site has information regarding data and policies developed to meet the needs of children. Recently, in 1990s, the organization has provided therapy for children traumatized by war and genocide.

### UN Department of Peacekeeping Operations (UNDPKO)

http://www.un.org/Depts/dpko

This site is an important one for it is the public face of the UN's efforts to organize and direct peacekeeping operations across the world. Between 1988 and 2000, there were 46 peacekeeping operations. Since 2000, there have been nearly two dozen peacekeeping missions.

### UN Documentation Center

http://www.un.org/en/documents/index.shtml

The site includes full text resolutions and decisions, selected documentation, speeches, and press releases from the General Assembly, the Security Council, and the UN's Economic and Social Council.

### UN Human Rights Documents

http://www.un.org/Depts/dhl/resguide/spechr.htm

This site provides detailed information about the human rights documentation of the UN and presents key documents of the Charter-based bodies, such as the UN's Human Rights Council.

### UN International Labor Organization (ILO)

http://www.ilo.org

This Web site provides the researcher with data and policies of the ILO regarding the condition of workers in military and industrial industries who contribute to a nation's war efforts. Its major goal is to provide social justice for workers.

## UN International Law Commission (ILC)

http://www.un.org/law/ilc

The ILC, a creation of the UN General Assembly, "shall have for its object the promotion of the progressive development of international law and its codification." The ILC's work on a topic usually involves some aspects of the progressive development as well as the codification of international law, with the balance between the two varying depending on the particular topic. Its Web site provides the reader with a comprehensive presentation of all of the ILC's sessions and accomplishments in international criminal law since its creation in 1949.

## UN NGO Global Network

http://www.ngo.org

This site is the home page for the UN's global NGO community. Its aim is to help promote collaborations between NGOs throughout the world, so that together they can more effectively partner with the UN and each other to create a more peaceful, just, equitable, and sustainable world for this and future generations.

## UN Office for Coordination of Humanitarian Affairs (OCHA)

http://www.reliefweb.int/dha_ol/about/cont.html

This site offers readers an understanding of the dynamics of the UN's efforts to address the myriad of humanitarian dilemmas that crop up across the world, including emergency responses to critical humanitarian issues.

## UN Office of the High Commissioner for Human Rights/ Commission on Human Rights

http://www.ohchr.org

The OHCHR is the principal human rights office of the UN. The OHCHR spearheads the UN's human rights efforts. Its Web site educates and encourages individuals to take action and assist States in upholding human rights.

### UN World Food Program (WFP)

http://www.wfp.org

This site enumerates the varied activities of the organization to provide food aid to people living in areas where poverty is rampant—due to civil war and natural disasters.

### U.S. Agency for International Development (USAID)

http://www.usaid.gov

This Web site is a resource for those interested in how U.S. foreign assistance works, who the beneficiaries are, and what impact assistance has on countries all over the world.

### U.S. Holocaust Memorial Museum, Washington, D.C.

http://www.ushmm.org

This site contains extensive information about the museum, library, collections, and archives and the U.S. Holocaust Memorial Council. Using the site, a researcher can do a search from the collections and archives online; help is available.

### U.S. Institute of Peace (USIP)

http://www.usip.org

The U.S. Institute of Peace (USIP) is an independent, nonpartisan, national institution established and funded by Congress. USIP provides the analysis, training, and tools that prevent and end conflicts, promotes stability, and professionalize the field of peace building. It is essential that the United States, working with the international community, play an active part in preventing, managing, and resolving conflicts. Fragile states, ethnic and religious strife, extremism, competition for scarce resources, and the proliferation of weapons of mass destruction all pose significant challenges to peace. The resulting suffering and destabilization of societies make effective forms of managing conflict imperative. The USIP is dedicated to meeting this imperative in new and innovative ways. Its goals are to help prevent and resolve violent international conflicts; promote postconflict stability and development; and increase conflict management capacity, tools, and intellectual capital worldwide.

The Institute does this by empowering others with knowledge, skills, and resources, as well as by directly engaging in peace-building efforts around the globe.

**USAID Directory of Registered NGOs**

**http://www.pvo.net/usaid**

This is a link to a list of all private voluntary organizations (PVO) registered with USAID. Many groups find it beneficial to partner with other NGOs, including groups registered with USAID as PVOs.

**Yad Vashem Home Page, Yad Vashem, Jerusalem**

**http://www1.yadvashem.org/yv/en/visiting/index.asp**

This site contains extensive information on the Yad Vashem museum and library, International Campaign for Gathering and Commemorating the Names of Holocaust Victims (one can submit testimonies online), Task Force for International Cooperation on Holocaust Education, Remembrance and Research, Teacher Training Seminars in North America and more.

# NGOs Affiliated with the UN and Its Agencies or Affiliated with Other IGOs

A number of NGOs have cooperative relationships with governmental agencies, at both national and international levels. The following enumeration of such groups illustrates the breadth of these NGOs and their cooperation with governmental organizations.

**Association for the Prevention of Torture (APT)**

**http://www.apt.ch**

The APT is the international NGO, based in Geneva, behind the ground-breaking Optional Protocol to the UN Convention against Torture (OPCAT). The APT believes that the risk of torture and other ill treatment exists everywhere in the world. The challenge and mission of the APT is how to prevent it. For 30 years the APT has been a leading force in prevention by promoting three integrated elements: (1) transparency of detention institutions through regular visits by independent experts; (2)

the capacity strengthening to reform practices of detention; and (3) effective legal frameworks.

### Center for Justice and International Law (CEJIL)

http://www.civil-society.oas.org

The Center for Justice and International Law (CEJIL) is a regional NGO that defends human rights in the Americas and the Caribbean. It operates offices in Costa Rica, Brazil, the United States, and the Caribbean and has representatives in Argentina, Chile, and Paraguay.

### Coalition for Women's Human Rights in Conflict Situations

http://www.womensrightscoalition.org

The mandate of the Coalition for Women's Human Rights in Conflict Situations is to ensure that crimes committed against women in conflict situations are adequately examined and prosecuted. The Coalition seeks solutions to the invisibility of women's human rights abuses in conflict situations, to condemn the practice of sexual violence and other inhumane treatment of women as deliberate instruments of war, and to ensure that these actions are prosecuted as war crimes, torture, crimes against humanity, and crimes of genocide, where appropriate. Working at the local and international levels, Coalition members act as a resource for consultation and debate on substantive issues related to the integration of a gender perspective in postconflict transitional justice systems. Coalition efforts also seek to strengthen international and regional capacity to monitor the respect of women's human rights in conflict and postwar situations through the creation of appropriate mechanisms of accountability and the assessment of their transferability to other contexts.

### Doctors without Borders/Médecins Sans Frontières (MSF)

http://www.doctorswithoutborders.org

Doctors without Borders/Médecins Sans Frontières (MSF) is an international medical humanitarian organization created by doctors and journalists in France in 1971. It provides aid in nearly 60 countries to people whose survival is threatened by violence, neglect, or catastrophe, primarily due to armed conflict, epidemics, malnutrition, exclusion from health care, and natural disasters. MSF provides independent, impartial assistance to those most in need. MSF reserves the right to speak out to bring attention to neglected crises, to challenge inadequacies or abuse of the aid system, and to advocate for improved medical treatments and protocols. In 1999, MSF received the Nobel Peace Prize.

### Human Rights Advocates (HRA)

http://www.humanrightsadvocates.org

HRA is a human rights organization based in Berkeley, California. It is dedicated to promoting and protecting international human rights in the United States and abroad. HRA participates actively in the work of various UN human rights bodies, using its status as a fully accredited NGO. HRA is most involved at the UN Council on Human Rights, the Commission on the Status of Women, the Commission on Sustainable Development, and several treaty bodies, including the Human Rights Committee and the Committee on the Elimination of All Forms of Racial Discrimination

### Institute of World Affairs (IWA)

http://www.iwa.org

Founded in 1924, IWA is an NGO working across cultural and political boundaries to advance creative approaches to conflict analysis, conflict management, and postconflict peacebuilding. Since its founding, it has been actively engaged in studying the sources of conflict in the international arena and in developing approaches to conflict management that attempt to address root causes. IWA's efforts focus on critical issues in access, participation, rule of law, and security along a pre- to postconflict continuum.

### International League for Human Rights

http://www.ilhr.org

The International League for Human Rights (ILHR) is a human rights organization with headquarters in New York City. The oldest human rights organization in the United States, the ILHR defines its mission as "defending human rights advocates who risk their lives to promote the ideals of a just and civil society in their homelands." In 1947, the League was granted consultative status with the UN Economic and Social Council

(ECOSOC), giving it the right to testify before that body about human rights abuses.

**Lawyers without Borders**

http://www.lawyerswithoutborders.org

Lawyers without Borders' mission is to protect the integrity of legal process, serve the underserved, and promote the culture of pro bono service in the legal profession—all with a neutral orientation. It fulfills its mission through advocacy training, cultivating lawyer skill sets to create effective strategies in the human rights and development sectors, neutral observation and engagement in programs that provide capacity building, and technical assistance in developing regions and regions emerging from conflict.

**Organization for Defending Victims of Violence (ODVV)**

http://www.idealist.org

The ODVV's goals are to promote a culture of nonviolence and to defend and support victims of violence. The Organization is active in Iran and in the Middle East. It publishes a monthly bulletin entitled *Defenders' Newsletter*, which covers information about human rights violations and articles on specific issues.

# Intergovernmental Organizations (IGOs), Other Than the UN and Its Agencies, with a Focus on Human Rights and Peacekeeping Operations

An IGO is created when two or more governments sign a multilateral treaty to form such an entity, agree to the goals and purposes of the IGO, and agree on a formula for financing its operations. IGOs are recognized in international law; they can enter into treaties and conventions, and the staff of an IGO possess diplomatic status. What follows are examples of these regional intergovernmental organizations.

### Association of Southeast Asian Nations (ASEAN)

http://www.asean.or.id

The task of this regional organization of 10 member states has been to safeguard the political and economic stability of the members. It has also been tasked to resolve conflicts between the members, by peaceful means if possible.

### Commonwealth

http://www.thecommonwealth.org

This site provides data and policies developed by this 54 nation organization of former members of the British commonwealth. The major goals are conflict prevention and to strengthen democratic values.

### Commonwealth of Independent States (CIS)

http://www.cis.minsk.by/main.aspx?uid=74

This IGO, made up of 12 former Soviet Republics who created the organization in 1991, has as its primary focus, maintaining peaceful relations between the member states, including the creation of peacekeeping operations if they are necessary. The Web site is for the Executive Committee of the CIS (English version).

### Council of Europe

http://www.coe.int/

Created in 1941 to provide political and social protection for the 41 member nation-states. It also is tasked with addressing and resolving human rights issues that emerge in the organization.

### Economic Community of West African States (ECOWAS)

http://ecowas.int/

This site provides information about the efforts of 16 West African nations to provide collective self-reliance, maintain peace, and protect human rights within this regional IGO.

### European Union (EU)

http://europa.eu/index_en.htm

Created in 1957 for the 15 member states to mediate disputes in their region of Europe. It has been involved in the reconstruction of the former Yugoslavia. The Web site provides annual data and policies that have been created to fulfill its mission.

### Gulf Cooperation Council (GCC)

http://www.globalsecurity.org/military/world/gulf/gcc.htm

This site, reflecting the goals and policies of six states, was created in 1981, in response to the war between Iran and Iraq. It has made efforts, so far unsuccessful, to create a regional peacekeeping force.

### League of Arab States

http://www.arableagueonline.org

This site provides data and policy making of the 22 member states' efforts to handle disputes between its members.

### North American Treaty Organization (NATO)

http://www.nato.int

This organization, which now has more than two dozen member states (including nations that were formerly part of the Soviet Union's regional defense and economic organization), provides military protection to member states and has intervened in Yugoslavia and Kosovo to end genocide and ethnic cleansing. The site provides information about the structure and the general goals of this IGO.

### Organization for Security and Cooperation in Europe (OSCE)

http://www.osce.org

This pan-European security organization, with 55 member states, has developed policies on arms control and human rights problems that have surfaced in the region.

### Organization of African Unity (OAU)

http://www.african-union.org

This organization, created in 1963, provides its 53 member states with policies that seek to defend sovereign territorial integrity after colonialism ended after World War II. Its goal is the peaceful resolution of conflicts between member states and that has meant, at times, mediation, military action, and peacekeeping operations.

**Organization of American States (OAS)**

http://www.oas.org

This Web site provides data on the structure of the OAS, as well as policies that have been created since 1951 to protect the sovereign integrity—maintenance of peace and security—of the 35 member states. It is committed to the peaceful settlement of disputes between the members.

# 8

# Resources

As one can image, there are many thousands of resources—print and nonprint—whose focus is on genocide, genocides, efforts to explain the social, psychological, religious, political aspects of genocide, prevent genocides from occurring, and steps taken to provide justice for the victims after genocide ends. This listing includes books, journal articles, essays in newspapers, documents, films, television and videos, and genocide websites on the Internet. The materials enumerated in this chapter merely touch the surface. However, they give the reader a starting point for further research. I have listed some of the more important resources that focus on genocide.

## Print Resources

Print resources provide readers and researchers with an abundance of materials on genocide, both general scholarship on the meaning of genocide and genocides as well as books written about major genocides such as the Turkish genocide of their ethnic Armenians, the German slaughter of millions of Jews, Pol Pot's effort to create a new Cambodian society by killing millions of his countrymen who did not have a place in his new world. In addition, I have presented examples of the type of coverage given to the subject of genocide in the daily press and in scholarly journals.

## General

Aall, Pamela, Daniel Milternberger, and Thomas G. Weiss. *Guide to IGOs, NGOs, and the Military in Peace and Relief Operations.* 3rd ed. Washington, D.C.: U.S. Institute of Peace Press, 2003.

This is a very useful book that provides the reader and researcher with succinct observations about the major intergovernmental organizations and NGOs.

Anderson, Martin E. *Dossier Secreto: Argentina's Desaparecidos and the Myth of the "Dirty War."* Boulder, CO: Westview Press, 1993.

This scholarly book examines the brutal events that took place in Argentina in the second half of the 20th century when the country was ruled by a right-wing military junta and their opposition was slaughtered and tortured, and many of their bodies "disappeared."

Arendt, Hannah. *Eichmann in Jerusalem: A Report on the Banality of Evil.* New York: Penguin Classics, 2007.

Now a classic, and controversial study, of the trial of Adolph Eichmann in Jerusalem after he was abducted by Israeli agents from his home in Argentina and brought to Israel. Arendt was captivated by the bland, banal, and thoroughly bureaucratic behavior of Eichmann and others who participated in the roundup, transportation, and killing of millions of Jews in Nazi Germany's killing centers.

Ball, Howard. *Prosecuting War Crimes and Genocide.* Lawrence: University Press of Kansas, 1999.

One of many scholarly books written about the genocides of the 20th century, beginning with the slaughter of the Herreros by Germany through the bloody events in Bosnia and Rwanda. It also focuses on the ways in which the international community responded to these tragedies.

Ball, Howard. *War Crimes and Justice.* Santa Barbara, CA: ABC-CLIO, 2002.

This is a reference book that provides the reader with information about war crimes that have occurred in the 20th century and the international community's responses to these actions. It contains a chronology of events and a bibliography.

Bass, Gary Jonathan. *Stay the Hand of Vengeance: The Politics of War Crimes Tribunals.* Princeton, NJ: Princeton University Press, 2000.

This book focuses on the intense interactions between law and international politics that accounted for the creation of the two ad hoc war crimes tribunals, the ICTY and the ICTR. It is also a history of the clash between law and politics as nations attempted to create tribunals from after the First World War through the military tribunals after World War II ended.

**Becker, Jasper. Hungry Ghosts: Mao's Secret Famine.** *New York: Henry Holt, 1998.*

This book examines the brutal 1958–1962 starvation of millions of Chinese by the Communist leadership in order to swiftly move the society forward as an industrial behemoth. This effort was called "The Great Leap Forward." It raises the question, as do so many books, whether intentionally creating the conditions of famine is itself the intent to destroy a group within society prohibited by the 1948 Genocide Convention.

**Berry, Nicholas O.** *War and the Red Cross: The Unspoken Mission.* **New York: St. Martin's Press, 1997.**

This book examines the role of the International Committee of the Red Cross (ICRC) as it has evolved since its creation in the middle of the 19th century in Switzerland. The mission he describes is that of the ICRC secretive efforts to stop genocides.

**Brackman, Arnold C.** *The Other Nuremberg: The Untold Story of the Tokyo War Crimes Trials.* **New York: William Morrow, 1987.**

Although the German leaders trial in Nuremberg in 1945 was a major event—and story—the War Crimes Trial of the leading Japanese military men and political leaders was not covered as extensively and was very different from the Nuremberg trial. This book examines the similarities and the differences between these first two ad hoc international military tribunals.

**Cameron, Maxwell A., Robert J. Lawson, and Brian Tomlin, eds.** *To Walk without Fear: The Global Movement to Ban Landmines.* **Toronto: Oxford University Press, 1998.**

Ths book examines the strategy of advocate NGOs to convince the international community of the human rights benefits of banning land mines from manufacture, sale, and use by armed groups—both state and insurgent groups.

**Chang, Iris.** *The Rape of Nanking.* **New York: Penguin, 1998.**

This is a powerful account of the Japanese slaughter and rape of half the Chinese population of Nanking, China (300,000 dead) at the start of the 1937 war against China.

**Chang, Jung, and Jon Halliday.** *Mao: The Unknown Story.* **New York: Knopf, 2005.**

This massive book touches on every aspect of the Chinese Communist leader's life and rise to power. It is an excellent—and savage—political biography of a major tyrant of the 20th century.

**Charney, Israel W., ed.** *The Encyclopedia of Genocide. 2 vols. Santa Barbara, CA: ABC-CLIO, 1999.*

This is a useful reference work on the subject of genocide, although somewhat dated.

**Dedijer, Vladimir.** *The Yugoslav Auschwitz and the Vatican: The Croatian Massacre of the Serbs during World War II.* **New York: Prometheus Books, 1992.**

The author, a close ally of Marshall Tito and the Yugoslav ambassador to the United Nations, writes about the long history of enmity between the Croats (Catholic) and the Serbs (Orthodox) and how this hatred led to the World War II killing of more than 200,000 Serbs by the Croatian government—which was allied with Nazi Germany against the Serbs and Tito's partisans. These historic insights go far toward explaining the continuing wars between the Croats and the Serbs in the early and mid-1990s.

**Drechsler, Horst.** *Let Us Die Fighting: The Struggle of the Herrero and Nama against German Imperialism, 1884–1915.* **London: Zed Press, 1980.**

This is a translation from the German of a historical account of the German military slaughter of most of the Herreros in what is now Namibia. It is, the author concludes, another example of Western imperialism in the 19th and early 20th centuries that led to the mass murder of the African native tribes at that time.

**Durch, William J., ed.** *UN Peacemaking, American Policy, and the Uncivil Wars of the 1990s.* **New York: St. Martin's Press, 1996.**

This is a well-documented account of the failure of both American foreign policy and the weakness and lack of will on the part of the United Nations in the face of brutal civil wars in Rwanda, Somalia, Bosnia, and Kosovo.

Ebrahim, Alnoor. *NGOs and Organizational Change: Discourse, Reporting, and Learning*. Cambridge, U.K.: Cambridge University Press, 2003.

This is a scholarly examination of the relationship between NGOs and their funding problems, including examples of how different NGOs have successfully maintained the stream of funds needed for their operations to continue.

Fein, Helen. *Genocide: A Sociological Perspective*. London, England: Sage, 1993.

The author has presented a succinct examination of genocide from a sociological perspective.

Fromkin, David. *A Peace to End All Peace: The Fall of the Ottoman Empire and the Creation of the Modern Middle East*. New York: Henry Holt, 1989.

The author, a noted historian, has carefully examined the rise and fall of the Ottoman Empire (at the end of the First World War) and how that led to the devastating problems of war, peace, and genocide that confront the world community in the 21st century.

Gellately, Robert, and Ben Kiernan, eds. *The Specter of Genocide: Mass Murder in Historical Perspective*. New York: Cambridge University Press, 2003.

This book of collected essays provides the reader with the latest scholarship on the history—as well as acute analyses—of the nature of genocide as well as data bases explaining the many genocides that have occurred in the 20th century. The essays discuss the Armenian genocide, Stalin's use of terror, Japan's mass murders of its enemies during the World War II, the Holocaust, Yugoslavia, Cambodia, Ethiopia, Rwanda, East Timor, and Guatemala.

Ghiglieri, Michael P. *The Dark Side of Man: Tracing the Origins of Male Violence*. Cambridge, MA: Perseus Books, 2000.

A very interesting book, based on monkey social behavior and psychological experiments, that argues that men are born to form bonds with their kin and fight and kill other men from different communities.

Goldhagen, Daniel Jonah. *Worse Than War: Genocide, Eliminationism, and the Ongoing Assault on Humanity*. New York: Public Affairs Press, 2009.

This controversial book attempts to argue that genocide, as defined in the Convention and international law, does not fully explain and account for man's cruelty to man. He posits that the concept of eliminationism is the most appropriate term to use in the effort to understand crimes against humanity.

**Goldstone, Richard J.** *For Humanity: Reflections of a War Crimes Investigator.* **New Haven, CT: Yale University Press, 2000.**

This book, written by an international lawyer who has participated in national (South Africa's Truth and Reconciliation Commission) and international (the initial prosecutor for the ICTY) actions that attempt to deal with the consequences of mass murder and genocide, provides the reader with insights based on Goldstone's experiences.

**Gutman, Roy, and David Rieff.** *Crimes of War.* **New York: Norton, 1999.**

This is an excellent reference book—accompanied by brutal photographs—on war crimes committed in the 20th century. There are succinct essays that cover the range of such crimes—for example, child soldiers, death squads, just and unjust wars, and humanitarian intervention—with acute assessments of the consequences of these actions.

**Hewitt, William L., ed.** *Defining the Horrific: Readings on Genocide and Holocaust in the Twentieth Century.* **Upper Saddle River, NJ: Pearson, 2004.**

**Hinton, Alexander L., ed.** *Annihilating Difference: The Anthropology of Genocide.* **Berkeley, CA: University of California Press, 2002.**

This is another excellent social science and anthropological effort to explain the nature of 20th-century genocide.

The author has put together a series of articles that focus on the major genocides of the 20th century.

**Iles, Greg.** *The Devil's Punchbowl.* **New York: Scribner's, 2009.**

A novel that, in part, explores man's capacity for doing evil.

**Jones, Adam.** *Genocide: A Comprehensive Introduction. New York: Routledge, 2006 (3rd ed. 2010).*

This book is an outstanding starting point for anyone interested in an all-embracing examination of the multidimensionality of genocide. It exposes the reader to social science explanations of the concept as well as providing clearly written explanations of specific genocides and the world community's efforts to prevent or stop genocides from occurring.

**Jones, Adam, ed.** *Genocide, War Crimes and the West: History and Complicity.* **London: Zed Books, 2004.**

This book is, much like Jones' book *Genocide*, an extensive and very comprehensive examination of Western responsibility for mass atrocity.

**Jones, Adam, ed.** *Gendercide and Genocide.* **Nashville, TN: Vanderbilt University Press, 2004.**

Jones has placed in this book a wide variety of articles that examine specific case studies of gender select murders in genocides occurring in the last half of the 20th century.

**Jones, Adam, ed.** *New Directions in Genocide Research.* **New York: Routledge, 2010.**

This book contains the latest set of scholarly essays that focus on theories of comparative genocide. Its essays also focus on core issues associated with genocide, including humanitarian interventionism, gender and genocide, and the use of children to achieve the destruction of a targeted group. The final section of this book focuses on a number of case studies of genocide. It is an excellent resource for those researching genocide and core issues associated with genocide.

**Kiernan, Ben.** *Blood and Soil: A World History of Genocide and Extermination from Sparta to Darfur.* **New Haven, CT: Yale University Press, 2007.**

This large important book by a noted genocide scholar provides the reader with an absorbing presentation of the global history of genocide and mass murder from the time of the Greeks to the continuing tragedy of Darfur in the Sudan. Lying beneath these tragedies is the burning desire of tyrannical leaders to acquire new territories or to build the New Serbia or the New Germany, as well as the mad desire to purify their race by exterminating all those who foul it.

**Klee, Ernest, Willi Dressen, and Volker Riess, eds.** *The Good Old Days: The Holocaust As Seen by Its Perpetrators and Bystanders.* *New York: The Free Press, 1991.*

This book's contribution is to present firsthand accounts of the perpetrators of the Holocaust as well as the voices of bystanders who witnessed aspects of state genocidal policy.

Kornbluh, Peter. *The Pinochet File: A Declassified Dossier on Atrocity and Accountability*. New York: The New Press, 2003.

This book, using recently declassified documents, presents a factual portrait of the Pinochet tyranny as well as chronicling two decades, 1970 to 1990, of American awareness of the tyrannical actions of the Pinochet government. In addition the book presents a clear case of American complicity in his efforts to eliminate communists and other enemies of the state.

Kuper, Leo. *The Prevention of Genocide*. New Haven, CT: Yale University Press, 1985.

This book offers a critical examination of the United Nations' efforts to prevent, stop, and punish perpetrators of genocide.

Lemkin, Raphael. *Acts Constituting a General (transnational) Danger Considered as Offences against the Law of Nations*. Report presented at the 5th Conference for the Unification of Penal Law, Madrid, Spain, October 14–20, 1933. www.preventgenocideinternational.org.

This is the core article written by Raphael Lemkin that first raised the specter of mass murder, which he labeled "barbarity," and was his effort in 1933 to convince international lawyers that there must be international law written to prohibit what he would, in 1944, label as genocide.

Lewis, Paul H. *Guerillas and Generals: The "Dirty War" in Argentina*. Westport, CT: Praeger Publishers, 2002.

Another historic/political account of the actions of the brutal military junta that ruled Argentina for decades and their battles against the rebel guerilla forces that led to murder, "disappearances," and the repression of liberties in the nation.

Lipstadt, Deborah. *Denying the Holocaust: The Growing Assault on Truth and Memory*. New York: Plume, 1994.

An important book that provides readers with the views of those who deny that the genocide of Jews occurred.

McCormack, Tim, and Jann K. Kleffer, eds. *Yearbook of International Humanitarian Law. 2008*, vol. 11. The Hague: Asser Press, 2010.

This annual resource book provides a truly international forum for high-quality, peer-reviewed academic articles focusing on this highly topical branch of international law. It also includes a selection of documents from the reporting period, many of which are not accessible elsewhere. There is an excellent detailed index. It serves as a useful reference tool for scholars, practitioners, military personnel, civil servants, diplomats, human rights workers and students.

**Milgram, Stanley.** *Obedience to Authority: An Experimental View.* **New York: Harper Perennial, 1995.**

The book is the laying out of the "Milgram Experiments on Humans," which answered questions about why people accept orders to cause pain on other people.

**Munoz, Heraldo.** *The Dictator's Shadow: Life under Augusto Pinochet.* **New York: Basic Books, 2008.**

Another well-documented history of life in the Chile run by the dictatorial government led by General Pinochet.

**Nardin, Terry, and Melissa S. Williams, eds.** *Humanitarian Intervention: Nomos XLVII.* **New York: NYU Press, 2006.**

An excellent set of essays, written by political philosophers, that explore the scope of humanitarian intervention in international law and politics.

**Neier, Aryeh.** *War Crimes: Brutality, Genocide, Terror, and the Struggle for Justice.* **New York: Times Books, 1998.**

The author, who had been executive director of the ACLU and, after that, Human Rights Watch, has written a book that focuses principally on the creation and function of the two ad hoc international criminal tribunals created by the UN in the 1990s: the ICTY and the ICTR. His book raises disturbing questions regarding the trials outcomes: can a handful of trials establish individual criminal guilt and break the cycle of collective ascription?

**Newman, Leonard S., and Ralph Erber, eds.** *Understanding Genocide: The Social Psychology of the Holocaust.* **Oxford, England: Oxford University Press, 2002.**

Essays written by psychologists that attempt to explain the behavior of both the victims and the perpetrators of genocide.

**Patterson, James.** *Cross Country.* **New York: Vision, 2008.**

A novel that takes place, in great part, in Darfur in the Sudan during the early days of the mass murders by the Janjaweed.

**Power, Samantha.** *"A Problem from Hell": America and the Age of Genocide.* **New York: Basic Books, 2002.**

This book has quickly become the standard for those interested in understanding America's historic role in the effort to end mass murder and genocide. Her focus is to answer the fundamental question: Why have American foreign policy leaders—in the White House and Congress—after pledging "never again" repeatedly fail to use their power to stop genocide?

**Roberts, Adam, and Richard Guelff, eds.** *Documents on the Laws of War.* **3rd ed. New York: Oxford University Press, 2000.**

This is a basic text, containing documents, conventions, treaties, and military rules of engagement, from 1859 to the present.

**Robertson, Geoffrey.** *Crimes against Humanity: The Struggle for Global Justice.* **2nd ed. London: Penguin, 2002.**

This is an extraordinarily valuable book that discusses general themes associated with genocide—the context that gives rise to genocides, ending impunity, the legal mechanisms for dealing with the perpetrators of genocide, the ethical questions—as well as providing insights into specific genocides and mass killings such as the Pinochet era, the Balkan trials at the ICTY, and 21st-century terrorism.

**Schabas, William A.** *Genocide in International Law: The Crime of Crimes.* **Cambridge, England: Cambridge University Press, 2000.**

This huge reference book is a basic jump-off point for researchers who focus on the legal basis for the crime of genocide. It has an excellent bibliography and includes the three drafts—written over two years—of the 1948 Genocide Convention.

**Sewall, Sarah B., and Carl Kaysen, eds.** *The United States and the International Criminal Court: National Security and International Law.* **Lanham, MD: Rowman and Littlefield, 2000.**

The authors have collected a series of essays that examine, historically, America's antipathy for an international criminal court.

**Shaw, Martin.** *War and Genocide: Organized Killing in Modern Society.* **Cambridge, MA: Polity Press, 2003.**

This is an outstanding treatment of the symbiotic relationship between war (civil, regional, and world) and the genocides that have taken place during wartime.

**Shaw, Martin.** *What Is Genocide?* **Malden, MA: Polity Press, 2007.**

His focus in this book is on the structure of conflict situations, that is, attacks on the unarmed by the armed forces of the state. For the author, genocide is a type of war directed at "civilian enemies," and the book is an effort to explain his view of genocide.

**Sheldon, Dinah, ed.** *Encyclopedia of Genocide and Crimes against Humanity.* **Detroit: Macmillan Reference, 2005.**

This is a huge addition to genocide reference books, updating Charney's edited volume published in the 1990s.

**Sluka, Jeffrey A., ed.** *Death Squad: The Anthropology of State Terror.* **Philadelphia, PA: University of Pennsylvania Press, 2000.**

An anthology, also written by social anthropologists, that examines the nature and the use of state terror as policy to destroy undesirable residents of a country.

**Smith, Dan, Kristin Ingstad Sandberg, Pavel Baev, and Wenche Hauge.** *The State of War and Peace Atlas.* **New York: Penguin, 1997.**

This small atlas provides the reader with an excellent visual layout of the areas of the world where civil wars, mass murder, and genocide have taken place since 1945.

**Staub, Ervin.** *The Roots of Evil: The Origins of Genocide and Other Group Violence.* **Cambridge, MA: Cambridge University Press, 1989, 2007.**

This is an early examination of the psychology of those who participate in genocidal actions. Explaining the roots of genocide, according to the author, means the weaving of an explanatory mosaic containing descriptions of social, economic, cultural, political, and group patterns in a society, and how this knowledge can be used to prevent the outbreak of genocide.

**Stiglmayer, Alexandra, ed.** *Mass Rape: The War against Women in Bosnia-Herzegovina.* **Lincoln: University of Nebraska Press, 1995.**

This is a powerful book that examines how rape of enemy women became a tactic used by Bosnian Serbs to destroy the Bosnian Muslim culture.

**Tanaka, Yukiko.** *Hidden Horrors: Japanese War Crimes in World War II.* **Boulder, CO: Westview Press, 1997.**

This book focuses on the biological experiments and other crimes of the infamous Unit 731 whose men were never brought to justice after the Second World War ended in the Pacific.

Totten, Samuel, and William S. Parsons, eds. *Century of Genocide: Critical Essays and Eyewitness Accounts.* 3rd ed. New York: Routledge, 2009.

This is an important collection of essays, eyewitness accounts, and memoirs that account for the many crimes against humanity and genocides that have occurred in the 20th century and early 21st century (Darfur).

van den Berge, Pierre L., ed. *State Violence and Ethnicity.* Boulder, CO: University Press of Colorado, 1990.

An excellent book to begin research about the use of state terror and how it folds into a policy of genocide.

Varney, Steven, and Hunt Tooley, eds. *Ethnic Cleansing in Twentieth-Century Europe.* New York: Columbia University Press, 2003.

An anthology that contains various perspectives about the concept of ethnic cleansing—definitions and events—that was actualized in late 20th-century Europe.

Waller, James. *Becoming Evil: How Ordinary People Commit Genocide and Mass Killing.* 2nd ed. New York: Oxford University Press, 2007.

An important social psychologist's effort to explain why ordinary people willingly kill other people. He writes about his theory of "extraordinary human evil," his attempt to explain why seemingly ordinary men become willing participants in genocidal actions.

Weiss, Thomas G., and Cindy Collins. *Humanitarian Challenges and Interventions.* 2nd ed. Boulder, CO: Westview Press, 2000.

This small book provides a brief history of and an excellent analysis of the many problems associated with humanitarian intervention to end genocide.

Welsh, Claude E., Jr., ed. *NGOs and Human Rights: Promise and Performance.* Philadelphia: University of Pennsylvania Press, 2001.

An excellent source book for researchers and readers interested in the creation of and actions taken by advocacy organizations, NGOs, to confront human rights abuses and genocide. In the last quarter of the 20th century, these organizations have become major players in the effort to end human rights abuses by government. This book carefully examines their growth and development into forces for good in the international community.

**Wheeler, Nicholas.** *Saving Strangers: Humanitarian Intervention in International Society.* **Oxford, England: Oxford University Press, 2000.**

Since its publication in 2000, the book has become a major reference point focusing on the issue of humanitarian intervention.

**Whitaker, Benjamin.** *Revised and Updated Report on the Question of the Prevention and Punishment of the Crime of Genocide.* **New York: United Nations, 1985.**

This book/report was an effort to address the criticism leveled by critics of the 1948 Genocide Convention. The report did recommend some revisions of the Convention based on the perceived narrowness of the 1948 document's definitions of genocide.

**Ziegler, David W.** *War, Peace, and International Politics.* **7th ed. New York: Longman, 1997.**

This book, in its seventh edition, provides the reader with a realist's understanding of the fundamental interconnections between international relations and one of its primary realities: war. The author also spells out a variety of efforts taken by the world community that will end war and bring peace.

## Specific Genocides and Mass Murders

There have been thousands of books written on the major genocides of the 20th century, especially the Holocaust. Many of these books are memoirs by young persons, middle-aged adults, and senior survivors whose memories have been transcribed by their family members. Books that focus on genocides not enumerated, for example, the Chinese Silent Genocide (famine in 1958–1962) in this section of the bibliography are listed in the section above.

### Armenian "Genocide," 1915–1918

Ahmad, J. *The Young Turks.* Oxford, UK: Oxford University Press, 1969.

An early historic and political account of the radical movement in the Ottoman Empire at the turn of the 20th century that led to the overturn of the government by these revolutionaries called "Young Turks."

Balakian, Grigoris. *Armenian Golgotha: A Memoir of the Armenian Genocide, 1915–1918*. New York: Vintage Books, 2010.

A shocking, revealing memoir of an ethnic Armenian cleric who survived nearly two dozen arrests during the time of the Armenian Genocide. It is, at once, a moving, frank telling of the horrid story.

Balakian, Peter. *The Burning Tigris: The Armenian Genocide and America's Response*. New York: HarperCollins, 2003.

The book does an excellent job of focusing on the plight of the ethnic Armenians living in Turkey and the American reaction and response to the tragedy.

Bryce, James, and Arnold Toynbee. *The Treatment of Armenians in the Ottoman Empire, 1915–1916*. (British Blue Book) London, England, 1916. www.cilicia.com/bryce/a00c.htm.

This is an important document, written by two well-respected historians for the British government during the First World War, that describes in detail the beginning of the Armenian genocide.

Cetin, Fethiye. *My Grandmother: A Memoir*. New York: Verso, 1988.

This is another memoir that gives additional insight into the process of genocide as carried out by the state and its military.

Dadrian, Vahakin. *Warrant for Genocide: Key Elements of the Turko-Armenian Conflict*. New Brunswick, NJ: Transaction Press, 1999.

The reader is given a clear portrait of how the policy and the mechanics of the Turkish genocide against the ethnic Armenians was developed and implemented.

Hovannisian, Richard, ed. *Remembrance and Denial: The Case of the Armenian Genocide*. Detroit: Wayne State University Press, 1999.

An examination of the arguments presented by those who deny that there was ever an Armenian genocide during and after the First World War.

Hovannisian, Richard, ed. *The Armenian Genocide in Perspective*. New Brunswick, NJ: Transaction Publishers, 1987.

A collection of scholarly essays on the Armenian genocide before and during World War I.

Miller, Donald E., and Lorna Touryan Miller, *Survivors: An Oral History of the Armenian Genocide*. Berkeley, CA: University of California Press, 1999.

This book provides an oral history that examines the experiences of Armenian children who were not killed in the death marches.

Morgenthau, Henry. *Ambassador Morgenthau's Story*. Garden City, NY: Doubleday, Page, and Co., 1918. http://www.armeniapedia .org/index.php?title=Ambassador_Morgenthau%27s_Story.

Ambassador Morgenthau was America's Ambassador to the Ottoman Empire, stationed in Constantinople, and witnessed, firsthand and from reports to him from the field, the horrors of the genocide. The book contains his strained relationships with the leaders of the Young Turk Movement.

## Stalin's Terror: The Forced Famine in the Ukraine, 1929–1933

Applebaum, Anne. *Gulag: A History*. London: Penguin, 2003.

Another well-written historical account of the creation of the Gulag forced-labor camp system and its primary purpose in the first decades of the new Soviet system.

Conquest, Robert. *The Harvest of Sorrow: Soviet Collectivization and the Terror-Famine*. New York: Oxford University Press, 1986.

A powerful indictment of Stalin's successful effort to destroy seven million Kulaks brought on by the state-run Ukrainian famine of 1929–1933. The book also shows how the American Relief Administration and other NGOs fed more than 12 million starving Russians, which is one of the most successful humanitarian interventions in the history of the 20th century.

Davies, R. W., and Stephen G. Wheatcraft, *The Years of Hunger: Soviet Agriculture, 1931–1933*. Basingstoke: Palgrave Macmillan, 2004.

Another critical examination of the forced collectivization of Russian agriculture by Stalin that led to the starvation deaths of millions of Kulaks.

Dolot, Miron. *Execution by Hunger: The Hidden Holocaust*. New York: W.W. Norton, 1985.

A chilling memoir of the Ukrainian famine of the early 1930s that killed millions of Ukrainians.

Service, Robert. *Stalin: A Biography*. Cambridge, MA: Belknap Press, 2005.

A well-written biography of Stalin, one of the 20th century's most notorious dictators.

**Solzhenitsyn, Alexander.** *The Gulag Archipelago, 1918–1956.* **New York: HarperPerennial, 2002.**

This is a classic study by a noted author who survived Stalin's brutal concentration camp system. It was a cruel system where millions of prisoners—political, agricultural, military, and social enemies of the state—were sent to work and to die anonymously.

## Nazi Germany and the Jewish Genocide (Holocaust), 1939–1945

There have been thousands of books written about the Nazi genocide of the European Jews. More books have been written about this six-year tragedy than any other genocide that occurred in the 20th century. Included in this huge set are memoirs written by Jews who experienced the Holocaust, controversial history texts, and books that try to gauge the impact of sociology, psychology, law, politics, and anthropology in accounting for the mass slaughter of more than six million Jews across the whole of Europe. What follows are examples of the scope and multidimensionality of the writings that focus on the Nazi Germany efforts from 1939 to 1945 to destroy the Jewish communities in Europe.

**Hahn Beer, Edith, with Susan Dworkin,** *The Nazi Officer's Wife: How One Jewish Woman Survived the Holocaust.* **New York: Harper Perennial, 2000.**

This is a memoir of one German Jewish woman's survival in Nazi Germany—married to a German military person. Her story begins in prewar Germany and chronicles her escapes from capture by the Germans; it ends in postwar Germany where she is a judge with a small child and her husband, a military officer, is in a Russian gulag in Siberia.

**Bloxham, Donald. Genocide on Trial: War Crimes Trials and the Formation of Holocaust History and Memory. New York: Oxford University Press, 2001.**

This small book is based on a controversial premise. Bloxham argues that the Nuremberg War Crimes Trials "did little to clarify conceptualizations of Nazi criminality in the public sphere anywhere. . . . They drew away from the victims of Nazi genocide and onto much more ambiguous symbols of suffering."

**Bonhoeffer, Dietrich.** *Letters and Papers from Prison.* **New York: Touchstone, 1997.**

Bonhoeffer, a Lutheran clergyman, was imprisoned and eventually executed by the Nazis because of his sermons' condemnation of the brutality and immorality of the Nazi regime. This book is a collection of notes and correspondence covering the period from Dietrich Bonhoeffer's arrest in 1943 to his execution by the Gestapo in 1945.

**Browning, Christopher.** *Ordinary Men: Reserve Police Battalion 101 and the Final Solution in Poland.* **New York: Perennial, 1993.**

A book that, using newly uncovered documents, examines how ordinary German policemen had no difficulty participating in the brutal slaughter of Jews in conquered Eastern European and Russian territory. Browning underscores the importance of group dynamics and pressure as well as the shared anti-Semitism of these nonideological, ordinary men to account for their willingness to participate in the genocide of the Jews and other *untermenschen*.

**Burleigh, Michael.** *Ethics and Extermination: Reflections on Nazi Genocide.* **Cambridge, England: Cambridge University Press, 1997.**

The book contains essays written by the author on a variety of subjects, including Germany's euthanasia policy, the racial state, and the treatment of Russians, Poles, and Jews when the war began.

**Cornwell, John.** *Hitler's Pope: The Secret History of Pius XII.* **New York: Viking Press, 1999.**

This book explores a controversial piece of Holocaust history: the relationship between Hitler and the Catholic Pope, Pius XII (who served as papal nunciate in Germany from 1917 to 1929). The author argues that there was a conflict between the Pope's quest for power and the Church's spiritual beliefs and goals. The outcome was the Pope's collusion with Hitler's mad tyranny that led to increased violence without the Church's efforts to block the Nazi killing machine.

**Frank, Anne.** *The Diary of a Young Girl: The Definitive Edition.* **New York: Doubleday, 1995.**

This is the world's most familiar diary of a young Jewish woman during the Holocaust. Anne, who lived in Amsterdam, hid—with her family—for three years and wrote in her diary during all that time. She was captured by the Germans and sent to her death in a concentration camp.

Friedlander, Henry. *The Origins of Nazi Genocide: From Euthanasia to the Final Solution*. Chapel Hill: University of North Carolina Press, 1995.

This book examines the precursor of the genocide policy against Jews: Germany's euthanasia project begun as soon as Hitler became the Fuhrer in 1933. From this beginning, killing lives not worth living, the development of the Nazi genocide policy is traced by the author.

Gellately, Robert, and Nathan Stolzfus, eds. *Social Outsiders in Nazi Germany*. Princeton, NJ: Princeton University Press, 2001.

The authors bring together important essays on the "others" in Nazi Germany, the social outsiders, i.e., homosexuals, the infirm, mentally ill, gypsies, and Jews, who had to be eliminated in order for Nazi Germany to purify itself in the march toward the New Aryan Germany.

Goldhagen, Daniel J. *Hitler's Willing Executioners: Ordinary Germans and the Holocaust*. New York: Vintage, 1997.

Unlike Browning's argument that, given peer pressure dynamics, ordinary men found it easy to murder Jews, Goldhagen's book, using the same archival data, maintains that the single cause of the success of the Holocaust was the German citizen's deep-rooted hatred of the Jewish community.

Hilberg, Raul. *The Destruction of the European Jews*. 3 vol., 3rd ed. New Haven, CT: Yale University Press, 2003.

Hilberg's outstanding scholarship on the Nazi effort to destroy the Jewish communities in Europe has led to this classic set of books. It is an account, highlighting the bureaucratization of the slaughter across the continent, of the events that is the starting point for any serious understanding of the Nazi genocide. His account is based on a careful examination of the thousands of documents produced by the Germans. From these data, his book constructs a factual record of the Holocaust.

Hirschfield, Gerhard, ed. *The Politics of Genocide: Jews and Soviet Prisoners of War in Nazi Germany*. Boston: Allan and Unwin, 1986.

The book draws parallels between the Nazi treatment of Russian prisoners of war and the Jewish communities in Europe. Both were seen as *untermenschen* not worthy of life.

Hitler, Adolf. *Mein Kampf.* Mannheim, Ralph, trans. Boston, MA: Houghton Mifflin, 1943.

This book, written by Hitler while serving a year in prison, was first published in 1926. It lays out his grandiose plans for the New Germany as well as his virulent hatred of Jews and what he thought Germany must do to relieve the society of these parasites.

Kennealy, Thomas. *Schindler's List.* New York: Touchstone, 1993.

A fact-based story about a famous rescuer of Jews working in his factory in Crakow, Poland. A moving, Oscar-winning movie was made of this story.

Klemperer, Victor. *I Will Bear Witness: A Diary of the Nazi Years.* 2 vol. New York: Modern Library, 1999, 2001.

Klemperer's books are a memoir of a Jew living in Berlin during the war. He survived the horror because he was married to a non-Jewish woman and, under Nazi law, was treated differently. His book examines life in Nazi Germany during the entire Nazi period, 1933–1945.

Landau, Ronnie S. *The Nazi Holocaust.* Chicago, IL: Ivan R. Dee, 1994.

A well-written insightful examination of the origins of the genocide against the Jews.

Laskier, Rutka. *Rutka's Notebook: A Voice from the Holocaust.* Jerusalem, Israel: Yad Veshem, 2008.

This memoir is a diary written by a 14-year-old Polish Jewess over three months before her transportation to Auschwitz in 1943 where she perished. It accounts the horror of captivity and living in the Bedzin ghetto and the depravity of the German soldiers who guarded them.

Levi, Primo. *Survival in Auschwitz.* New York: Touchstone, 1996.

The author, a Jewish survivor of the Nazi death camps, provides the reader with a unforgettable account of his almost two years in these camps.

Lewy, Guenter. *The Nazi Persecution of the Gypsies.* Oxford, England: Oxford University Press, 2000.

A controversial examination of the Nazi extermination policy employed against European Roma (Gypsies).

Lifton, Robert J. *The Nazi Doctors: Medical Killing and the Psychology of Genocide.* New York: Basic Books, 1986.

The author examines the psychology behind the actions of medical doctors in Nazi Germany in order to explain their participation in inhumane killings of human guinea pigs (Jews, Russian prisoners, and other groups).

Marrin, Albert. *Hitler.* New York: Viking, 1987.

The book examines the childhood influences and failures as a young adult (including an aborted painting career) that led to Hitler's destructive, racist personality that emerged after World War I had ended.

Persico, Joseph E. *Nuremberg: Infamy on Trial.* London: Penguin Press, 1995.

A very readable account of the German leaders who stood in the docket and faced war crimes and crimes against humanity charges. The author was able to interview many of them during the trial and the reader is presented with insights into the minds of these Nazi murderers.

Plant, Richard. *The Pink Triangle: The Nazi War against Homosexuals.* New York: Owl Books, 1988.

The author, who survived the Nazi regime, has written a book that examines the Nazi persecution and extermination of homosexuals.

Schlink, Bernhard. *The Reader.* New York: Vintage Books, 1997.

This is an excellent, moving novel about a woman who was a concentration camp guard in the Crakow area of Poland and, years later, long after the war has ended, finds herself and other guards on trial for their actions against Jews at the camp.

Toland, John. *Adolf Hitler.* Garden City, NY: Doubleday, 1976.

Toland's book uses previously unpublished documents, diaries, notes, photographs, and dramatic interviews with Hitler's colleagues and associates to create his portrait of the Nazi leader.

Wander, Fred, and Michael Hofmann, trans. *The Seventh Well.* New York: Norton, 2005.

This is a novel about the lives of Jewish prisoners in Buchenwald, the last of the author's 20 concentration camps. It focuses on how survival in the camps is the task of more than one person, the community of prisoners is the key to survival.

Weiss, John. *Ideology of Death: Why the Holocaust Happened in Germany*. Chicago: Ivan R. Dee, 1996.

The book examines why Germany developed the Final Solution for the Jewish problem even though most European societies were generally anti-Semitic.

Weisel, Elie. *Night*. Boston: Schocken Books, 2001.

In this, his first book, the noted author describes his concentration camp experiences.

## Pol Pot and the Cambodian Genocide, 1975–1979

Becker, Elizabeth. *When the War Was Over: Cambodia and the Khmer Rouge Revolution*. New York: Public Affairs, 1998.

The book examines the rationale behind the grim reality of the killing fields. A very readable history of the Khmer Rouge years in power.

DePaul, Kim, ed. *Children of Cambodia's Killing Fields: Memoirs by Survivors*. New Haven, CT: Yale University Press, 1997.

Like so many collections of memoirs written by children and teenagers, this is a series of harrowing tales of human survival in the most difficult of conditions: the Killing Fields of Cambodia.

Hinton, Alexander L. *Why Did They Kill? Cambodia in the Shadow of Genocide*. Berkeley: University of California Press, 2005.

The author, an anthropologist, offers the reader an anthropological explanation of the killings during the Khmer Rouge era.

Kamm, Henry. *Cambodia: Report from a Stricken Land*. New York: Arcade Publishing, 1998.

This is a Pulitzer Prize–winning journalist's account of the Cambodian tragedy, from 1970 into the last decade of the 20th century. He also provides a history of the Khmer empire from the earliest time. He analyzes the history of revolution, invasion, government overthrow, and genocide in Cambodia on the basis of his personal knowledge of Cambodian leaders and many interviews. It is an excellent read.

Kiernan, Ben. *The Pol Pot Regime: Race, Power, and Genocide in Cambodia under the Khmer Rouge, 1975–1979*. New Haven, CT: Yale University Press, 1996.

Another fine, detailed study—based in part on more than 500 interviews with survivors of the Killing Fields—of the violent beginning of the Pol Pot years, written by a scholar who is an expert in the area of genocide and directs the Yale University genocide project. He sets out to answer a question raised in every genocidal event: Why did Cambodians—many highly educated—impose the cruelest genocide on fellow Cambodians.

Ung, Loung. *First They Killed My Father: A Daughter of Cambodia Remembers*. New York: HarperCollins, 2000.

A frightening memoir, written by a Chinese-Cambodian young woman, about her survival during the Pol Pot regime.

## Milosevic and the Bosnian Genocide, 1992–1995

Bass, Gary Jonathan. *Stay the Hand of Vengeance: The Politics of War Crimes Tribunals*. Princeton, NJ: Princeton University Press, 2000.

This book provides the reader with an inside view of the politics surrounding the creation of war crimes trials, beginning with an examination of the Nuremberg and Tokyo tribunals and ending with the politics of the creation of the ICTY and the ICTR.

Boyle, Francis A. *The Bosnian People Charge Genocide: Proceedings at the International Court of Justice Concerning BOSNIA V. SERBIA on the Prevention and Punishment of the Crime of Genocide*. Amherst, MA: Alethia Press, 1996.

The author was the legal advisor for the leaders of two breakaway nations, Croatia and Bosnia, in their legal proceedings in the International Court of Justice. This book presents the case he made for the people of Bosnia-Herzegovina in the effort to stop the killings.

Brkic, Courtney Angela. *The Stone Fields: Love and Death in the Balkans*. New York: Picador, 2004.

This is a very moving story of a young forensic anthropologist, part of a UN-sponsored forensic team sent to Bosnia after 1995 to find the missing bodies in the area of Srebrenica and, using forensic skills, to try to identify the bones of these victims of Bosnian-Serb ethnic cleansing. What makes this a special experience is that the author is a Bosnian Muslim whose family lived in the very area where she was doing her forensic work.

Crnobrnja, Mihailo. *The Yugoslav Drama*. 2nd ed. Montreal: McGill-Queen's University Press, 1996.

The author was the Yugoslav ambassador to the European Community before the nation deteriorated after Tito's death in 1980. His book, based on his experiences as a politician/diplomat, provides some new insights into the destruction of Yugoslavia and the emergence of nationalist leaders such as Slobodan Milosevic.

**Doder, Dusko, and Louise Branson,** *Milosevic: Portrait of a Tyrant.* **New York: Free Press, 1999.**

This biography of a key figure in the disintegration of Yugoslavia examines his upbringing that led to his uncanny ability to manipulate and to mobilize citizens in order to create a New Serbia. These actions include the ethnic cleansing of Croatia, Bosnia, and Kosovo, and the authors describe his 1999 actions and his indictment by the ICC.

**Filipovic, Zlata.** *Zlata's Diary: A Child's Life in Sarajevo.* **New York: Viking Penguin, 1994.**

This is another diary written by a young teenaged girl that describes the conditions in Sarajevo during the three years of bombardment, 1992–1995, by Bosnian Serb artillery and snipers in the mountains overlooking the city.

**Fromkin, David.** *Kosovo Crossing: American Ideals Meet Reality on the Balkan Battlefields.* **New York: The Free Press, 1999.**

This book by a noted historian examines the relationship between American ideals and the reality of events in Bosnia and the implications of this clash between values and brutal reality.

**Hagen, John.** *Justice in the Balkans: Prosecuting War Crimes in The Hague Tribunal.* **Chicago, IL: University of Chicago Press, 2003.**

Hagen's book argues that although the ICTY, at its inception, was seen as a throw-away institution that would have little lasting impact, it has become a major model and resource for providing justice to the victims of the genocide. A key to the change, for the author, has been the very high quality of its prosecutors and its judges. Their actions are written about in this book.

**Honig, Jan Willem, and Norbert Both.** *Srebrenica: Record of a War Crime.* **New York: Penguin Books, 1996.**

This small book provides the reader with a frank and brutal look, based on documents and eyewitness reports, at the Bosnian Serb march into Srebrenica, one of the six "safe areas" supposedly under the control and protection of UN peacekeepers. The roundup of nearly 30,000 Bosnian Muslims is recounted in grim detail, especially the murder of more than 8,000 boys and men.

**Malcolm, Noel.** *Kosovo: A Short History.* **New York: NYU Press, 1999.**

The author, a historian, provides the reader with an excellent overview of the history of the Balkan provinces from 850 ce, including their existence on the Ottoman Empire, the long-standing differences and clashes between Kosovars, Serbs, Albanians, Croats, and Bosnians, the impact of the First World War on these regions, and the tragedy of Kosovo while Milosevic was the Serbian president.

**Neuffer, Elizabeth.** *The Key to My Neighbor's House: Seeking Justice in Bosnia and Rwanda.* **New York: Picador, 2001.**

The author is a journalist who has covered the events in Bosnia and Rwanda for more than a decade. Her book depicts the events in those two areas through the telling of three stories of survivors of these genocides. She bases her writing on extensive interviews with perpetrators and victims of both tragedies, with forensic experts, and with judges who sat on the two ad hoc tribunals established by the United Nations in 1993 and 1994, respectively.

Organization for Security and Cooperation in Europe (OSCE). *Kosovo/Kosova: As Seen As Told.* October 1998–October 1999. http://www.osce.org/search/?displayMode=3&lsi=18q=kosovo%2Fkoseva%3Aas+seen+as+told&GO=GO

An excellent, very detailed report on the atrocities committed by the Serbs in Kosovo.

**Rohde, David.** *Endgame: The Betrayal and Fall of Srebrenica, Europe's Worst Massacre since World War II.* **Boulder, CO: Westview Press, 1998.**

The author has penned a moving story about the Serb devastation of Srebrenica, the brutal killing of nearly 8,000 boys and men, and the rape of thousands of Bosnian women.

**Sarhandi, Daoud, and Alina Boboc.** *Evil Doesn't Live Here: Posters from the Bosnian War.* **London: Laurence King Publishing, 2001.**

This is a shocking but visually stunning book that contains posters from the combatants in the Bosnian wars—Croatian, Bosnian, and Serbian art that presents the visual propaganda battle that was waged from 1992 to 1995.

Scharf, Michael P. *Balkan Justice: The Story Behind the First International War Crimes Trial since Nuremberg.* Durham: Carolina Academic Press, 1997.

Examines the events that led to the creation of the ICTY in 1993 by the United Nations as well as carefully explaining and describing the very first trial, that of Dusko Tadic.

Sell, Louis. *Slobodan Milosevic and the Destruction of Yugoslavia.* Durham, NC: Duke University Press, 2002.

An important historical account of the life of the most important of the radical nationalists who emerged as leaders after the death of Tito in 1980. It is a story of how men such as Milosevic, with their grand visions of a New Serbia, led to the bloody genocides in the former Yugoslavia during the 1990s.

Sells, Michael A. *The Bridge Betrayed: Religion and Genocide in Bosnia.* Berkeley: University of California Press, 1996.

In this book, Sells describes the genocide in Bosnia as a result of the clash of religious forces in the region: Orthodox Serb, Catholic Croat, and Muslim Bosnian. The leaders of these communities, especially the Serb nationalists (Milosevic) used these religious differences to mobilize the groups to wage war in the former Yugoslavia in the 1990s.

Silber, Laura, and Allan Little. *Yugoslavia: Death of a Nation.* New York: TV Books, 1995.

This is one of the first books about the Bosnian wars and remains an excellent starting point for those interested in this particular genocidal event. It does a masterful job of showing the literal breakdown of a nation into warring provinces.

Stiglmayer, Alexandra, ed. *Mass Rape: The War against Women in Bosnia-Herzegovina.* Lincoln: University of Nebraska Press, 1995.

Since its 1995 publication this collection of essays has become a basic starting point for research on sexual violence against women as genocide.

Stover, Eric, and Gilles Peress. *The Graves: Srebrenica and Vukovar.* New York: Scalo Zurich, 1999.

An amazing, frightening collection of stories about forensic excavations in Bosnia to find the Bosnian Muslims murdered by Bosnian Serb militias. The research and photographs in the book were collected in Bosnia and Croatia between 1992 and 1997.

### The Hutu Genocide of the Tutsi, Rwanda, 1994

Dallaire, Romeo. *Shake Hands with the Devil: The Failure of Humanity in Rwanda*. New York: Carroll and Graf, 2004.

This is a powerful indictment of the failure of the UN to use its on-station UN troops to stop the genocide from taking place. The author was the Commander of the peacekeeping force in Rwanda who tried unsuccessfully to convince the UN bureaucrats to allow his troops to act.

Des Forges, Alison. *Leave None to Tell the Story: Genocide in Rwanda*. New York: Human Rights Watch, 1999.

This is an important report on the destruction of human rights within the Rwanda genocide.

Gourevitch, Philip. *We Wish to Inform You That Tomorrow We Will Be Killed with Our Families: Stories from Rwanda*. New York: Farrar, Strauss, and Giroux, 1998.

This is a powerful—and best-selling—book, based on extensive interviews with Rwandans, that dramatically lays out the context within which the Rwandan genocide took place.

Prunier, Gerard. *The Rwanda Crisis: History of a Genocide*. New York: Columbia University Press, 1997.

This book, very carefully documented, has become the starting point for researchers and readers who focus on the 1994 genocide.

Scherrer, Christian P. *Genocide and Crisis in Central Africa: Conflict Roots, Mass Violence, and Regional War*. Westport, CT: Praeger, 2002.

This book is an expansive account of the many civil wars, mass killings, and genocides that have occurred in Africa over the past four decades.

### al-Bashir and the Darfur Genocide, Sudan, 2003–

De Waal, Alex. *Famine That Kills: Darfur, Sudan*. 2nd ed. Oxford, England: Oxford University Press, 2004.

The author has provided researchers on genocide and mass murder with a first-rate examination of the events that are taking place in the Sudan.

**Prunier, Gerard.** *Darfur: The Ambiguous Genocide.* **Ithaca, NY: Cornell University Press, 2005.**

The author, who has also written about the Rwanda genocide, has provided the reader with an excellent detailed examination of the Darfur genocide.

## Press Coverage

This listing provides the reader with the flavor of journalistic coverage of world events that have exhibited mass murder and genocide. Major newspapers, for example, *The New York Times, The Washington Post, The Guardian* (UK), always carry stories that examine outbreak of war and the mass killings that occur as a manifestation of these hostilities.

Anderson. Scott. "How Did Darfur Happen?" *The New York Times.* October 17, 2004.

Becker, Elizabeth. "U.S. Ties Military Aid to Peacekeepers' Immunity." *New York Times.* August 10, 2002.

Bellinger, John B., III. "A Global Quandary for the President." *The Washington Post.* August 10, 2009. www.washingtonpost.com.

Carl, Michael. "Obama May Put Americans under World Judges' Power." *World Net Daily.* November 19, 2009. www.wnd.com.

Crosette, Barbara. "US Budges at UN Talks on a Permanent International Criminal Tribunal." *New York Times.* March 18, 1988, A1.

Danner, Mark. "The Killing Fields of Bosnia." *New York Review of Books.* September 24, 1998.

Draculic, Dlavenka. "Rape after Rape after Rape [in Bosnia]." *New York Times.* December 13, 1992, A1.

Dworkin, Anthony. "Cambodian War Crimes Tribunal Given Go-Ahead." May 5, 2005. www.crimesofwarproject.org.

Franchi, Howard. "International Court Eyes Role beyond War-Crimes Trials." *Christian Science Monitor.* September 12, 2009, 1.

Goldman, T. R. "A World Apart, U.S. Stance on a New ICC Concerns Rights Groups." *Legal Times.* June 8, 1998.

Jackson, Donald W. "Creating a World Criminal Court Is Like Making Sausage—Except It Takes Longer." *Texas Observer.* June 30, 1998, 19.

Lake, Anthony. "The Limits of Peacekeeping." *New York Times.* February 6, 1994, D17.

Lynch, Colum. "U.S. to Attend Conference Held by War Crimes Court." *The Washington Post.* November 17, 2009. www.washingtonpost.com.

MacAskill, Ewen. "U.S. May Join ICC, Hillary Clinton Hints." *The Guardian.* August 6, 2009. www.guardian.co.uk/world/2009.

Mydans, Seth. "Cambodia's Leader Says Top Khmer Rouge Defectors Will Be Spared." *New York Times.* December 29, 1998, A1.

Mydans, Seth. "Two Khmer Rouge Leaders Spend Beach Holiday in Shadow of Past." *New York Times.* January 1, 1999, A1.

Ryle, John. "Disaster in Darfur." *New York Review of Books.* August 12, 2004.

Simons, Marlise. "International Court Begins First Trial." *New York Times.* January 29, 2009.

Schwammenthal, Daniel. "Prosecuting American 'War Crimes,'" *The Wall Street Journal.* November 26, 2009. www.online.wsj.com.

Stanley, Alessandra. "U.S. Specifies Terms for War Crimes Court." *New York Times.* July 10, 1998, A1.

Timberg, Craig. "Rwanda's Tormentors Emerge from the Forest to Haunt Congo: Hutu Guerillas Find New Victims." *The Washington Post.* February 10, 2005.

# Journals/Reports

Aksar, Yusuf. "'Victimized Group' Concept in the Genocide Convention and the Development of International Humanitarian Law through the Practice of Ad Hoc Tribunals." *Journal of Genocide Research* 5, no. 2 (2003): 211–24.

*Amnesty International Report 1998.* London: Amnesty International, 1999.

This report is published annually by this very important NGO.

Bassiouni, M. Cherif. "From Versailles to Rwanda in Seventy-five Years: The Need to Establish a Permanent International Criminal Court." *Harvard Human Rights Journal* 10 (1997): 11–17.

CBC News. "The Genocide Convention." September 18, 2006. www.cbc.org.

Frontline Special Report. "The Crime of Genocide." 1995. http://www.pbs.org/wgbh/pages/frontline/shows/rwanda/reports/dsetexhe.html.

Goldberg, Mark L. "Congress Reverses Bush-Era Policy on the ICC." March 12, 2009, *Report: Center for Strategic and International Studies*. www.csis.org.

Harff, Barbara. "No Lessons Learned from the Holocaust? Assessing Risks of Genocide and Mass Murder." *American Political Science Review* 97, no. 1 (February 2003): 57–73.

Howard-Hassman, Rhoda E. "Genocide and State-Induced Famine: Global Ethics and Western Responsibility for Mass Atrocities in Africa." *Perspectives on Global Development and Technology* 4, no. 3–4 (2005): 487–516.

Human Rights. 2008. "Five Controversies on Genocide (. . .But Not the Only Five)." http://humanrights.change.org/blog/view/5_controversies_on_genocide_but_not_the_only_five.

*Human Rights Tribune*. "Value of UN Genocide Convention Questioned." International Center for Transitional Justice, December 17, 2008. http://www.hrtribune.com.

International Committee of the Red Cross. "The Impact of Armed Conflict on Women." www.reliefweb.int/library/documents/2001/icrc-women-17oct.pdf.

This report examines how women have been treated during wars, especially civil wars that took place in Rwanda, the Congo, and the Sudan.

Kiernan, Ben. "The Demography of Genocide in Southeast Asia: The Death Tolls in Cambodia, 1975–1979, and East Timor, 1975–1980." *Critical Asian Studies* 35, no. 4 (2003): 585–97.

Kuperman, Alan J. "Provoking Genocide: A Revised History of the Rwanda Patriotic Front." *Journal of Genocide Research* 6, no. 1 (March 2004): 61–84.

Marcus, David. "Famine Crimes in International Law." *American Journal of International Law* 97 (2003): 245–81.

McDonald, Garbrielle Kirk. "The Changing Nature of the Laws of War." *Military Law Journal* 156 (June 1998): 9–29.

Menoz Report. Report of the Special Advisor on the Prevention of Genocide—Visit to Darfur, Sudan, September 19–26, 2005.

Powell, Colin. Testimony before U.S. Congress. U.S. Participation in UN Peacekeeping Activities. House Committee on Foreign Affairs, September 18, 2006. www.cbc.org.

Rudolph, Christopher. "Constructing an Atrocities Regime: The Politics of War Crimes Tribunals." *International Organization* 55, no. 3 (Summer 2001): 655–91.

Stahn, C. "The Ambiguities of Security Council Resolution 1422." *European Journal of International Law* 14 (2003): 85–104.

Stanley Foundation. "The UN Security Council and the ICC: How Should They Relate." Arden House, New York, February 20–22, 1988.

Stanton, Gregory H. *The 8 Stages of Genocide.* 1998. (Originally presented as a briefing paper at the U.S. State Department in 1996.) http://www.genocidewatch.org/aboutgenocide/8stagesofgenocide.html.

Straus, Scott. "Darfur and the Genocide Debate." *Foreign Affairs* 84, no.1 (2004): 123–33.

U.S. Department of State. Fact Sheet. "The International Criminal Court." *Office of War Crimes Issues*, Washington, D.C., May 6, 2002.

Varner, Bill. Obama's Envoy Voices Support for International Court. January 29, 2009. http://www.bloomberg.com/apps/news?pid=newsarchive&sid=aYK_ULgi3Ix0.

Wisner, Frank. Report Presented in U.S. Congress, *International Peacekeeping and Peace Enforcement*, U.S. Senate Committee on Armed Forces, 1993.

Zappala, Salvatore. "The Reaction of the US to the Entry into Force of the ICC Statute: Comments on UN SC Resolution 1422 (2002) and Article 98 Agreements." *Journal of International Criminal Justice* 1 (2002): 114–34.

# Nonprint Resources

There have been many dozens of films made—in America and in Europe—that tell about genocidal events in 20th-century history. Listed is a sampling of the available films. All are available on DVD.

## Films

**Armenia**
*Ararat, 2002*
*Lark Farm, 2007*
*Mayrig, 2000*
*Screamers, 2006*

**Bosnia**
*Behind Enemy Lines, 2001*
*Graffiti Street, 2007*
*Harrison's Flowers, 2000*
*No Man's Land, 2001*
**Cambodia**
*The Killing Fields, 1984*
**Nazi Germany**
*Defiance, 2008*
*Diary of Anne Frank, 1959*
*Escape from Sobibor, 1987*
*Europa, Europa, 1990*
*Everything Is Illuminated, 2005*
*Jakob the Liar, 1999.*
*Judgment at Nuremberg, 1961*
*Life Is Beautiful, 1998*
*Man in the Glass Booth, 1975*
*Night and Fog, 2003*
*Out of the Ashes, 2003*
*Playing for Time, 1980*
*Schindler's List, 1993*
*Sophie's Choice, 1982*
*The Black Book, 2006*
*The Couple, 2004*
*The Garden of the Finzi-Continis, 1970*
*The Grey Zone, 2001*
*The Juggler, 1953*
*The Last Stop, 1948*
*The Music Box, 1990*
*The Pawnbroker, 1964*
*The Pianist, 2002*
*The Reader, 2008*
*The Shop on Main Street, 1966*
*The Sorrow and the Pity, 1972*
*The Wall, 1982*
**Rwanda**
*Beyond the Gates, 2007*
*The Devil Came on Horseback, 2007*
*Hotel Rwanda, 2005*
*Munyurangabo, 2009*
*Shooting Dogs, 2005*
*Sometimes in April, 2005*

*A Sunday in Kigali, 2006*
**South American Military Juntas**
*Missing, 1984 (Chile)*

## Documentaries

**Armenia**
*Assignment Berlin, 1981*
*The Armenian Genocide: 1915–1923, 2007*
*The Greek Holocaust: 1915–1922, 2007*
*The River Ran Red, 1993*
*Voices from the Lake, 2007*
**Bangladesh**
*Earth, 1998*
**Bosnia**
*Beyond Reasonable Doubt, 2005*
*Human Tragedy: The Faces of Kosovo, 2001*
*Living in Emergency: Stories of Doctors without Borders, 2010*
*Milosevic on Trial, 2007*
*Resolution 819, 2008*
*Savior, 1998*
*Shot through the Heart, 1998*
*Srebrenica: A Genocide Foretold, 2005*
*Vukovar, 1994*
*Welcome to Sarajevo, 1997*
*Yellow Wasps: Anatomy of a War Crime, 1996*
**Cambodia**
*New Year Baby, 2006*
*Pol Pot: A Man of Genocide, 2002*
*Rain Falls from Earth, 2007*
*S-21: The Khmer Rouge Killing Machine, 2002*
*Scarred by History: Among the Disappeared, 2002*
**Darfur**
*A Journey to Darfur, 2007*
*Darfur Destroyed, 2009*
*Darfur Diaries, 2006*
*Darfur Now, 2008*
*God Grew Tired of Us, 2005*
*Sand and Sorrow, 2007*
*The Devil Came on Horseback, 2007*
*Unholy War: Christian Genocide in Sudan, 2008*

**East Timor**
*Death of a Nation, 1994*
**Iraq**
*Chemical Ali's Anfal, 2005*
*In the Name of Honor, 2000*
**Japan**
*Declassified: Human Experimentation, 2008*
*The Rape of Nanking: China and Japan at War, 2005*
**Nazi Germany**
*A Day in October, 1991*
*All My Loved Ones, 2000*
*And the Violins Stopped Playing, 1988*
*Kaddish, 1984*
*KZ, 2005*
*Out of the Ashes, 2003*
*Shanghai Ghetto, 2002*
*Shoah, 1985*
*Sobibor, October 14, 1943, 4 p.m., 2001*
*The Children Remember the Holocaust, 1995*
*The Eternal Jew, 1940*
*The Lost Children of Berlin, 1997*
*The Memory of Justice, 1976*
*The Warsaw Ghetto, 1966*
*We Live Again, 1946*
**Russia**
*Alexander Solzhenitsyn's First Circle, 1989*
*The Soviet Story, 2010*
**Rwanda**
*As We Forgive, 2009*
*Keepers of Memory, 2005*
*100 Days, 2001*
*Rwanda—Do Scars Ever Fade? 2008*
*Rwanda—Hope Rises, 2010*
*Shake Hands with the Devil: The Journey of General Dallaire, 2004*
*Triumph of Evil, 1998*
**South American Military Juntas**
*Pinochet's Last Stand, 2006*
*Romero, 1989 (El Salvador)*
*Social Genocide, 2005 (Argentina)*
*Sweet Country: The 1973 Chile Coup d'état, 1976*
*The Disappeared, 2007 (Argentina)*

*The Hour of the Furnaces, 1968 (Argentina)*
*The Official Story, 1985 (Argentina)*


## Television/Videotapes

ABC News Classic: *Cambodia: This Shattered Land*, 2008
ABC News Nightline: *Starvation in Srebrenica*, 2007
ABC News Nightline: *The Sudan*, 2007
ATV: Year Zero: *The Silent Death of Cambodia*, 1979
BBC: *The Death of Yugoslavia*, 2002
BBC Miniseries: *QBVII*, 1974
CBC: *Nuremberg*, 2000
CNN: *Scream Bloody Murder*, 2008
NBC: *Diary of Anne Frank*, 1967, 1980
NBC Miniseries: *The Holocaust*, 1979
PBS Bill Moyers' Journal: *Srebrenica: A Cry from the Grave*, 1999.
PBS Frontline: *Ghosts of Rwanda*, 2004
PBS Frontline: *Memory of the Camps*, 2006
PBS Frontline: Special Report, *"The Crime of Genocide."* 1995
PBS Frontline: *The Armenian Genocide*, 2006
PBS Frontline: *Valentina's Nightmare in Rwanda*, 1997
PBS: *Playing for Time*, 1980
PBS The American Experience: *The Nuremberg Trials*, 2006
Touchstone: *Anne Frank: The True Story*, 2001 (TV mini-series)
WNET: *Srebrenica: A Cry from the Grave*, 1999.


## Databases/Web Sites

Anne Frank Center USA at www.annefrank.com.
Armenian Genocide Museum-Institute at www.gen-mus.am/eng/index.php.
Armenian Genocide at www.armenian-genocide.org.
Armenian National Institute at www.armenian-genocide.org.
Armenian Research Center at www.umd.umich.edu/dept/armenian.
Bangladesh Genocide Archive at www.genocidebangladesh.org.
Bosnia Genocide Research at www.cco.caltech.edu/-bosnia.
Cambodia Genocide Project at www.yale.edu/cgp.
China Famine Study at www.genocideproject.net.
Coalition for the ICC at www.iccnow.org/documents/usandtheicc.html.

Committee on Conscience at www.ushmm.org/conscience.
Council on Hemisphere Affairs (focus on South America) at www
.coha/org.
Crimes of War at www.crimesofwar.org.
Cybrary of the Holocaust at www.remember.org.
East Timor Genocide Project at www.yale.edu/gsp/east_timor.
Gendercide Watch at www.gendercide.org.
Genocide and Human Rights Institute at www.niu.edu.
Genocide Documents Center at www.ess-uwe.ac.uk/genocide
.htm.
Genocide Intervention at www.genocideintervention.net/index.php.
Genocide Research Project at www.people.memphis.edu/
genocide.
Genocide Studies Program at www.yale.edu/gsp.
Genocide Watch at www.genocidewatch.org.
Holocaust Education through Art at www.holocaust-art.org.
Holocaust History Project at www.holocaust-history.org.
Holocaust New at www.h-net.org.
Holocaust Teachers Resource Center at www.holocaust-trc.org.
Human Rights USA at www.hrusa.org.
Human Rights Watch at www.hrw.org.
IDEA: Journal of Social Issues at www.wiley.com/bw/journal
.asp?ref=0022-4537
International Association of Genocide Scholars at www.
instituteforthestudyofgenocide.org.
International Criminal Tribunal for Rwanda (ICTR) at www.ictr.org.
International Criminal Tribunal for former Yugoslavia (ICTY) at
www.icty.org.
International Law-Genocide at www.in_law.site.weslyn.an.edu/
tag/genocide.
International Military Tribunal for Germany, at http://avalon
.law.yale.edu/subject_menus/imt.asp.
Nizkor Project at www.nizkor.org.
Posen Bibliographic Project on Antisemitism at www.sicsa.huji.ac-il.
Prevent Genocide International at www.preventgenocide.org.
Russian Famine at www.infoukes.com/hist/famine/index.html.
Rwanda Development Gateway at www.rwandagateway.org.
Rwanda Genocide at www.hrw.org/reports/1999/rwanda.
Simon Wiesenthal Center at www.wiesenthal.com.
Special Court for Sierra Leone, SCSL at www.sc-sl.org.
Sudan Genocide at www.unitedhumanrights.org/sudan_geocide_
genocide_in_sudan.php.

Sudan Research, Analysis, and Advocacy at www.sudanreeves.org.

The Armenian Genocide at www.unitedhumanrights.org/ Genocide/armenian_genocide.htm.

The International Criminal Court (ICC) at www.icc-cpi.int/ MENUS/ICC?lan=en-GB

Ukrainian State Archives of Ukrainian Genocide Famine at www .archives.gov-ua.

UN Human Rights page at www.un.org/en/rights/index.shtml.

U.S. Department of State at www.state.gov.

U.S. Department of State Bureau of Democracy, Human Rights, and Labor at www.state.gov/g/drl.

U.S. Department of State Office of War Crimes Issues at www.state .gov/s/wci.

U.S. Department of State Office of Special Envoy to Monitor and Combat Antisemitism at www.state.gov/g/drl/seaa.

U.S. Holocaust Memorial Museum at www.ushmm.org.

Yad Veshem, The Holocaust Martyrs' and Heroes' Remembrance Authority at www.yadveshem.org.

Yale Avalon Project at www.avalon.law.yale.edu.

# Glossary

**Ad Hoc International Criminal Tribunals** These are criminal courts that hear cases involving major crimes universally condemned by the civilized world community. These crimes are crimes against humanity, war crimes, and genocide. The first two such ad hoc courts were convened by the victorious Allies after the end of World War II: the Nuremberg, Germany International Military Tribunal and, in Tokyo, Japan, the International Military Tribunal. Judges heard testimony regarding the actions of major German and Japanese political and military leaders. At the present time, ad hoc courts are created by UN resolutions to indict, arrest, and try persons accused of committing one or more of the major crimes enumerated above, in wars that took place in the former Yugoslavia (the ad hoc International Criminal Tribunal for the former Yugoslavia, 1993) and in Rwanda (the ad hoc International Criminal Tribunal for Rwanda, 1994). The UN Security Council sets the parameters for these courts, including dates and scope of the tribunal's coverage, its organization, and its judicial processes before, during, and after trial.

**Age of Impunity** This term reflects the primacy of the sovereign nation-state. It covers the period from the late 18th century to the present time and is the basis for the present-day dilemma surrounding the failure of the world community to halt genocide before it can be implemented by a nation's leaders or the leaders of armed forces engaged in a civil war within a nation. Leaders who engage their military forces in genocidal acts against a group or groups within the nation have been immune from any international intervention to stop the genocide because of the respect given to the notion of national sovereignty. Tyrants such as Hitler in Nazi Germany, Stalin in the Soviet Union, Idi Amin in Uganda, and Pol Pot in Cambodia exterminated their enemies with impunity.

**Bilateral Immunity Agreements** These are bilateral treaties that were entered into by the United States and another sovereign nation between 2002 and 2008. The nation agrees not to enforce an International Criminal Court (ICC) arrest warrant against any American personnel even though the nation has formally ratified the ICC. It reflects the concern on the part of American leaders that U.S. military leaders and personnel and political leaders would face partisan efforts by other nation-states to indict and arrest Americans for alleged war crimes, crimes against humanity, or genocidal actions.

**Collectivization of Agriculture**   This process, which has occurred in nations led by tyrants (Stalin in the Soviet Union, Mao Tse-Tung in China, and Pol Pot in Cambodia), is a brutal process of forming agricultural collective communities, where the agricultural products and property are controlled by the state. Ostensibly introduced as a method of creating greater efficiency in agricultural production than in the privately owned agricultural property, in reality, wherever collectivization was introduced, famine—the silent genocide—occurred.

**Command Responsibility**   This term was first made part of the international law of war in the 1945 trial of major Nazi leaders at Nuremberg, Germany. It was codified in the 1949 Geneva Conventions. Although troops under the command of a military leader had committed genocide or war crimes or crimes against humanity *without* a general's orders or even his *knowledge*, that military commander was not absolved "from penal disciplinary responsibility" for the actions of his subordinates in the field.

**Complementarity**   This term reflects the relationship between a nation's criminal justice system and the newly created, 1998, ICC. Paragraph 10 of the Rome Statute states that "the ICC established under this Statute shall be complementary to national criminal jurisdictions." Therefore, the initial legal actor in bringing before the bar of justice those persons accused of committing genocide, war crimes, or crimes against humanity is a nation's own courts and judges. If that nation cannot or will not so act, then the ICC can take whatever legal action necessary to bring the perpetrators to justice.

**Crimes against Humanity**   Such crimes are defined in the 1998 Rome Statute that created the ICC. They are "particularly odious offenses in that they constitute a serious attack on human dignity or grave humiliation or degradation of one or more human beings." These crimes are an aspect of a government policy aimed at destroying a group; they are not isolated instances of atrocities. They usually occur in concert with genocide and war crimes. The Nuremberg and Tokyo tribunals concluded that the leaders of these Axis powers had committed crimes against humanity.

**Dehumanization**   This is a social, psychological process in which members of a national ethnic or racial group target another group within the region for extermination. An initial stage in the genocidal process is to perceive the targeted group—racial, ethnic, foreign, or religious—as an *inferior* one that jeopardizes the health and future development of that society. The inferiority of the targeted group becomes reflected in discriminatory laws, the use of vile names such as "cockroach" (in Rwanda), parasite and vermin (in Nazi Germany), and other propaganda, the goal of which is to deprive the offensive group of all human qualities.

**Ethnic Cleansing**  This term was first heard by the international community during the Bosnian War between Serb and Bosnian Serb forces on one side and Bosnian Muslims on the other. President Milosevic of Serbia and Radovan Karadzic, the Bosnian Serb leader, spoke about the need to purify Bosnia of its Muslim population in order to create a "Greater Serbia" free of that religious group. Functionally, the concept has existed and has been practiced for centuries. Generally, it connotes the idea of literally moving ethnic or religious groups out of—or eliminating them from—a particular region. The ethnic cleansing actions, for example, of Albanians from Turkey, of Hindus from Pakistan, of Tutsis from Rwanda, and of Jews from Europe were part of an overarching state policy of genocide.

**Final Solution**  This was the term used by the Nazi government when, in 1940, its leaders developed the policy of mass extermination of Jews in areas occupied by the German forces in Europe. The Final Solution was to kill all those, Jews and other inferior groups, who were unworthy of life.

**Genocide**  The 1948 Genocide Convention said that genocide was a formal state policy made "with intent to destroy, in whole or in part, a national, ethnical, racial or religious group, as such."

**Grave Breaches**  The 1949 Geneva Conventions enumerated the ways wars were fought on land and on the sea, how civilians were to be treated in war, and how prisoners of war had to be handled by their capturers. Grave breaches are violations committed by an enemy against civilians and belligerents and include killing, torture, inhumane treatment, and willfully causing great, unnecessary suffering.

**The Hague Conventions**  These were a series of international treaties signed by a number of nations in 1899 and 1907 that tried to limit military excesses during war.

**Hybrid International Criminal Courts**  These courts are similar to ad hoc international courts except for the makeup of the prosecutors' office and the judges. They are called hybrid because they are composed of national judges as well as jurists and prosecutors from other nations sitting alongside the domestic contingent. Sierra Leone, East Timor, Cambodia, and Afghanistan are four nations that have used such a court or have contemplated using such a court.

**Interhamwe**  These were civilian death squads of Hutus who, in the 1994 Rwanda genocide, were tasked by their leaders with the extermination of the Tutsi enemy.

**Janjaweed**  These are armed Arabic Muslim militias in Sudan who are largely responsible for the murders of nearly 400,000 Africans, the destruction of hundreds of villages, and the rape of thousands of women living in the Darfur region.

*Kristallnacht*   On the night of November 9, 1938, the beginning of the
end of life as they knew it for German Jews began. It was to lead to
the Final Solution. Across Germany and Austria, Nazis burned synagogues, smashed stores owned by Jews, plundered homes of Jews, and
killed many Jews during the night. It was called *Kristallnacht* because of
all the broken glass littering the streets in front of the destroyed synagogues. It was followed by more brutal and discriminatory laws that
targeted Jewish assets and freedom to travel and denied them basic
human rights.

**Military Immunity from Prosecution**   Until the end of the Second
World War, military leaders charged with war crimes argued successfully
that they were obeying orders from their superiors and were immune
from prosecution. With Nuremberg and Tokyo, that concept ended. They
could be tried and punished for failing to prevent illegal actions by their
troops or for obeying orders that violated international laws of war.

**PrepCom**   In 1988, the UN secretary-general, in anticipation of the
convening of nations to create an ICC, created preparatory committees—PrepComs—to begin to draft a proposed treaty for review and ratification. Ten years later, in 1998, the Rome Statute for the creation of the
ICC was debated by more than 120 nations and was ratified. It came into
force in 2002.

**The "Disappeared"**   These are civilians who opposed a military regime
and who "disappeared" from society, having been killed by the regime;
most of their bodies were never found. It has been a term used in military
junta–controlled states such as Argentina, Guatemala, and Chile. However, in any genocide, there are thousands of dead who have disappeared,
having been buried in mass graves known only to the perpetrators.

**The "Other"**   This is a term used to define enemies of a dictatorship.
They are inferior outsiders not considered an integral element in that
society and are targeted for dehumanization, discrimination, and the
Final Solution.

**Unit 731, Japanese Army**   This was a highly secret medical-military
unit in the Japanese Army that functioned in China from 1937 to 1945.
They conducted medical experiments, including those with chemical and
biological materials, on Chinese civilians and Allied prisoners of war.
The unit developed and implemented chemical gas attacks on Chinese
populations during the war. The leaders of this unit were never charged
with war crimes or crimes against humanity. Instead, in return for this
immunity, the medical personnel turned over all their data to American
forces after the war ended.

**Universal Jurisdiction**   The Nuremberg and Tokyo war crimes tribunals
concluded that there were certain crimes—war crimes and crimes against
humanity (and, after 1948, genocide)—that were universally condemned.

Therefore any national court could claim jurisdiction and bring to the bar of justice those accused of committing such universal crimes against persons—even though the crimes were not committed in that nation.

**War Crimes**   This is considered a crime subject to universal jurisdiction. A war crime is a grave breach of the laws of war because of excessive and cruel actions taken against civilians and military personnel.

# Index

# About the Author

**Howard Ball** is Professor of Political Science Emeritus, University Scholar, at the University of Vermont. He is the author of 34 books on the U.S. Supreme Court, war crimes, and domestic and international justice. He has also taught at Hofstra University, Mississippi State University, The University of Utah, and Dartmouth College. Overseas, he has been Fulbright Distinguished Professor at Sofia University Law School in 2002 and John Marshall Distinguished Professor at the University of Szeged, in Szeged, Hungary, in 2006–2007.